Margaret Fuller's
New York Journalism

Margaret Fuller's New York Journalism

A BIOGRAPHICAL ESSAY AND KEY WRITINGS

Edited by Catherine C. Mitchell

The Poynter Institute
For Media Studies

The University of Tennessee Press
Knoxville

Copyright © 1995 by The University of Tennessee Press / Knoxville.
All Rights Reserved. Manufactured in the United States of America.
First Edition.

Parts of this book have previously appeared as "Greeley as Journalism Teacher: 'Give Us Facts, Occurrences,'" in *Journalism Educator* 44, no. 3 (Autumn 1989): 16–19.

The paper in this book meets the minimum requirements of the American National Standard for Permanence of Paper for Printed Library Materials. ∞   The binding materials have been chosen for strength and durability.

Library of Congress Cataloging in Publication Data

Fuller, Margaret, 1810-1850.
  Margaret Fuller's New York Journalism: a biographical essay and key writings/ edited by Catherine C. Mitchell.—1st ed.
        p.   cm.
  Includes bibliographical references and index.
  ISBN 0-87049-870-3 (cloth: alk. paper)
  1. Fuller, Margaret, 1810-1850—Knowledge—Journalism.
  2. Women journalists—New York (N.Y.)—Biography.
  3. United States—Social conditions—To 1865.
  4. New York (N.Y.)—Social conditions.
  5. Journalism—New York (N.Y.)
    I. Mitchell, Catherine C. II. Title. III. Title: New York Journalism.
PS2502.M56   1995
818' .309—dc20   94-18710
{B}   CIP

Contents

Preface	VII
I. Margaret Fuller's Work Life	
1. Introducing Margaret Fuller	3
2. A Journalist at the *Tribune*, 1844–1846	14
3. The Denigration of Margaret Fuller	43
II. Margaret Fuller's Journalism: Forgotten Writings	
4. The Rich and the Poor	51
The Rich Man—An Ideal Sketch	55
Prevalent Idea That Politeness Is Too Great a Luxury to Be Given to the Poor	62
Consecration of Grace Church	65
The Poor Man—An Ideal Sketch	68
5. Prison and Asylum Reform	76
St. Valentine's Day—Bloomingdale Asylum for the Insane	79
Twenty-fifth Annual Report of the Bloomingdale Asylum for the Insane	83
Our City Charities	88
Asylum for Discharged Female Convicts	94
Report and Documents of the New-York Institution for the Instruction of the Deaf and Dumb	97
Prison Discipline	105
Condition of the Blind in This Country and Abroad	113
Floral Fete for the Children of the Farm Schools on the Fourth July	120
Caroline	121
6. Equality for Women and African Americans	125
The Wrongs of American Women, The Duty of American Women	128
School of the Misses Sedgwick	135
Narrative of the Life of Frederick Douglass, an American Slave	136

First of August, 1845	139
The White Slave; or, the Russian Peasant-Girl	145
What Fits a Man to Be a Voter? Is It to Be White within, or White Without?	147
Lyceum of New-Bedford, Mass.	151
"Darkness Visible" [1]	152
"Darkness Visible" [2]	161
7. The Irish	163
The Irish Character [1]	165
The Irish Character [2]	168
The Irish Character [3]	174
8. A Miscellany	175
Thanksgiving	176
Wonders Have Not Ceased in Our Times	181
Peale's Court of Death	182
The Grand Festival Concert at Castle Garden	185
Leopold de Meyer	188
Physical Education and the Preservation of Health	190
The Beethoven Monument	194
Study of the German Language	199
Instruction in the French Language	201
Discoveries	202
Farewell	204
Notes	207
Bibliography	219
Index	227

Illustrations

Margaret Fuller, c. 1846	4
Horace Greeley, c. 1841	28

Preface

This book represents an effort to reclaim an often overlooked aspect of the important nineteenth-century intellectual, Margaret Fuller: her work as a journalist. All of the scholarship on Fuller mentions her occupation, but most authors have concentrated their efforts on studying her contributions to American literature and her inspiration of the campaign for woman's rights. As a young woman in the 1960s studying journalism among a sea of men, I assumed I was slightly odd because I wanted to enter a predominantly male field. I had no idea of the rich history of the many women who had preceded me working in journalism. As a college professor, the discovery of all these women and most particularly Margaret Fuller has been a joy that I wanted to share with others—thus this book.

In researching this book, I set out to answer one main question: What was Margaret Fuller's life like at work? Along the way, I came upon several other research questions that really need answering but would have taken me far from my main question. Although there has been much scholarly writing about Margaret Fuller in the last twenty years, I found many possible routes left for studying her involvement with journalism. Study is needed of Fuller's influence on her friend George Ripley. He succeeded her as book editor at the *New York Tribune* and was for twenty years the dean of American literary critics. A researcher might well ask whether Fuller established the standards for book reviewing at the *New York Tribune* in its infancy, the standards that Ripley applied as book editor of the *Tribune* in its maturity. Also, although several authors have made a passing comparison of Fuller's criticism and that of her contemporary, Edgar Allan Poe, no one appears to have done a detailed analysis.

Fuller's news reporting has been studied as an important step in the evolution of her personal thinking, but no one has pondered the effect of this writing. A future study could look at her reforming articles in the context of New York City's journalism and social history. One could also examine Fuller's role as editor of the *Dial,* the transcendentalist literary magazine. The ideas published in this magazine had a major impact on America's intellectual thought. As an editor, how did Fuller contribute to the development of this body of thought? How heavily did she edit?

Although the study of Great Men is currently out of fashion in the scholarly community, journalism historians have perhaps abandoned the topic too hastily. For instance, a needed contribution to scholarship on Horace Greeley is the publication of a definitive version of his letters. These are housed in library special collections around the country, and Greeley was infamous for his poor handwriting. Francis Nicoll Zabriskie reports the following tale: Greeley fired one of his employees, but the man found that no one could read the letter of dismissal, so he gave the letter his "own interpretation as a letter of recommendation, and got several first rate situations by it."[1] Reading Greeley's letters is an arduous task that requires much travel and eyestrain.

In the history of journalism a topic for further study concerns the influence of the Mexican War on front-page makeup. This author found that page 2 of the *New York Tribune* carried the most newsworthy items. The Mexican War, though, moved literature off page 1 to make more space for foreign news. Maps of troop movements broke up the front-page makeup.

And finally, a tantalizing source for study is a deteriorating, leather-bound, vellum volume in the New York Public Library's special collections. This assignment log of the *New York Tribune* kept by the city editor in 1867–68 lists all the reporters and their story assignments plus clippings from articles. It is an invaluable primary source for research on the typical assignments on a major American newspaper in the 1860s.

Many people have helped me in the preparation of this manuscript. Since it originated in my Ph.D. dissertation on Margaret Fuller, I want particularly to thank Paul Ashdown, who directed my dissertation, and committee members Jim Crook, Ed Caudill, and William Shurr. I greatly appreciate their help and interest throughout my graduate studies. I also want to thank Robert N. Hudspeth, who photocopied a prepublication galley proof of the entire fourth volume of his *Letters of Margaret Fuller* for me. Without this aid, plus the bibliographic work on Fuller done by Joel Myerson, this research would have been infinitely more difficult to complete. In the preparation of this manuscript, I received very thorough, detailed, and kind suggestions from Maurine Beasley and Dwight Teeter. I want to thank them for the care they took with the project. I also want to thank Christie Waters for the superb job of preparing an accurate typescript of Margaret Fuller's articles and the University of Tennessee Press, particularly acquisitions editor Meredith Morris-Babb, for their enthusiasm and efficiency. Special thanks must also go to the University of North Carolina at Asheville for giving me release time from teaching to complete this project and to the staff of the D. Hiden Ramsey Library at the University of North Carolina at Asheville, particularly interlibrary loan librarians Mary Brown and Nancy Hayes. I also want to thank the New York Historical Society and the New York Public Library for allowing me access to their Special Collections. Then, of course, there is all the friendship, support, and encouragement I received from Jane Casto, Brian Baldwin, Evelyn Brannon, Pam Nickless, Peggy Parris, Kathryn Long, and Chris Streppa. Thanks, guys.

Part I.
Margaret Fuller's Work Life

1
Introducing Margaret Fuller

Sarah Margaret Fuller was single, thirty-three years old, and a highly respected New England intellectual when she joined Horace Greeley's *New York Tribune* on December 7, 1844. She was well read in French, Italian, and German literature and could read Latin and some Greek. Edgar Allan Poe called her a person of "high genius" who had "only one or two dozen" equals "on the whole face of the earth." Literary critic Marie Urbanski has called her the most important woman in nineteenth-century America.[1]

Fuller was a witty woman. Beman Brockway, one of Horace Greeley's reporters, described an encounter between Greeley's wife and Fuller. Molly Greeley refused to wear kidskin gloves because she opposed killing animals. One day the two met on the street. Mrs. Greeley touched Fuller's gloved hand and exclaimed, "Skin of a beast, skin of a beast!" "Why, what do you wear?" asked Fuller. "Silk," said Mrs. Greeley. Then Fuller touched Molly Greeley's hand and exclaimed, "Entrails of a worm!"[2]

At the *Tribune* Fuller wrote at least 250 articles, mostly about American literature, but she also wrote articles and essays about social and political issues. Horace Greeley had at least four good reasons to offer Fuller a job. First, her intellectual abilities were already well recognized. When Greeley announced the hiring of Fuller, he called her a writer "already eminent in the higher walks of literature" and predicted "decided and gratifying change" for his newspaper. Second, Molly Greeley recommended Fuller. She had attended several "Conversations," a popular series of lecture/encounter groups on woman's rights that Fuller led in Boston beginning in 1839. Third, Fuller had gained editorial experience from 1840 to 1842 as editor of the *Dial,* the literary magazine founded by Ralph Waldo Emerson to publish transcendentalist literature. Fourth, Greeley liked Fuller's 1844 travel book, *Summer on the Lakes.*[3]

Fuller's work, bylined with a star, inspired the contemporary pun that she was the "star" of the *Tribune.* Greeley made the pun in a letter: "The * of the *Tribune* is Miss S. Margaret Fuller, . . . the most thoroughly learned woman on this continent and of capacious intellect." *Graham's Magazine* made the same pun in a September 1846 social notice of Fuller's depar-

Margaret Fuller, c. 1846. Courtesy, Metropolitan Museum of Art, gift of I. N. Phelps Stokes, Edward S. Hawes, Alice Mary Hawes, Marion Augusta Hawes, 1937 (37.14.10).

ture for Europe. "Miss Margaret Fuller, the 'Star' of the *New York Tribune* . . . sailed a few days ago for Europe, intending to spend a few months in Italy."[4]

After two years of writing in New York, Fuller became *Tribune* European correspondent. In a "Farewell" essay (see Chapter 8), Fuller said her years in New York had provided her "a richer and more varied exercise for thought and life than twenty years could in any other part of these United States." She said she had learned two things in New York: education was important for the future of the country, and woman's role in society would keep expanding. In New York she modified her romantic transcendentalist idealism after observing the poor living conditions forced upon inhabitants of the city's slums, prisons, and almshouses. She turned from literary criticism to practical essays on how to solve social problems. In Europe Fuller met Thomas Carlyle, George Sand, Elizabeth Barrett Browning, and Italian revolutionary Giuseppe Mazzini. She also met Italian count Giovanni Ossoli (ten years her junior), bore him a son, and, perhaps, married him. She got caught up in a revolution in Italy, covered it for the *Tribune,* and ran a hospital for the rebels. In 1850 she sailed back to the United States with Ossoli and the baby, but her ship wrecked at the entrance to New York harbor within sight of scavengers on the shore. The entire family drowned. A manuscript she had written about the Italian revolution was also lost in the shipwreck.[5]

Margaret Fuller's primary importance in American history derived from her contributions to the movement for women's rights. Elizabeth Cady Stanton said that when Fuller organized her discussion groups, called "Conversations," in Boston she became one of the first people to engage women in philosophical discussions. "These conversations . . . were in reality a vindication of woman's right to think," said Stanton. Fuller's most important contribution, *Woman in the Nineteenth Century,* derived from an essay, "The Great Lawsuit," which first appeared in the *Dial.* In both pieces she argued that women should have the same rights and opportunities as men. Women have the same intellectual capacity as men, should exercise that capacity, and could do physically demanding work, she said.[6]

Fuller's fame also grew from the outstanding literary criticism she wrote at the *Tribune.* The high quality of the literary essays comes from two factors. First, she based her writing on a carefully thought-out critical philosophy. Second, she used European, particularly Continental, works to argue the possibility of creating a national literature for Americans. Fuller reviewed books at a time when the first real geniuses had begun to publish in the nascent field of American literature. Fuller reviewed new works by Herman Melville, Edgar Allan Poe, Henry Wadsworth Longfellow, and Nathaniel Hawthorne. She also wrote critical essays on prominent European writers including Robert Browning, Honoré de Balzac, Alexandre Dumas, Johann Goethe, Percy Bysshe Shelley, Benjamin Disraeli, Thomas Carlyle, and Charles Dickens. Lurton Ingersoll credited her with introducing Americans to George Sand. Of course, she also critiqued much more pedestrian works like J. Stanley Grimes's *Etherology; or, the Philosophy of Mesmerism and Phrenology*.[7]

"What Did She Do?"

Although many scholars have written Fuller biographies and even more have examined her literary criticism, very few have discussed her career as a journalist.[8] When scholars have looked at Fuller's New York work, they have paid far too much attention to her personal life. Almost every biography has devoted most of its New York space to a description of her romance with James Nathan. All the attention to Nathan may have come about because Fuller's love letters to him form the bulk of her surviving correspondence from that period.[9]

The other major focus of scholarship on the New York period has been the personal relationship between Margaret Fuller and Horace Greeley. Fuller lived at the home of Molly and Horace Greeley during her first year in New York. Without a doubt, the editor and his book reviewers were close, but scholars looking at Greeley and Fuller have asked, Just how close? Greeley biographer William Harlan Hale, for instance, noted the editor's unhappy marriage and his close friendship with Fuller, but concluded they were not sexually intimate; however, Hale reached this conclusion while titling his chapter on Fuller "Lover." Some Fuller scholars have even hinted on very little evidence that Greeley fired her as a foreign correspondent, perhaps out of jealousy, when he learned of her involvement with Ossoli.[10]

In a 1986 poem Amy Clampitt asked the modern question about Fuller, "What did she do?" Clampitt's poem described Fuller's Italian years and then contrasted the reality with a flippant summary of Fuller's life. What Margaret Fuller did was journalism, but scholars have usually described Fuller's duties at the *Tribune* only in scanty one-line asides. William Harlan Hale, for instance, summarized them in one sentence, "She conducted a book column whose critical standards and style stood well above any other in America," then he dropped the subject. While scholars have happily pursued the possibility of scandal, they have ignored the important business collaboration that helped create one of America's great newspapers.[11]

About This Book

Here I draw on new primary sources to argue with the received history that Margaret Fuller did not work very hard. Most Fuller biographers have reported this charge as fact because Horace Greeley repeatedly claimed that Fuller failed to work diligently. However, he made similar statements about almost everyone who worked for him.

I also argue that Fuller edited the literary section of the newspaper, doing much more work than just writing the three columns a week which most biographers have described as her total work output. I base my belief on two quotations from the *Tribune* placing Fuller "in charge of the literary department" and a comparison of the literary content of the newspaper with the rest of the publication. This information does not exist elsewhere in the Fuller literature.

Since this information about Fuller's work life comes from the *New York Tribune* and documents concerning its editor, Horace Greeley and his newspaper receive almost as much space here as does Margaret Fuller herself. A better understanding of Fuller's journalism can come through knowledge of her editor and the publication in which her writing appeared. Fuller herself left little information about her life as a journalist. Her letters from 1844 to 1846 dealt mainly with friendship and familial matters while her essays contained only the barest of references to the work of doing journalism.

This book draws its inspiration from a genre of photography called the environmental portrait. Instead of framing a picture close-up on the subject's face, the photographer moves back. The picture includes the subject's cluttered desk, coat rack with coat, pictures on the wall, books, mementos, potted plants—everything in the subject's office. In an environmental portrait a photographer trades the ability to reveal a person's face in detail for the opportunity to portray aspects of the subject's surroundings. This work presents an environmental portrait of what Margaret Fuller called her "business life" at the *New York Tribune*.[12] This book does not give a fully rounded biography of Fuller's two years in New York. Instead, it provides a contextualization. It analyzes her work environment to bring Fuller herself into sharper focus.

In the first half of this book, I focus on two years of a great newspaper rather than on Fuller's personal life. This section describes the *New York Tribune* from 1844 to 1846, its editorial positions, economic health, competition, circulation, and staff. I assess Fuller's value to the newspaper as an employee and describe the major news stories the *Tribune* covered during her time there. This section looks at Fuller's salary, byline, and work space and outlines the two distinct versions of Fuller's public image that originated among her contemporaries.

The second half of the book contains a selection of Fuller's essays on social conditions in New York City from 1844 to 1846. Many editions of Fuller's work have appeared, including four nineteenth-century and four twentieth-century volumes. The twentieth-century books concentrated on publishing Fuller's important work as a critic of American literature and included only the occasional piece of reporting. This is the first book to focus on Fuller's journalism.[13]

This book includes many articles never before reprinted in full from the *New York Tribune*. To avoid redundancy, I have included only twelve articles that have appeared in other twentieth-century volumes. Another eight were reprinted in the nineteenth century.[14] Some of the wording in the essays included here varies slightly from that which has appeared in other reprints. I have taken the text directly from the daily editions of the *New York Tribune*. I have preserved nineteenth-century spellings, but I have corrected obvious typographical errors such as the ending of a sentence with a comma.

The Great Moral Organ

The *New York Tribune* was THE major American newspaper throughout much of the second half of the nineteenth century. When noted British war correspondent E. L. Godkin immigrated to the United States in the late 1850s, he found the *Tribune* established at the height of its influence and reputation. He said that "farmers in New England and in the Western Reserve" adored Greeley and "believed he wrote every word of the *Tribune,* not excepting the advertisements." Godkin's contemporary, Beman Brockway, described the *Tribune* he worked for in the 1850s as having "an influence such as no other paper has ever wielded in this country. Its earnest words went down to the popular heart, producing an impression that forced people to think and act."[15]

The weekly edition earned the *Tribune* its national fame and influence by functioning like a news magazine today and bringing national news to rural subscribers. Greeley did the "thinking & theory" for the people in the West, Ralph Waldo Emerson wrote to Thomas Carlyle in 1854, but readers did not seek out the *Tribune* for the thoroughness of its news gathering. Emerson said westerners saw the editor as "the right spiritual Father of this region." They wanted the essays on philosophy that Greeley ran in his paper, making it a forum for all thought on the important issues of his day. In 1873 one of the first journalism historians, Frederic Hudson, noted, "The *Tribune* has always been remarkable for its peculiar penchant for isms of all sorts." Many writers have romanticized the *Tribune*. For instance, one of Greeley's first biographers, Lurton Ingersoll, wrote in 1873: "Wherever humanity struggled against oppression; wherever a contest was being waged for freedom, for labour, for progress, . . . the *New York Tribune* was sure to have its representative."[16]

History has remembered this newspaper, at the height of its fame, but in the 1840s the *Tribune* was still struggling for a footing. James Parton, writing in 1855, called 1845–47 "the fighting years of the *New York Tribune*. If it was not at war with all the world, all the world seemed to be at war with it." For instance, editors in the 1840s hired marksmen to shoot down pigeons carrying messages for rival newspapers. Shortly after the *Tribune* began publication in 1841, Greeley had to defend his delivery people from assaults by employees of the rival *Sun*.[17]

Fuller scholars have assumed she worked for Horace Greeley when his paper had attained national prominence,[18] but a look at the circulation, the size of the staff, and the size of the newspaper itself shows a much smaller and less influential *Tribune*.

Margaret Fuller was hired in 1844 to work for a young newspaper. Greeley had begun the *Tribune* in April 1841 at the urging of politicians to present a Whig party viewpoint for working-class readers. A penny paper meant to circulate through street sales rather than through subscriptions, the *Tribune* had an initial press run of 5,000 copies but only 600 subscribers. The paper met with quick success. By the winter of 1842 the paper had settled into a circulation of 10,000 daily. The weekly edition, begun September 18, 1841, had a circulation of 13,000. In 1842 the *Tribune* was one of twenty-seven newspapers and 250 printing offices in New York City. These twenty-seven newspapers had a combined circulation of 131,200 with the 1.5 cent *Tribune* ranking third behind the 1 cent *Sun*'s 20,000 circulation and the 2 cent *Herald*'s 15,000.[19]

Twenty-Eight Thousand Readers

Historians have difficulty determining the accuracy of newspaper circulation figures because publishers can inflate their numbers. For the mid 1840s, though, a reasonably accurate statement existed. In 1847 the editors of the *Herald* and the *Tribune,* in a dispute about the accuracy of their circulation claims, hired a neutral auditor, who verified his audit using such measures as each newspaper's consumption of paper over a four-week period. The conclusion of the auditor: The *Tribune* in 1847 had a total circulation of 28,115: 11,455 daily, 15,700 weekly, and 960 semiweekly. The *Herald*'s circulation totaled 28,946: 16,711 daily, 11,455 weekly, and

780 for a presidential edition. Historian Frederic Hudson noted the high weekly circulation revealed by this audit may have pushed Greeley to promote his national weekly edition.[20]

Fuller informed her brother in 1845 that she addressed 50,000 readers. The paper actually had little more than half that circulation. Of course, two readers per printed copy of the newspaper would explain this figure. Perhaps this is how Greeley inflated his circulation claims. Ralph Waldo Emerson offered a more accurate estimate of the *Tribune*'s circulation in an 1846 letter to Thomas Carlyle, in which he reported the newspaper's circulation at about 30,000.

In March 1845, Fuller described the *Tribune* to an English friend as "a journal as widely circulated as any in this country." Although this is technically true, a person reading this sentence from the vantage point of history, knowing what the *Tribune* became, might tend to give the newspaper even more importance than it had in 1845. The *Tribune* competed that year with two other leading newspapers for dominance in America's largest city and therefore circulated as widely as any in the country.[21] Ten years later the *Tribune* had grown into THE most important publication in the country, and its strong national influence endured for more than thirty years. The *Tribune* Margaret Fuller worked for, though important in New York City, was a mere seedling compared to the enormous tree it became.

From 1844 to 1846 the paper consisted of four pages with copy set seven columns wide, but by the mid 1850s the newspaper regularly ran eight pages. By 1852 the *Tribune* claimed an "aggregate circulation" of 83,000—triple its circulation in 1847—and offered special subscription rates for readers in Europe and California. The weekly edition had 200,000 readers, although in New York City the *Tribune* never achieved a dominating circulation.[22]

Margaret Fuller worked at the *Tribune* when it began its transition to prosperity. After a fire destroyed its original office in 1845, the newspaper moved to a five-story brick building where it remained until 1873. In 1846 the newspaper was worth $100,000 with a yearly profit of $30,000. Success came partially from ignoring grand moral principles in the sale of advertising. Although Greeley supported the temperance movement, his newspaper contained many advertisements for liquor and patent medicines.[23]

The *Tribune*'s Staff

The *Tribune* became famous because Horace Greeley attracted and trained an exceptionally talented staff. One *Tribune* writer, John Russell Young, called his coworkers "resolute, brilliant, capable, irresponsible, intolerant—not above setting things on fire for the fun of seeing them burn."

E. L. Godkin recalled that "admission to the columns of the *Tribune* almost gave the young writer a patent of literary nobility."

Greeley staffed his paper with intellectuals including many transcendentalists who, like Margaret Fuller, had Brook Farm connections: George William Curtis, William Fry, George Ripley, and Charles Anderson Dana.[24] Here he took a risk. The *National Cyclopedia* said the editors of the transcendentalist *Dial* had a reputation for being "zanies, Bedlamites, and considerably madder than the Mormons."[25]

Beman Brockway, a *Tribune* staffer from 1853 to 1855, described the editorial staff in 1854 as a managing editor, ten associate editors, and forty reporters and correspondents. In 1867–68 the newspaper had a city-side editorial staff of seventeen including one city editor, two assistant city editors, and fourteen reporters. In 1866 the *Tribune* grossed more than $900,000 and had a payroll of $100,000 for writers and editors. By 1871 it ranked among the largest newspapers in the world, with 400 to 500 employees and weekly production costs of $20,000.[26]

For fifteen years Charles Anderson Dana was the much celebrated city editor of the *Tribune*. Lurton Ingersoll called him "a man of liberal culture, enthusiastic nature, untiring energy; a brilliant, dashing writer upon a great variety of topics; with a fine genius for journalism." Before joining the paper in 1846, Dana worked as general instructor and managing trustee at Brook Farm; he later became assistant secretary of war under Edwin Stanton. He was succeeded at the *Tribune* by Sidney Howard Gay, John Russell Young, and Whitelaw Reid.[27]

Another well-known writer from the early years, agriculture editor Solon Robinson, helped create the *Tribune*'s nationwide success among rural readers. He joined the paper in 1852.[28]

Travel writer Bayard Taylor began working for the *Tribune* in 1844 as a foreign correspondent, paid by the article. With $144 in cash he sailed to Europe July 1, 1844, on the promise that the *Tribune* might run some of his letters. He published his first book of travel writing, *Views Afoot,* in 1846, and in 1848 joined the *Tribune* full time.[29]

George Ripley succeeded Fuller as book editor in 1849. His thirty-one influential years at the *Tribune* have tended to overshadow Fuller's literary work. Many have dubbed him the father of literary criticism. Ripley may deserve this title because he wrote book reviews of high quality for America's most influential newspaper at the height of its importance and influence, but Margaret Fuller had set the standard. Ripley and Fuller were old friends: he had hosted one of her Boston Conversation series in his home and worked as the *Dial*'s business manager when she was its editor. Fuller's work at the *Tribune* may have influenced the way Ripley chose to do book reviews when he became literary editor.[30]

Another newspaper great, Henry J. Raymond, preceded Fuller as literary editor and general news reporter at the *Tribune,* beginning in 1841 at the age of twenty. Greeley praised Raymond's work: "I never found another person, barely of age and just from his studies, who evinced so signal and such versatile ability in journalism as he did." In 1843 Greeley and Raymond fought over money, and Raymond went to the *Courier and Enquirer,* where he worked during Fuller's years in New York. In 1850 he founded the *New York Times.*[31]

Raymond, Ripley, Taylor, Robinson, and Dana were giants from the early days of the *Tribune,* but none of them worked with Fuller.

Margaret Fuller's Coworkers

The *Tribune* eventually had a large and highly respected staff of writers, but from 1844 to 1846 Greeley operated the newspaper with an editorial staff of only four people. A two-part *Tribune* article in April 1845 described their duties. An assistant editor collected "commercial transactions, Sales of Stocks, City Intelligence, &c." "In the department of General Literature and Criticism, we have secured assistance of the highest order." Two reporters covered "the proceedings of the various Courts of our City . . . noting every thing deemed interesting to our readers." Greeley also hired correspondents as needed to cover stories in other cities, including Washington, D.C. Based on this report then, the staff of the *Tribune* consisted of a commercial editor, a literary editor, and two local reporters, plus correspondents filing occasional articles from out of town.[32]

One can with some confidence name Fuller's editorial coworkers at the *Tribune.* Assistant editor George Snow wrote financial news for the *Tribune* for twenty-two years starting in 1843 or earlier, and when Greeley incorporated the *Tribune,* Snow became a major stockholder. Very little information is available about him.[33]

City reporter Oliver Johnson was the *Tribune*'s Boston correspondent from 1842 to 1844. In his early thirties, Johnson then worked as Greeley's assistant from 1844 to 1846 or 1848. In 1870 Johnson returned to work for Greeley, editing the weekly *Tribune* for two years. Philosophically in sympathy with Fuller, Johnson had a long career as a reformer. He believed in equal rights for women and, as an early backer of abolitionist William Lloyd Garrison, Johnson advocated full participation of women in anti-slavery societies as early as 1838.[34]

William Ellery Channing, Fuller's brother-in-law, may have been the second reporter mentioned in the April 1845 article. A poet, Channing was a member of Emerson's transcendentalist circle. When Greeley hired Fuller, she persuaded him to hire Channing as well. When Channing arrived, Greeley gave him instructions, then went on vacation. Emerson commented that Channing had a "very tender & delicate nature as poets are wont to be" and disliked being on his own in the newspaper office. At first, Channing did an acceptable job. In a letter dated January 9, 1845, Fuller reported that "both Mr. Greeley and Mr. Johnson have spoken of Ellery as doing well in the office." Channing didn't like clipping articles from exchange papers and running errands, and he either quit or was fired in March or April 1845. At any rate, he worked only briefly at the *Tribune*. If Channing worked on the paper at the time of the April 15, 1845, publication of the prospectus that described the newspaper's staff, he was making his final contribution.[35]

Business manager Thomas McElrath created the newspaper's financial success in the 1840s. According to Greeley, the *Tribune* needed much "ready money for a time, . . . but early in the fall a kind of providence brought T. McElrath to propose a partnership." McElrath kept to the business side and away from editorial policy. During their ten-year partnership, Greeley recalled, McElrath "never once even indicated that my anti-Slavery, anti-Hanging, Socialist, and other frequent aberrations from the straight and narrow path of Whig partisanship, were injurious to our common interest." Greeley may have dominated the paper's personality, but McElrath himself made an impression. "He was a strikingly handsome man, with a dignified and commanding presence; considerate, kindly and just; genial and sympathetic in social intercourse; interested and interesting," reads his entry in the *National Cyclopedia*. A bank director and an alderman for the third ward in New York City, McElrath was deeply religious, well read, and a figure in society.[36]

From 1844 to 1846, then, the *New York Tribune,* still a small newspaper far from the national stature it later attained, did rate as one of three leading newspapers in New York City. Horace Greeley had a staff of only four editorial employees: Margaret Fuller, in charge of the literary department; Oliver Johnson, assistant editor; George Snow, financial editor; and one other reporter, perhaps William Ellery Channing. None of the other giants from the early days of the *Tribune* worked there during Fuller's tenure, but the mechanisms for the *Tribune*'s great future had gone into place. The *Tribune* published its weekly national edition, although not at this time to a vast audience, but the newspaper had begun to prosper.

2
A Journalist at the *Tribune,*
1844–1846

Historians have underestimated Margaret Fuller's contribution to the day-to-day production of the *New York Tribune.* For example, historian Bernard Weisberger called her an "occasional contributor," while Glyndon Garlock Van Deusen said she "wrote brilliantly, if somewhat scantily, for the *Tribune.*" Contemporaries did not give specific descriptions of Fuller's duties at the newspaper. Edgar Allan Poe said she worked as "assistant editor of the New York 'Tribune,' or rather a salaried contributor to that journal, for which she has furnished a great variety of matter, chiefly notices of new books." Ralph Waldo Emerson described Fuller as a "critic of all new books, critic of the drama, of music, & good arts in New York." In March 1845, Fuller described her job as "in care of the literary department of the N.Y. Tribune."[1]

Fuller's starred articles suggest that her writing duties varied. She wrote literary criticism, but in addition she did music reviews, essays on questions of philanthropy, and translations from the foreign press. Although she generally wrote in-depth essays, when she did translations she dealt with more mundane topics. For instance, one translation described the dedication of a memorial to German writer Johann Goethe. "Some Items of Foreign Gossip" reported a famine in Hungary, a London exhibit of pickpockets' tools, and the tale of a Parisian lady who masqueraded as a man so that she could participate in "high play."[2]

It is unclear whether she worked as a full-time employee or as an occasional contributor. Parton, in 1855, reported that Fuller wrote three articles a week. Most scholars have followed Parton's lead and described Fuller's contribution to the *Tribune* as her 250 bylined articles, yet a look at the *Tribune* as a whole from 1844 to 1846 would suggest that Fuller did much more than contribute occasional pieces. For instance, Parton did not say, and no one else has pointed out, that the *Tribune* from 1844 to 1846 was a very small newspaper. On the days when Fuller's long pieces appeared, Fuller was, by herself, providing at least one quarter of the editorial copy in that edition.[3]

The Literary Department

The *Tribune* ran four pages in each edition, and each seven-column page contained ads and editorial material. Fuller's copy usually began at the top of the first column on the front page and filled almost all the editorial space (three and often four columns of type). Advertising filled approximately 50 percent of each edition, including 3 to 4.5 columns on the front page. Page 2 carried half a column in the bottom right corner. On pages 3 and 4, however, five of the seven columns ran to advertising.

Fuller's articles alone, then, occupied a substantial part of the newspaper, and she contributed more than just the starred essays. Her work was labeled "in care of the literary department." The content of the *Tribune* during Fuller's twenty months in residence showed a clear attempt on Horace Greeley's part to departmentalize his publication. Literature, on page 1, was one department.

Page 2 featured Greeley's views on Whig party politics. Page 2 usually led off in the upper left corner with what twentieth-century newspaper readers would call an editorial by the publisher. Besides political news, page 2 contained reports on state legislatures and the U.S. Congress plus reprints of news stories from other newspapers. Court reports, police calls, coroner's calls, marriages, deaths, and financial news dominated page 3. Usually page 4 contained one short article or poem in the upper left column. On February 4, 1845, page 4 of the *Tribune* reprinted "The Raven" by Edgar Allan Poe.

Greeley seems to have assumed people read page 2 before they read page 1. Routinely page 2 carried a small box in the upper left corner labeled "Today's Outside." This box listed the articles published on pages 1 and 4 and probably had the same goal as front-page boxes in twentieth-century newspapers that list stories inside the newspaper. Today editors want people to read more than page 1. Greeley evidently wanted people to read more than pages 2 and 3. The importance of page 2 placement in 1844 shows in the March 4, 1845, issue. Page 1 carried a five-column essay by Margaret Fuller: "English Writers Little Known Here. Milnes . . . Landor . . . Julius Hare." Meanwhile, page 2 reported the inauguration of President James K. Polk.

Page 1, the intellectual showcase of the paper, featured Fuller's essays plus foreign news, travel writing, and essays on social issues. Occasionally political or city news would make it onto the front page but only rarely. Fuller's starred pieces ran in two or three of the six issues a week. With her work, or taking its place, other articles on page 1 discussed either literature or events outside New York City.

During the spring and summer of 1845 the *Tribune* had a peripatetic correspondent bylined C.D.S. On March 1, 1845, C.D.S. appeared on the front page reporting "Things in the South." On April 25 the paper published the first of a series of C.D.S. articles from Havana, Cuba. The May 3 issue features a C.D.S. piece from New Orleans. On June 16 the correspondent reported on a Fourier Association in Northwestern Kentucky. The C.D.S. story on July 12 came from Boston, and on July 29, from Saratoga.[4]

Besides travel writing, page 1 regularly featured European news. The heading "Fifteen Days Later from Europe" or "Seven Days Later from Europe" signaled the docking of a ship carrying European newspapers. When this happened the *Tribune* would devote much of its front page to a synopsis of the contents of these papers. Page 1 also routinely reprinted interesting pieces from other publications, including several short stories by abolitionist Lydia Maria Child. Often the *Tribune* ran complete texts of speeches and articles that addressed Greeley's social causes.

Page 1 was not a haphazard construct. Horace Greeley had a formula for the types of articles that should go there. He outlined this formula in a November 1845 ad announcing plans to begin a new publication with five sections:

> The plan of this paper will combine—
> 1. ORIGINAL LITERATURE—Reviews, Poems, etc.
> 2. SELECT LITERATURE—Tales, Sketches, extracts from new Books, etc.
> 3. MISCELLANY—Letters from Europe and different parts of our Country, Statistics, Anecdotes, &c.
> 4. HINTS ON DOMESTIC ECONOMY—Agriculture, Inventions, Recipes, &c.
> 5. GENERAL INTELLIGENCE—Foreign and Domestic, including Political events, Proceedings of Congress &c, &c.

The ad called the new publication a family newspaper "from which Political essays and all matter of a partisan character will be carefully excluded." This ad actually described the composition of the *Tribune*'s front page, as edited by Margaret Fuller.[5] Partisan political news plus local New York City news and financial news ran on pages 2 and 3. The *Tribune*'s literary department, then, occupied a substantial amount of space, and the editor saw this department as important to the total editorial mix.

The News in the *Tribune*

From the newspaper's inception, Horace Greeley planned to take a reform stance. In the prospectus for the *Tribune* Greeley said he intended to "advance the interests of the people, and to promote their Moral, Political and Social well-being." Greeley favored Fourieristic socialism and labor unions, wanted to ban the sale of liquor, and campaigned for the emancipation of slaves. He had a "deep desire to improve the lot of the poor, the unemployed, the suffering and the degraded," said historian Luther Mott.[6]

Greeley began the *Tribune* in April 1841 at the urging of Whig politicians to present the Whig viewpoint to working-class readers. Whig politics dominated page 2 of the newspaper. For example, on December 16, 1844, a 450-word editorial urged Whigs in New York to attend ward caucuses that evening to vote for delegates to the General Assembly.[7]

Because a great deal of information has already been written on the *Tribune*'s reform ideas, its positions on national issues, and its devotion to Whig politics, to avoid redundancy that information does not appear here, but a description of the major news covered by the *Tribune* outside Fuller's columns could help place her essays in context.

The copy in the *Tribune* from 1844 to 1846 showed a newspaper actively involved with both national and local issues. Both of Greeley's major interests, the Whig party and politically liberal idealism, appeared in his coverage of THE major news story during Margaret Fuller's time at the newspaper, the war with Mexico over the annexation of Texas by the United States.

"The Guilt of Wholesale Slaughter"

In 1836 Americans in Texas had declared independence from Mexico and fought the Battle of the Alamo. Just after Margaret Fuller's arrival at the *Tribune* in December 1844, the United States officially annexed Texas, and in May 1846 the United States and Mexico began a war that lasted until 1848. In article after article, the *Tribune* adamantly opposed the annexation of Texas and as adamantly opposed the war itself. In December 1844 in an editorial entitled "The Texas Iniquity," the *Tribune* objected to saber rattling by the U.S. government. It described a government "bent on picking a quarrel with Mexico, on any grounds or on no grounds. Such a string of unjust fault finding we never before read." When war arrived, the newspaper warned, "People of the United States! your Rulers are precipitating you into a fathomless abyss of crime and calamity! . . . Awake and arrest the work of butchery ere it shall be too late to preserve your souls from the guilt of wholesale slaughter!"[8]

The *Tribune* hated the annexation of Texas and the war partly for political reasons. Greeley had campaigned vigorously for Henry Clay, the Whig candidate who lost the 1844 presidential election. The editor disliked the Democratic victor, James K. Polk. He even accused the Democrats of using ballot fraud in Louisiana to throw the election to Polk. The *Tribune* lamented what Greeley saw as the president's irresponsibility. In July 1845, the *Tribune* charged, "President Polk is now pouring the troops of the United States into Texas, at a season when the lower part of that country is most unhealthy and when its Vice President has just died of fever." The *Tribune* also hated the war for idealistic reasons. The abolitionist *Tribune* did not want Texas, where slavery was legal, admitted to the Union. Commenting on the new state's constitution, the *Tribune* mourned that slavery had become the "fundamental, irrepealable law of a region larger than Italy, never yet trodden by a Slave."[9]

In 1845 and 1846, President Polk also considered war with Great Britain over the Oregon Territory. In November 1845, the *Tribune* saw no reason to go to war "over the comparatively valueless territory of Oregon." A month later, the newspaper counseled, "There are yet many ways in that Justice may be obtained, War avoided—Wo to those who shall disregard these and plunge two mighty nations in horrible carnage and desolating crime!" On June 11, 1846, the *Tribune* reported with great relief a treaty negotiated with Great Britain to solve the Oregon problem.[10]

The United States emerged from these two foreign controversies with the land that would become most of the Southwestern states and the states of California, Oregon, and Washington, but the expansion of the United States caused pain. A description published in the *Tribune* of a skirmish with American Indians in Florida contained in an excerpt from a book, *Sketches of the Florida War,* which chills the twentieth-century reader: "The Indians had not escaped entirely unscathed, for five of their warriors lay stretched upon the field, and the tracks of the fugitives were marked with blood, while one young girl, wounded mortally by some random shot, lay weltering in agony. Tears filled every eye, as she uttered probably the only English words she knew—'me sick!'"[11]

Hints of a future conflict also appear in the *Tribune* between 1844 and 1846. The Civil War was sixteen years in the future, but the seeds of that war had begun sprouting. For instance, the December 10, 1844, issue contained a story about a dispute between the states of Massachusetts and South Carolina about African-American sailors. The state of Massachusetts had protested a South Carolina law under which the *Tribune* said, "Colored Seamen of Free States, not charged with or suspected of any crime, are imprisoned on arriving within these States, and kept in jail until this vessel is ready to sail, when they are liberated only on the payments of costs." The *Tribune* protested the expulsion of Massachusetts negotiator Samuel Hoar from the city of Charleston: "Is slavery not merely paramount but the only law in the country? Is there any other State in the Union but South Carolina?"[12]

The slavery issue came up regularly. For instance, one article pointed out the hypocrisy of a preacher who attacked former president John Tyler for holding dances at the White House. The newspaper commented sarcastically, "The Rev. gentleman must have been hard run for a subject, but he could not probably have been induced by any consideration to say a word against those democratic trifles[,] the slave pens in the Federal District." In another 1846 article, freed slave Frederick Douglass described his speaking tour of Great Britain. Douglass reported enthusiastic crowds for his speeches and much "warm and generous cooperation" from the English. He said this reception "contrasted so strongly with my long and bitter experience in the United States, that I look with wonder and amazement on the transition."[13]

Anti-Rent Violence

All these national issues—slavery, Oregon, and Texas—look to the future of the United States, but the major regional news in the *Tribune* from 1844 to 1846 involved an issue from the American Revolution—the anti-rent controversy.

In 1844 hereditary landlords still owned large tracts of land ranging from 1,000 to 100,000 acres in upstate New York. Although their ancestors had received royal land grants from the British crown before the Revolutionary War, the landlords did not actually work their land. Instead, many small families rented parcels and farmed them. Some renters had farmed the same land for generations. Their ancestors had felled the forest and cleared the land for farming in the first place. In the early 1840s hereditary landlords, citing nonpayment of rent, had begun forcing farmers from land their families had worked for decades.[14]

Upstate New York farmers, who had decided to fight eviction, formed anti-rent associations and began vigilante action. In early 1845, the *Tribune* reported, American Indians supposedly threatened to kidnap a woman, but it turned out the would-be kidnappers were really anti-renters who had dressed up as Indians. From this early play-acting, the anti-rent troubles led to the murder of a sheriff who had helped with forcible evictions. The *Tribune* ran many articles and letters to the editor about anti-rent meetings and anti-rent violence.

In the winter of 1845, the *Tribune* sided with the landlords. They owned the property. Under law, they had the right to collect rent, argued the newspaper. Besides, the *Tribune* disapproved of the anti-renters' violence. By September, the newspaper was changing its position. The "Anti-Rent Controversy" in the newspaper's headlines of 1845 became in 1846

"Manorial Tenure." The *Tribune* began expressing sympathy for people who had developed and farmed the same land for generations. The *Tribune* explained the renters' plight. "On the side of some ridge or mountain, in the most rugged and sterile of the inhabited portions of our State, lives a poor farmer . . . in the house built by his father and on the farm which he inherited from his father—such farm having been first taken on a perpetual lease when entirely wild by some ancestor of the family." The newspaper explained the anti-renters' argument that "the laws which give some men a thousand times as much land as they can use and thus deprive millions of any at all, are invalid."[15]

In 1846, New York's governor and legislature found a solution to land reform. New legislation converted rental contracts into mortgage contracts upon the death of the manor owner. The landlord's heirs would still derive income from the land, but the income come from mortgage payments from farmers who could now buy their family land.[16]

"Utterly Sad and Pitiful"

Three big news stories—Texas, Oregon, and anti-rent—dominated the *Tribune* during Fuller's time, but fire dominated the ongoing news about New York City. Routinely the *Tribune* carried articles about fire consuming entire city blocks.

Eyewitness accounts give a firsthand feel for the tragedy of fire. On June 2, 1845, the *Tribune* reported a fire that destroyed one hundred buildings, killed twenty-five horses, and left four hundred families homeless. A reporter, who spent two hours walking among the ruins interviewing people, wrote, "Nothing can be conceived so utterly sad and pitiful as the condition of these three thousand men, women and children, . . . reduced to absolute want and hunger—shelterless and many of them unclad and with only a blanket about their shoulders. They are sitting weeping and starving under the fences and in the vacant lots—crowded into cow-pens and out-houses—the middle-lifed, the young, the decrepid aged, the helpless infant—what a scene!" This tragedy also shows that violent revenge by former employees did not begin in the late twentieth century. A boy who had recently lost his job started this fire in the stables where he had worked.[17] Another stable fire caused the *Tribune* less grief. This one destroyed nine buildings including "the notorious den of Pete Williams." The *Tribune* rejoiced to see the dive "completely cleaned out—a process that nothing short of fire could have ever accomplished."[18]

Tribulations of the *Tribune*

The *Tribune* itself made major fire news on February 6, 1845, when the newspaper's offices burned to the ground. A clerk who slept on the counter at night found the early morning fire, which had spread from a heating stove. A blizzard made the streets impassable for fire fighters, and the editor lost all his "own manuscripts, correspondence, and collection of valuable books, some manuscripts belonging to friends."[19]

Besides fire, the *Tribune* also fought two libel suits filed by James Fenimore Cooper, author of *Last of the Mohicans*. Horace Greeley's *Tribune* was one of several American newspapers the famous novelist sued for libel after the 1838 publication of *Home as Found*. Originally, Cooper objected to the insulting language newspapers used to review his novel. The two lawsuits he filed in 1842 and 1843 against Greeley objected to satirical language in *Tribune* commentaries on the other libel suits. Greeley, representing himself, lost the first lawsuit and received a judgment of $200. Then Cooper sued again over the jesting coverage Greeley gave his own trial.[20]

A third crisis for the *Tribune* came in 1846, when the U.S. House of Representatives banned all *Tribune* reporters and correspondents from covering Congress because one congressman, a Mr. Sawyer, disliked a story about the way he ate his lunch on the floor of the House. According to a correspondent, Sawyer wiped his greasy fingers on his coattails and through his hair. The Congress did not intimidate the *Tribune*. Said an editorial, "We shall continue to have regular reports, as heretofore, full, fair and (when Justice shall require it) caustic."[21]

Everyday Life

The newspaper from 1844 to 1846 also ran hundreds of little articles that give a fascinating peek at life in the United States. Two stories showed the hazards of New York streets. In one article, a bullterrier was the problem. After a man kicked it, the dog "instantly seized the gentleman's leg, and maintained his grip with a tenacity that for a time defied all attempts to loose it. . . . Finally the gentleman thrust his hand into his pocket, pulled out a snuff box and emptied the contents into the eyes and nose of the dog. The effect was miraculous." Another article encouraged people not to drop peach skins or orange peels on city streets. The newspaper told of a young man who had been rushed to a surgeon after slipping and falling. "The young husband and father had died under a surgical operation— a victim to a piece of orange-peel, thoughtlessly thrown upon the sidewalk."[22]

Another article spoke to the nature of justice in the 1840s. The *Tribune* reported, "Cornelius Driscoll was tried for keeping a disorderly house, at No. 31 Orange street, the resort of the vicious and vile of both sexes, where drinking, rioting, fighting, and other immoral practices were permitted daily and nightly, and even on the Sabbath." Driscoll was found guilty, but "the prisoner in his defence said he had given $10 to officer Cochrane, $10 to officer Sitler, and $10 to Henry Jenkins to settle this matter and not to appear against him on trial, but to have the affair arranged." The judge said he would look into Driscoll's charges before passing sentence.[23]

An article in praise of hats addressed standards for men's clothing. The article contained an earnest attack on "that effeminate invention, the umbrella. . . . This utensil is truly a disgrace to the manhood of the times; and its existence, by allowing people to dispense with warm cloaks and other anti-rain appliances, has caused more disease, in letting them catch cold, than anything else we know of. . . . Umbrellas are only fit for men-milliners, Cockney travelers, and women."[24]

Page 3 reported financial material similar to the inside pages of today's *Wall Street Journal*. For example, on January 6, 1845, page 3 listed exchange rates for foreign currency, exports from the port of New York, and a financial statement of the revenues and expenditures of the State of Massachusetts for the year 1844. It included market reports: "COTTON.—The Market continues rather active, and the sales today are 1,200 bales at steady prices, mostly for shipment. The sales of the week . . . Friday evening were 5,150 bales, at Upland and Florida." Another commodity report noted: "FEATHERS.—The stock of Live Geese is large, and the market is dull. We notice sales of 2,000 lbs. prime Western at 30 cents, and 2,500 lbs. fair 28 1/2, cash."

"It Is Universally Believed"

A twentieth-century reader, who knows how history turned out, sometimes longs to shout advice to these nineteenth-century citizens. For example, one article praised experiments using wooden pavement on Broadway. "The advantages of wooden pavements are that carriages create less noise in passing over them, and their first cost is much less than granite blocks," said the article. In the experiment, the wood "cracked" and "decayed." Urging that the experiments with wood be continued, the author argued the wood deteriorated because the experimenters had failed to lay down a good substratum to carry away water.[25]

From the point of view of history, a more frighteningly erroneous article ran on June 24, 1845. The newspaper announced a speech by Capt.

Lansford W. Hastings, who was in New York City recruiting people to join a wagon train to the Oregon Territory. He planned to leave Independence, Missouri, on August 1, 1845. According to the *Tribune* reporter, it was "now universally believed to be utterly impossible for emigrants, starting after the month of May, to cross the mountains with any degree of safety. Capt. Hastings, however, having conducted the emigrants of 1842 to Oregon and California, and having thereby acquired a thorough knowledge of both the route and the method of traveling, confidently assures all those who may join him in his contemplated excursion, that he will be able to conduct them, with entire safety either to Oregon or California." The same year Hastings published a book, *Emigrants' Guide to Oregon and California,* used by many emigrant wagon trains. A year later, the Donner Party planned to join Hastings, but his wagon train left before they could rendezvous, so the Donner Party proceeded west using Hastings's book as a guide. They starved in the snows of the Sierra Nevada in October 1846.[26]

Advertising

Large display ads did not run in the *Tribune* of the 1840s. Instead, advertisers used short notices to recommend their wares. Wistar's Balsam of Wild Cherry, a patent medicine made of "wild cherry bark and tar," regularly ran its ad on page 1 just after Margaret Fuller's column. The ad described the product as the "best remedy known to the world for the cure of coughs, colds, asthma, croup, bleeding of the lungs, whooping cough, bronchitis, influenza, shortness of breath, pain and weakness in the breast or side, liver complaint, and the first stages of CONSUMPTION." After this laudatory subhead, the ad went on for three inches of detailed claims about the medicine.[27]

Also with prominent placement on the front page just beneath Wistar's Balsam and therefore next to Fuller's work for several months in late 1844 and early 1845 ran the following:

> LEECHES! LEECHES! LEECHES!
> THE best of SWEDISH LEECHES, large and medium size, imported by G. A. & H. Witte, 38 John street, for sale from this date, AT ONE SHILLING EACH. . . .[28]

Front-page ads were not classified. On December 7, 1844, for instance, an ad announcing that the A. W. Spies & Co. had just received "a large assortment of Gothic and Sandwich Tea Trays in sets" followed a notice of a dividend of 3.5 percent on Howard Insurance Company capital stock. Other front-page ads that day described watches, hats, "reams of newsprinting paper," "wires covered for magnetic machinery," raw silk, a room to let, and Ingoldsby's Black and Blue Reviver, which made "old clothes bright and new." These ads ran about one column by half an inch. They began with a capitalized word or two and then continued in body type.

Classified ads filled half of page 3 and all of page 4. Categories included Dry Goods, Wanted, New Publications, Amusements, Auction Sales, Schools, Real Estate, Medicines, For the North (notices of train and ship schedules), For the South, For the East, For Foreign Ports, Legal, Coal, Boots and Shoes, and Daguerreotypes. The existence of this last classification in 1844 testified to the quick spread of technology. The daguerreotype had become public knowledge in 1839. Five years later, E. White, "upstairs at 178 Broadway," advertised in the *Tribune* that he had a gallery displaying "his splendid collection of Daguerreotype portraits." He also sold "Imported German cameras, also French and American instruments of the very best quality." The cameras came equipped with plates, chemicals, and polishing materials.

The December 21, 1844, edition, on page 4, carried two more ads of interest in publishing history. One advertised reprints of the first edition of the *London Lancet*, "the most Popular Medical Journal in the World." (The *Lancet* is still an extremely influential medical journal.) A second ad announced: "THE BROADWAY JOURNAL THE FIRST NUMBER OF A NEW WEEKLY PAPER" for sale starting in January 1845. (Edgar Allan Poe was one of its literary critics.)

Margaret Fuller's work then coexisted amid war, fire, goose feathers, leeches, and the other items about daily life that run in most daily newspapers.

"Ample and Able Literary Assistance"

Most scholars have described Fuller's job as writing three articles a week to run on page 1 of the newspaper, but published comments in the newspaper suggested Fuller's work "in care" of the literary department was more extensive. Horace Greeley said he could consider starting a second publication because he now had "ample and able Literary assistance"—presumably from Margaret Fuller. Soon after Greeley announced his plans in a November 1845 advertisement, Fuller began preparing to go to Europe. Greeley stopped the ad, and the planned publication never appeared. In another house ad the *Tribune* boasted, "In the Department of Literature and Criticism, we have secured assistance of the highest order." In a third house ad, Greeley praised the assistants who handled each editorial department including the department of literature and criticism. Fuller's letters contained comments that show her importance to the production of the newspaper. Particularly as summer approached, Greeley urged her to produce more work. Without a major contribution from Fuller, she said, he could not go on vacation.[29]

To receive this kind of appreciation, Fuller must have done other work for the *Tribune* beyond writing three starred essays a week. Contemporary descriptions of Fuller's job title said she was in charge of two different categories: criticism and literature. The bylined reviews made clear her contribution in the way of criticism, but the word *literature* usually also appeared in these definitions of her work. The second half of her job was most likely selecting, excerpting, and introducing literature to the *Tribune*'s readers. Fuller wrote the 250 starred pieces in the *New York Tribune,* but the front-page literary section of the *Tribune* during Fuller's tenure contained at least as many more unstarred pieces of a literary nature.

It seems highly likely Fuller wrote or edited/selected much of this unstarred material, including a regular column, "New Publications." This consisted of six to fifteen paragraphs, each describing a new book but offering no analysis. "New Publications" typically ran alongside one of Fuller's starred pieces, typographically designating the book section.

In addition, the *Tribune* regularly published what twentieth-century journalists would call book briefs, 150- to 400-word analyses of books. These would usually stack on top of each other, three or four in a column. Occasionally these book briefs carried a star.

Fuller probably wrote some, but not all, of the unstarred short pieces as well. An example of a series of unstarred book briefs probably written by Fuller appeared on the front page on December 24, 1844. A series of brief essays reviewed different children's books. Internal evidence suggested Fuller's work. A one-paragraph discussion of *Mary Howitt's Picture and Verse Book* (a translation of German stories for children) referred to the reviewer's familiarity with German. Horace Greeley clearly wrote some of these unstarred brief articles. For example, on January 18, 1845, a 500-word review of an Iowa newspaper followed a starred piece. The ideas in the article suggest an author who had given some thought to what the content of a newspaper should be. The *Tribune* also contained longer unsigned essays on books.[30] Fuller may well have written some of these long unbylined essays. Most intriguing of the longer unstarred essays on books were four bylined with "F." These four pieces did not appear in Joel Myerson's descriptive bibliography of Fuller works, but the "F." combined with the fact that they were lengthy book reviews suggests that Fuller wrote them.[31]

The other major assignment most likely done by Fuller was excerpting from longer literary works. Here an editor wrote a brief introduction and transitions between excerpted sections. The editor's work ran in larger type than the excerpted material.[32]

Fuller probably produced another category of unsigned work, translations of articles from non-English language newspapers. Some of her starred pieces were translations from the *Deutsche Schnellpost* and the *Courrier des États-Unis*. Many other unstarred translations from these publications appear on the upper left front page.[33]

At the *Tribune*, then, Fuller did much more than merely contribute literary essays. She edited its literary section. She produced much of the work that appears in the literary department of the newspaper without her star byline. This work included a regular column "New Publications," 500-word book reviews, lengthy essays not previously identified as Fuller's, introductions and transitions in literary excerpts, and translations not previously identified as Fuller's. Add this work to the starred items and it becomes clear that Fuller was, as Greeley called her, an important contributor to the production of the newspaper.

"Friendly Antagonism"

Margaret Fuller and Horace Greeley did not have a totally peaceful working relationship. They were both thirty-three in 1844, but he was a plebeian workaholic while Fuller was a genteel lady with only an intermittent commitment to newspapering. He wrote quickly and efficiently. She wrote slowly and carefully. "Each was dogmatic and opinionative, and neither inclined to admit error or mistake. Each held personal convictions in high reverence, but Miss Fuller was especially disposed to resent any interference with her own methods of thought and action," recalled Charles T. Congdon. Greeley observed, "Fortune seemed to delight in placing us two in relations of friendly antagonism,—or rather, to develop all possible contrasts in our ideas and social habits."[34]

Scholars have described Fuller as a difficult employee and a weak writer. Francis Nicoll Zabriskie labeled her "incapable of incessant or even regular labor." Henry Luther Stoddard said she threw "temperamental sulks." Ishbel Ross took the general view of Fuller as an employee: "She was always late with her copy, suffered from violent headaches and was less adaptable than Mr. Greeley had hoped."[35]

These descriptions stem from several belittling comments Horace Greeley made about Margaret Fuller and her work. He said she had "no capacity for incessant labor" partially because of "headaches and other infirmities." He also argued she wrote far too slowly. "If quantity only were considered, I could write ten columns to her one." Greeley complained Fuller spent far too much time pondering over the books she reviewed. While acknowledging the "rare intellectual wealth and force" of Fuller's work, Greeley complained she too often produced her work "a day after the fair." Sometimes while she sought just the right words, a rival journal beat the *Tribune* into print with an important review. If the competition had already reviewed the book, Greeley argued, "the ablest critique would command no general attention."[36]

"Always at Work"

These potent complaints lose their strength when viewed in context. Horace Greeley's contemporaries saw him as an impatient workaholic. Recalled Beman Brockway, one of his reporters: "He was always at work. He worked because he could not help it." Former *Tribune* war correspondent Junius Browne concurred: "In respect to work he was positively fanatical." Browne credited Greeley's death to overwork.[37]

Greeley differed with the rest of the world on the definition of good, hard work. In 1844, while campaigning for Clay's election as president, Greeley each day filled an average of four newspaper columns, answered twenty letters, gave a speech, and conferred with politicians. Even when he was not part of a political campaign, he regularly worked until 2 or 3 A.M. In a letter to Schuyler Colfax, Greeley reported working into the night. "It is after 11 o'clock at night and I am very heavy with hard work and lack of sleep." Anyone this tired should have gone home to bed, but Greeley wrote that, after he finished this letter, he intended to turn to proofreading the newspaper. In part, the newspaper's printing schedule caused Greeley's late hours. The *Tribune* went to press at midnight. While his assistant editor took a six-week vacation, Greeley complained that his fifteen-hour days gave him "pains through the back and shoulders caused by the excessive work.... This is too hard and I have often been unable to sleep after it." Horace Greeley saw a fifteen-hour workday as too much, but he probably defined the length of a good workday as at least ten hours. That is what the *Tribune* typesetters regarded as a minimum workday. The typesetters' union in New York in 1836 negotiated two standard rates of pay, one for an eleven-hour day and one for a ten-hour day.[38]

Margaret Fuller was often denigrated for her moods, but Greeley was equally volatile. "He had his ups and downs, and the distance between the two extremes was immeasurable," recalled Brockway. Junius Browne saw him as a combination of "sterling manhood" and "unconquered childishness." Ralph Waldo Emerson found Greeley restless and pushy: "I saw my fate in a moment & that I should never content him." Charles Dana

Horace Greeley, c. 1841. Courtesy, Library of Congress.

saw this moodiness stemming from Greeley's intense convictions: "He had that peculiar courage, most precious in a great man, which enables him to adhere to his own line of action despite the excited appeals of friends and the menaces of variable public opinion." Brockway agreed Greeley's convictions caused his irritability. "He thought the world might be reformed in a day—in his day." Brockway recalled a visit to the newspaper by the governor of New York. As the governor talked, Greeley continued to work on his writing. "When he reaches a period, Mr. Greeley stops writing, turns around in his chair, and gives his views [to the governor] in the fewest possible words; and this he does repeatedly during the interview."[39]

Greeley harshly criticized Margaret Fuller, but he was no less kind to the many famous men who worked for him. He called poetry by his great travel writer, Bayard Taylor, "gassy stuff." He complained of H. J. Raymond (who later founded the *New York Times*): "He doesn't feel the grave importance of our vocation." The easygoing George Ripley, who replaced Fuller as book editor, wrote a friend in 1849: "Greeley is a hard case personally, and as coarse, sharp and gritty as a flint."[40]

Horace Greeley, then, was a moody, impatient workaholic taken to making crusty comments to and about everyone including his employees and even the governor of New York. Therefore, one cannot take at face value his observations on anyone's character.

Fuller's Work Effort

Greeley accused Fuller of being undependable, blocked from writing for days at a time, yet Margaret Fuller published an average of three bylined essays a week and wrote, edited, or excerpted at least twice that much copy in a week. As already noted, from examining the *New York Tribune* itself one must conclude she made a substantial contribution to the production of the newspaper. Her section ran daily. Her basic job got done. This does not mean she was a perfectly dependable employee, especially in the eyes of a perfectionist like Horace Greeley.

Fuller did linger over her copy and on at least one occasion this caused her to get scooped. The rival *Courier and Enquirer* beat her to press with a review of a book on capital punishment. Fuller said she had to write this review in "short stages with long intervals of rest and refreshment between" because the idea of capital punishment so repelled her.[41]

Fuller had nowhere near Greeley's dedication to newspapering. From the start she made only a tenuous commitment to the *Tribune.* She planned to work for Greeley for a year and a half and then go to Europe. When she first took the job, she wrote a spate of spirited letters about what she called her "business life." She planned visits to the city's insane asylums and prisons to gather information for articles. After working at the *Tribune* for four or five months, she went through a period of ambivalence. Two things reduced her enthusiasm for her work: preparation of her book, *Woman in the Nineteenth Century,* and a romance with James Nathan. This relative lack of devotion would have irritated the demanding Horace Greeley.[42]

Physical problems did interfere with Fuller's writing. After she had worked barely a month for the *Tribune,* she said her life had become crowded with activities, and she complained of pains in her side and spine. "I am obliged," she said, "to be especially careful not to write too much." Still, Fuller could work very long hours. When rewriting *Woman in the Nineteenth Century,* she reported finishing the manuscript in a marathon day. She took a long early morning walk and then wrote until 9 P.M. Another time, she described working on a piece for the *Tribune* solidly from 11 A.M. to 5 P.M., taking a break for a walk, and then going back to work. Thomas Wentworth Higginson, her first biographer, maintained Fuller did work "very hard in her own way, which was not always Mr. Greeley's method. Her researches into poverty and crime took many of her leisure hours."[43]

Greeley also castigated Fuller for being too slow at the act of composition. Again it is necessary to view this disparagement in the context of Greeley's idea of writing quickly. A fast, efficient writer, Horace Greeley refrained from long pondering and extensive revision. Brockway reported that Greeley wrote his first draft exactly as he "intended it should read when put in type, every comma, semicolon or other mark of punctuation being precisely where he wished it." Greeley normally filled three columns of type with copy he had written by hand on fifteen pages of foolscap[44] a day. Working as an assistant editor for Bennett's *Herald* in 1836 and 1837, Thomas L. Nichols produced a similar amount of copy. He corrected proof and wrote "three newspaper minion[45] columns" a day on "light and lively" topics like social matters and fashion. Three columns of type a day, then, seem to have been the standard work product. Since the *Tribune*'s literature section ran three and often four or five columns a day, Fuller met this standard. In addition, Fuller wrote, for the most part, carefully constructed essays, the kind of writing that takes twice as long to produce. Given the difference in the type of writing, Fuller certainly worked as hard at the *Tribune* as Nichols had worked at the *Herald*.[46]

One must conclude that Margaret Fuller was a hard worker, serious about her writing and devoting much time to it, but she was no Horace Greeley. Her definition of hard work did not meet Greeley's exaggerated standards. He criticized her caustically, just as he reprimanded the other great journalists who worked for him. In one area, Fuller benefited from these criticisms just as others did. She received tutelage in writing from Horace Greeley, himself a fine stylist.

Horace Greeley, Journalism Teacher

Charles Dana described Greeley's writing as "plain, clear, striking. His illustrations were quaint and homely, sometimes even vulgar, but they never failed to tell." Francis Nicoll Zabriskie praised its "directness, its unhalting and unswerving progress from the first sentence to the equally abrupt yet complete close." By all accounts, Greeley was an active and involved editor who would have given Fuller detailed comments on her work. Writers who worked for Greeley described him as a sometimes rough but valued critic. Zabriskie recalled many different friends telling him how they had been picked "from the very dust and door sill of the *Tribune* office in . . . boyhood, and put in the path of self-improvement and advancement in journalism." Commented George William Curtis, "I rejoice that I took my first degree in journalism in such a school and under such a master."[47]

Margaret Fuller studied in that school of journalism. Greeley had criticisms of her writing style.[48] He said he did not at first "prize" Fuller's work at the paper. He saw her writing as always fresh and vigorous, but not always clear, and he speculated that her knowledge of German "seemed to have marred her felicity and readiness of expression in her mother tongue." In the obituary he wrote at Fuller's death, Greeley observed caustically: "Her great thoughts were seldom irradiated by her written language—they were more often clouded and choked by it." In another essay, though, Greeley said at the *Tribune* Fuller developed a style "characterized by a directness, terseness, and practicality, which were wanting in some of her earlier productions."[49]

Fuller's writing improved because at the *Tribune* she developed a sense of audience. Greeley understood this concept of couching one's writing for a specific audience. He called Fuller's essays at the *Dial* "more elaborate and ambitious," but said her *Tribune* work aimed to reach "the great majority of readers." Many of Fuller's letters also show her thinking about her newspaper readers. She acknowledged the need to bend content and style for a specific audience.[50]

"Write Impulsively, but Revise with Great Labor"

One can see Greeley at work as a teacher of journalism in a series of letters he wrote in 1843 and 1844 to H. Hubbard, who was considering a newspaper career. In these letters Greeley described good newspaper writing. In addition, Greeley printed an article in the *Tribune* telling correspondents what kind of writing he wanted from them. In the Hubbard correspondence Greeley acknowledged his role as a teacher of journalism. He saw tough criticism as part of that role. He said he would help Hubbard "with harsh advice if I can do no more."[51]

The key to good writing, according to Horace Greeley, was careful revision. He advised correspondents not to submit their first drafts: "If you send us word that you 'have written in great haste, and have no time to correct,' we shall put your manuscript quietly in the fire." He advised Hubbard, "Write impulsively, rapidly, but revise with great labor and love."[52]

Greeley liked tight writing. He advised Hubbard, "Write slowly, write sparingly; and be sure that every line is such as will tell." He told correspondents:

> When you have written what you have to say, run it over and see if there are not *some* sentences that could be spared without serious injury. If there are, out with them! We are compelled to decline good articles because we cannot make room for them. A half column has ten chances where two columns have one and three columns none.[53]

He advised correspondents to eliminate superfluous words from their copy. "Oblige us by omitting all such flourishes as 'your interesting and valuable paper,' 'your able and patriotic course,' &c. . . . If you think by this to improve your chances of insertion, you mistake ruinously." Greeley also wanted unemotional, logical writing. "Try to disparage as little as possible, and where you must condemn, let your facts be stronger than your words. . . . Give us facts, incidents, occurrences, at the earliest moment." He also insisted that his correspondents take responsibility for what they wrote. He gave out the names of his writers to people who complained about the newspaper's content. "He is a sneak and a coward who could ask us to bear the responsibility of his attacks on others," Greeley said.[54]

Although Greeley clearly cared about good, responsible writing, the editor was realistic. He cautioned that writing ability alone would not bring success in newspapering. He said New York City housed more than one thousand skilled writers but fewer than fifty would make it in the field of journalism. The difference between the fifty and the thousand, he said, was "the immensity of minute knowledge required." An editor, he said, has to know a myriad obscure facts or else he will accidentally publish "a gross and mischievous blunder."[55]

"A Sagacious and Good Man"

Greeley's caustic advice on writing did not seem to disturb Fuller. Ripley, Dana, and Brockway complained about Greeley's treatment, but Fuller did not. Her letters discussed Greeley admiringly and contained only the gentlest of criticism. She called him "a sagacious and a wonderfully good man." She said, "His abilities, in his own way, are great. He believes in mine to a surprising extent. We are true friends." Fuller only complained about Greeley's rough manners, but she forgave them. She called him "a slattern and plebeian" who was "in his heart a nobleman."[56]

When Fuller did mention criticism from Greeley, it usually concerned his wish for a larger volume of copy. For instance, in July 1845 she wrote that "the paper when I attend to it as much as Mr. G. wishes, takes all the time I feel disposed to read or write. He is now quite content again. I write often and at length." Margaret Fuller handled Horace Greeley's criticism and tutelage with equanimity. She only complained about Greeley's "plebeian" ways. Despite Greeley's crustiness, Fuller liked her work. "I like the position; it is so central, and affords a far more various view of life than any I ever before was in," she reported shortly after going to work for the *Tribune*. Journalism allowed her to address a large audience, but she shared Greeley's realism about its effects. She did "not expect to do much, practically, for the suffering," but at least her work would let readers know about conditions. Fuller felt respected by her colleagues at the *Tribune*. "My associates think my pen does not make too fine a mark to be felt, and may be a vigorous and purifying implement." Fuller's articles often "attracted a good deal of attention," she said. In her farewell column she said she had enjoyed the "degree of sympathetic response" her work had generated.[57]

"The Loftiest, Bravest Soul"

In evaluating the quality of Fuller's work at the *Tribune*, one other piece of information needs mentioning. While Horace Greeley made several cruel comments about Margaret Fuller, he also praised her extravagantly. When he announced her hiring, Greeley called Fuller a writer "already eminent in the higher walks of literature" and predicted "decided and gratifying change" for his newspaper. He wrote enthusiastically about *Woman in the Nineteenth Century,* which he published. "Margaret's book is going to *sell*. I tell you it has the real stuff in it." Greeley said he had found himself "drawn, almost irresistibly, in the general current" of admiration for Fuller. Commenting on the tragedy of her death, Greeley ended his recollections: "So passed away the loftiest, bravest soul that has yet irradiated the form of an American woman."[58]

There is one puzzling letter in the material that pertains to the relationship between Margaret Fuller and Horace Greeley. On September 3, 1850, two months after Fuller's death, Greeley refused to write a piece on Fuller for Sarah Josepha Hale, editor of *Godey's Lady's Book,* saying he did not know Fuller well enough to write about her. "Though she lived in my house a year and a half, I . . . only met her at breakfast, leaving soon after for my office and not returning til long after the whole family had gone to rest," Greeley told Mrs. Hale. Interpreting this letter is difficult given the great weight of evidence indicating Greeley knew Fuller very well.

In his comments for the *Memoirs of Margaret Fuller Ossoli* prepared by her friends, Greeley observed that he had tried to "escape the fascination which she seemed to exert over the eminent and cultivated persons. . . . But as time wore on, and I became inevitably better and better acquainted with her, I found myself drawn, almost irresistibly, into the general current." Lurton Ingersoll reported that Greeley, on his deathbed in 1872, spoke "with great admiration and kindness" for Margaret Fuller, although she had passed away more than twenty years earlier.[59]

Despite his protestations to Hale, Greeley did write several memorial descriptions of Fuller, most notably in his *Recollections of a Busy Life,* in the *Memoirs of Margaret Fuller Ossoli,* and in an obituary in the *Tribune.* On July 27, 1850, just after Fuller died, Greeley urged Emerson to produce a book of *Memoirs.* He wanted the book "got out before the interest excited by her sad decease has passed away." Greeley told Emerson he had neither the time, the capacity, nor "the knowledge essential to a proper Memoir of our departed friend." In his obituary of Fuller, Greeley called for a publication of a memoir of Fuller with a collection of her writing. Greeley thought someone should write a memorial book on Fuller, but he did not want to do it. Probably Greeley denied his friendship with Fuller in his letter to Sarah Hale because he did not want to write a piece for Hale. In the same letter he also refused to make a contact she had requested of him, explaining that he was "hurried out of reason."[60]

Horace Greeley did disparage Margaret Fuller's work on occasion, but he also said very complimentary things. The derogatory comments he made about Fuller do not mean that she failed to fulfill her duties as an employee nor that she could not write. Greeley made similarly harsh observations about the men whose work he edited. The harshness of Greeley's comments instead suggest the powerful editing that Fuller's writing received. Fuller was not a perfect employee. Her commitment to newspapering did not reach Greeley's exceptional standards, but one must call Margaret Fuller a serious writer who devoted much time to her compositions. Although her definition of hard work did not reach Greeley's exaggerated expectations, she seems to have handled Horace Greeley's criticism and tutelage with equanimity.

A balanced summary of Fuller as an employee might best come from Horace Greeley. He observed that her "faults and weaknesses were all superficial and obvious to the most casual, if undazzled, observer." Yet when one knew her, these faults "took on new and brighter aspects in the light of her radiant and lofty soul."[61]

A Woman Working in Journalism in 1844

With the industrial revolution of the 1830s, the introduction of machines to do much of mankind's work, came a redefinition of woman's role in the American workplace. Before the industrial revolution a family produced most goods on its own farm. In these days of cottage industry, neither men nor women had an occupation beyond the homestead. As men began leaving the household to work, the home became woman's sphere while activity in the larger public world belonged to man. This new concept of the home as woman's sphere was a middle-class idea because, after the industrial revolution, only women of the upper and middle classes could afford to stay at home. Economic necessity forced other women out of the home to work mostly as servants or in the textile mills.[62]

By the 1840s, when Fuller went to work at the *Tribune,* some middle-class women had begun to resent their new position as decorative pieces in the drawing room. Unmarried ladies of good family faced an especially tedious fate. While married women had a house and family to care for, single women became "maiden aunts" traveling from relative to relative and friend to friend, visiting for a few weeks and then moving on. After Fuller left the *Dial,* her letters suggest she lived this life. One of her hosts, Ralph Waldo Emerson, described her as "everywhere a welcome guest," a great talker who could establish deep friendships quickly.[63]

Middle-class women who wanted a more active life in the antebellum era had to find their occupation within what society defined as woman's sphere, and writing for publication lay within woman's sphere. At the start of the nineteenth century women wrote 20 percent of best-selling novels, and by the 1850s and 1860s they wrote 36 percent. Women writing books and magazine articles between 1820 and 1860 usually addressed the topic of woman's place in society. They urged women to be religious, humble, moral, and skilled in the running of a household.[64]

In 1855, Nathaniel Hawthorne made his famous attack on women writers. "America is now wholly given over to a d——d mob of scribbling women, and I should have no chance of success while the public taste is occupied with their trash—and should be ashamed of myself if I did succeed." Some critics have attributed Hawthorne's comments to jealousy at the volume of the women's book sales, but Margaret Fuller did not align herself with these popular women novelists. Five years earlier, she also had attacked "female scribblers," calling them "the paltriest offspring of the human brain." In choosing to write essays about literature instead of writing romances or housekeeping advice, Fuller avoided joining the mainstream of women writers. She produced more serious work than most of her contemporaries. Still the writers of more sentimental work did make a contribution. By the act of successfully publishing, they defined writing as a part of the woman's sphere and therefore an acceptable activity for a woman like Fuller.[65]

Society in the 1840s also began to accept an interest by women in reform with women taking part in the temperance and abolition movements. The sphere of women included reform because nineteenth-century ideology considered women more pure and moral than men, but society did distinguish between writing about reform and participating in reform activities. Although women could write about topics within their proper sphere of interest, a woman who took a position in the broader public arena dared scandal. For instance, when members of the Female Moral Reform Society in the 1830s marched in the streets of New York City to stop prostitution, they shocked proper society. Activist Jane Grey Swisshelm described the angst she suffered in 1844 while trying to decide whether to begin writing publicly about abolition. She expected social disgrace. "No woman had ever done such a thing, and I could never again hold up my head under the burden of shame and disgrace which would be heaped upon me."[66]

Margaret Fuller advocated radical ideas, but, at least while she lived in New York, this advocacy came in the genteel form of essays on literature and philanthropy published in a mainstream newspaper. She did not march in the streets. She did not write for a radical abolitionist organ, as Swisshelm did. Fuller stayed on the edge, but not over the edge, of polite, ladylike behavior within woman's sphere. Fuller, then, behaved in a socially acceptable way by writing for the *Tribune,* but society saw her as singular.

In 1853 Sarah Josepha Hale, the quite traditional editor of *Godey's Lady's Book* who wrote the poem "Mary Had a Little Lamb," published an encyclopedia listing distinguished women. She admired Fuller's intellect and defended her right to publish *Woman in the Nineteenth Century.* However, Hale predicted Fuller's works were not "destined to hold a high place in female literature. There is no true moral life in them."[67] Fuller did not write sentimental, moralistic poetry. She wrote intellectual discourses, and this made her different. Still she addressed the topics of literature and philanthropy, and this legitimized her journalism.

The *Norton Anthology of Literature by Women* calls Fuller "the first self-supporting American woman journalist." This is not accurate. Women preceded Fuller in American journalism, some by more than one hundred years. Margaret Fuller had many women contemporaries in the working press including Cornelia Walter, editor of the Boston *Transcript* from 1842 to 1847; Jane Grey Swisshelm, editor of the Pittsburgh *Saturday Visiter* [*sic*] from 1848 to 1852; and Anne Royall, publisher of a weekly newspaper in Washington, D.C., from the 1830s to the 1850s. Fuller is exceptional not for being first but for being extraordinarily talented. In 1889, the great woman's rights advocate, Elizabeth Cady Stanton, wrote an excellent summary of Fuller's importance as a woman in journalism:

> It has been declared not the least of Horace Greeley's services to the nation, that he was willing to entrust the literary criticisms of the *Tribune* to one whose standard of culture was so far above that of his readers or his own. Margaret Fuller opened the way for many women, who upon the editorial staff of the great New York dailies, as literary critics and reporters, have helped impress woman's thought upon the American mind.[68]

Five Hundred Dollars a Year

At the *Tribune* Fuller worked as a full and equal member of the staff earning a salary equivalent to her male coworkers. Fuller earned $500 a year plus room and board at Greeley's home. Both Ralph Waldo Emerson and Evart Duyckinck considered Fuller's salary good pay. In Greeley's eyes this must have seemed a generous salary. He said as editor of the *Dial* Fuller was supposed to earn $200 a year, but that publication never made enough money to pay her.[69]

In 1846, after Fuller moved from the Greeley home to a boarding house and began planning to leave for Europe, her salary proved less adequate. At the end of 1845, Greeley and McElrath told Fuller she would receive a raise. Later as she planned to leave for Europe to become a foreign correspondent for the *Tribune,* Fuller negotiated a new salary with firmness. She told her brother that McElrath did not seem interested in the second edition of her book and might not offer her enough pay for European correspondence. She said she planned to deal with this disinterest by avoiding the issue of salary for foreign correspondence until the last minute and then threatening to jump to another newspaper. This strategy evidently worked well. Greeley said he paid her $10 per column, "twice what we pay for any other European correspondence, but we are very well aware that the quality justifies this." In 1848 Greeley paid Jane Grey Swisshelm $5 per column for letters from Washington, D.C.[70]

Fuller went to the *Tribune* not for purely altruistic reasons. She needed employment. Fuller had known better and worse times financially. After her father died in 1835, leaving very little money, she had handled the family finances. For two years she supported the family by teaching school, at one point earning $1,000 a year. She continued the Conversations in Boston because she needed money. Ticket prices were $20 for ten of Fuller's Conversations, "a very high price for that time," said Caroline Dall, who attended.[71]

A salary of $500 a year was extraordinarily better than the average working woman's. In 1845 mill workers drew $1.75 a week ($91 a year), and in the 1830s women weaving palm hats for a living made 25 to 30 cents a day ($78 to $93 a year). At the model Lowell, Massachusetts, textile mills women earned $1 to $2 a week ($52 to $104 a year) plus room and board for a seventy-five-hour workweek. Elementary teachers made $2.50 a week ($130 a year) while their male counterparts took home $5 a week ($260 a year).[72]

Fuller's salary also compared favorably with her coworkers. In 1844, typesetters at the *Tribune* received an $11 weekly ($572 yearly) guarantee. They could try to exceed this guarantee at piece work rates. This was considerably above the going rate for New York printers, who usually earned from $300 to $450 a year. Writers at the *Tribune* in the 1840s earned around $500 a year. Henry J. Raymond started at the *Tribune* in 1841 at $416 a year. As city editor for Greeley in 1847, Charles Dana's starting salary was $416 a year. George Ripley began as a part-time literary assistant in 1849 at $260 a year. Bayard Taylor began as assistant editor at $625. Greeley's craft workers and writers made almost twice what workers in other shops earned. In 1842, Godwin at the *Evening Post* offered Walt Whitman $75 for three months ($300 a year) to write for him. Greeley himself between 1841 and 1843 averaged $15 a week, or $780 a year.[73]

Women writing for newspapers in the 1840s seemed to do as well as men. Cornelia Walter, editor of the *Boston Transcript,* earned $500 a year, the same salary drawn by her brother, the paper's previous editor. The *Transcript*'s two reporters each made $11 a week ($572 a year). In the same period Lydia Maria Child was promised $1,000 a year for her work at the *National Anti-Slavery Standard* but received much less. Fiction writers received very little per story. Hawthorne in the same period made $20 a story; Poe received $10 for the publication of "The Tell-Tale Heart."[74]

Just how far would $500 go in 1844? The average family spent about $543 a year. Fuller, therefore, made about what the average family would have earned. This average family spent 57 percent of its total income on food, 17 percent on rent, 7 percent on fuel and light, and only 19 percent on expenses other than room and board. Fuller's salary of $500 a year, then, provided a more than reasonable middle-class income, and the supplement of room and board with the Greeley family made her salary exceptionally good. The arrangement had special advantages for Fuller. By living with the Greeleys she could preserve the status of a respectable lady visiting and save a considerable amount on expenses.[75]

The Star Byline

In terms of salary Fuller received equal treatment with her male coworkers. What of her byline, the star? There is much documentation to show that the star in the *Tribune* represented Fuller's work, but neither Fuller nor her contemporaries left any explanations for the star. Did the newspaper use a star instead of Fuller's name to hide her gender?

When radical abolitionist Jane Grey Swisshelm in 1844 chose to sign the first articles she published (in the abolitionist newspaper, *The Spirit of Liberty*) with her initials instead of her full name, she cited two reasons: "My dislike and dread of publicity and the fear of embarrassing the Liberty Party with the sex question." Through her writing Fuller took a prominent part in public affairs, and she wanted her ideas heeded, but nothing suggests she deliberately avoided using her name on articles to conceal her gender. While the *Tribune* ran Fuller's work marked with a star, it regularly reprinted pieces bylined "L. Maria Child." *Tribune* editorial policy then included printing a reform article by a woman and giving it a byline.[76]

Most of the editorial copy in the paper lacked bylines. However, four types of bylines appeared in the *New York Tribune* from 1844 to 1846: initials, noms de plume, complete names, and Fuller's star. These different types of bylines appear on different types of work. Reprints from other publications usually had a complete name as a byline. Correspondents used initials, noms de plume, or complete names.[77] The rest of the copy in the paper ran without a byline and appeared to be in-house work. From 1844 to 1846 the *Tribune* ran no bylines of George Snow, G.S., or S. or of Oliver Johnson, O.J., or J., though both men worked full-time for the paper during this period. Business writer Snow's work stood out clearly. A great deal of unbylined financial news ran regularly on pages 2 and 3.

Byline policies like the use of noms de plume and initials stemmed from the personal nature of nineteenth-century journalism. Tradition credited every article in a newspaper to its editor. "In America nearly every paper of any importance is identified with its leading editor," explained Thomas L. Nichols in 1864. "In France, every article must bear the signature of the writer, or some one who takes responsibility for the article. In America, as a rule, the opinions of a paper are attributed to the responsible editor." From 1844 to 1846 the noms de plume, initials, and full-name bylines label material not produced in-house, under the editor's direction. Complete bylines always went to material reprinted from other publications while material receiving its first publication but not written in-house received initials or a nom de plume. (An occasional but rare piece in the *Tribune* from 1844 to 1846 is signed G. or H.G., clearly Greeley's in-house work.)[78]

By 1849 Greeley was working out a formal byline policy for his paper. He instructed Bayard Taylor to:

> sign your own initials or some distinctive mark at the bottom [of articles]. I want everybody connected with the "Tribune" to become known to the public (in some unobtrusive way) as doing what he does, so that in case of my death or incapacity it may not be fancied that the paper is to die or essentially suffer.[79]

Fuller then probably used the star as a byline, not to keep her female name out of print but because Horace Greeley asked her to label her work with either initials or a distinctive mark to distinguish it from his unbylined essays. The newspaper from 1844 to 1846 did not byline in-house material, but Fuller's essays differed from the unbylined financial and city news written anonymously by other staffers.

"The White Foam of Gossip"

In one major way Margaret Fuller's work life differed from that of the men at the *Tribune*. Fuller did not work in the office. Instead she wrote at home and dropped her writing off at the newspaper office. Many scholars have argued that Fuller did not work in the *Tribune* offices because she was too temperamental, too flighty, and too emotional to handle such a situation.[80]

This argument seems farfetched, especially considering a much more powerful reason for Fuller to avoid the office. In the 1840s a woman risked her reputation if she worked in an office because offices were a part of the public sphere reserved for men. Not until the Civil War, fifteen years later, did office work become socially acceptable for women. With so many men joining the army, the Union government brought in women to staff its offices. When Margaret Fuller went to New York in 1844 she had a role model. Cornelia Walter edited the *Boston Transcript* for five years from her home to avoid participating in man's rightful sphere.[81]

In 1848 abolitionist Jane Grey Swisshelm caused a scandal when she began working side by side in an office with her publishing partner, Robert M. Riddle, producing the *Saturday Visiter*. She called working in the office an "appalling prospect." She had only known one woman who worked in an office, a daughter who clerked for her lawyer father. Swisshelm called that woman's experience "remarkable and very painful." Because Swisshelm was "publicly asserting the right of woman to earn a living as book-keepers, clerks, sales-women," she decided to risk "the crimson waves of scandal, the white foam of gossip" and go to work in an office.[82] When Swisshelm in 1850 arrived in Washington, D.C., to write for the *New York Tribune,* "no woman had ever had a place in the Congressional reporter's gallery," she recalled. She asked Vice President Millard Fillmore for a seat assignment in the gallery, but he tried to talk her out of it. "The place would be very unpleasant for a lady, would attract attention, I would not like it; but he gave me the seat," she reported. Her first day in the gallery was exciting. She watched Senator Foot draw "a great horse pistol and cocking it" threaten to shoot Senator Benton.[83]

Society frowned on women who worked in offices, but one might argue mere convention would not have blocked the way of the intrepid Margaret Fuller. After all, in *Woman in the Nineteenth Century* she argued women should captain ships at sea.[84] A mere four years later she covered a revolution in Italy, riding to battlefields on horseback. She had a romance with a man ten years her junior and bore him a child, perhaps out of wedlock. These events describe a woman freed of convention, but all radical thinkers still follow most of the conventions of their day.

Swisshelm went to the office only with great hesitation, and Fuller was no less conventional. For example, Fuller explained in a letter to a friend how she would go about getting tickets to review a theater performance if the box office had closed. She said she would "have gone down to our office and one of the gentlemen would have gone with me to the Theatre door and probably got us in." Fuller did not feel she could or should go to a theater door by herself to ask for tickets. Instead, propriety demanded she go out of her way to find a male coworker to escort her.[85] Despite what later writers have said, for Margaret Fuller to work in an office in 1844 would have caused a scandal.

Fuller also had to endure some abuse from Horace Greeley because she was a woman. He said of her: "Noble and great as she was, a good husband and two or three bouncing babies would have emancipated her from a deal of cant and nonsense." Greeley made this comment while acknowledging that he himself was not "wholly exempt from the vulgar prejudice against female claimants of functions hitherto devolved only on men." Greeley had mixed views on woman's rights. While he did hire Fuller and brag on her work, he also reported "much perfectly good-natured, but nevertheless sharpish sparring between us." Greeley complained that while demanding for women "the fullest recognition of Social and Political Equality with the rougher sex," Fuller also sought deference. When a woman demands a "gentleman's arm to conduct her properly out of a dining room," he observed, "I cannot see how the 'Woman's Rights' theory is ever to be anything more than a logically defensible abstraction." Greeley, then, endorsed and actively supported woman's rights by, among other things, hiring Fuller, but he also pointed out the logical fallacy of granting women equal rights while simultaneously deferring to them, and Greeley did make unprogressive comments about woman's place in society.[86]

In summary, Margaret Fuller worked at the *New York Tribune* when the concept of woman's sphere defined socially acceptable activities for women. Writing for publication, especially about literature and reform, fit within woman's sphere, although working actively to achieve reform did not. On the job Fuller received pay equal to her male colleagues. Her use of a star as a byline followed the custom for writers of both sexes in the 1840s. Fuller did not work in the office, because to do so was to leave the woman's sphere, and Horace Greeley did make abusive comments to her about her sex.

3
The Denigration of Margaret Fuller

Controversy surrounded Margaret Fuller in her day and follows her still today. Two drastically different schools have labeled Margaret Fuller and her importance to history. One interpretation has described her as silly, selfish, and egotistical. The other has called her an extraordinary intellect, the most outstanding woman of the nineteenth century. While most people have tried to explain the contrasting views of Fuller in American history by discussing the personal motivations of the men who created Fuller's image in history, a further reason exists for the denigration of Fuller. She worked in journalism, publishing bold and independent criticisms. The very fact that she wrote journalism and not poetry made her controversial.

The modern debate about Fuller's worth centers on several hostile analyses published by Harvard English professor Perry Miller in the late 1950s and early 1960s. Miller seemed to enjoy writing in an outrageous style. He referred to Fuller as "grandiose," "ludicrous," and "operatic." He praised her extravagantly and then insulted her egregiously. Miller called Fuller the embodiment of "an ideal womanly genius" but noted she was also "patently a dream-image of a plain, monstrously learned, tempestuous, and tormented Germaine." Miller begrudgingly acknowledged Fuller's abilities. "She possessed the only mind among her contemporaries that could have conversed on a place of equality (though she brashly self-assumed this) with Rousseau and Goethe." Ignoring the popularity of *Woman in the Nineteenth Century* and testimony from Elizabeth Cady Stanton, Miller argued that Fuller made only a "slight contribution to the campaign for women's rights."[1]

Marie Urbanski has refuted Miller's evaluations, but Miller remains influential because he wrote so prolifically. Two of his books and one article feature Fuller prominently and disapprovingly. Miller's influence appears as recently as 1986 in Richard Kluger's history of the *Tribune*. Kluger based the Fuller section primarily on Miller despite the wealth of more recent scholarship.[2]

Most studies of Fuller's negative image have concentrated on comments by her celebrated contemporaries. Fuller's detractors find their ammunition primarily in the *Memoirs of Margaret Fuller Ossoli,* edited by Ralph

Waldo Emerson, William Henry Channing, and James Freeman Clarke. For example, in the *Memoirs* Emerson wrote this widely quoted description:

> Margaret occasionally let spill, with all innocence imaginable, some phrase betraying the presence of a rather mountainous ME, in a way to surprise those who knew her good sense.[3]

This phrase, "mountainous ME," has supported the impression of an egotistical Fuller who had an inflated vision of her own intellectual prowess.

An early example of the impact the *Memoirs* had on Fuller's public image comes from an 1852 English review. After reading the *Memoirs* the anonymous reviewer called Fuller a "he-woman" who "understood Socrates better than Plato did, Faust better than Goethe did, Kant's Philosophy better than Kant did."[4]

Emerson, Channing, and Clarke prepared the *Memoirs* shortly after Fuller's death. Bell Gale Chevigny has documented extensive censorship by the three editors as they prepared their "literary monument" to Fuller. To protect Fuller for history, the editors condensed her wording, corrected her grammar, and omitted individual names and "unflattering opinions" about individual people. They defaced Fuller's private papers, using scissors and crayon to delete passages.[5]

"The Haunting Margaret-Ghost"

The argument made by Urbanski and many other scholars about Fuller's image has problems. First it assumes history has censored Fuller. This viewpoint ignores the continuous strand of admiring literature that exists through time alongside the derogatory remarks. In 1903, some fifty years after her death, Henry James identified the two conflicting views of Margaret Fuller. Calling her the "haunting Margaret-ghost," he wondered how the world of 1903 would have responded to her. Would people see her as a "formidable bore" or as an impressive genius?[6]

In her day Fuller was an admired celebrity. Before she even joined the *Tribune,* newspapers wrote about her work in the *Dial.*[7] The most often quoted praise of Fuller comes from Edgar Allan Poe. He noted the "high genius she unquestionably possesses" and called a review of Longfellow "frank, candid, independent . . . giving honor *only* where honor was due." Thomas Carlyle found Fuller's writing "the undeniable utterances . . . of a true heroic mind." (Carlyle's observation, however, was not published until the twentieth century.) Walt Whitman read a collection of Fuller's essays to learn about literary criticism. Fuller's celebrity combined with the tragedy of her early death inspired much adoration in the 1850s. For example, twenty-two-year-old Alfred Janson Bloor wrote eighteen pages of sentimental verse memorializing Fuller's death. "In her the world lost a rare scholar, linguist, writer and critic; a true reformer and enlarged philanthropist; and in every respect a great woman," he commented in his introduction.[8]

Throughout the nineteenth century Fuller merited admiration from ordinary people. For example, in 1869 Edwin Studwell of New York and R. A. Canby of Iowa published a small volume, *Dottings from the Writings of Margaret Fuller Ossoli*. "I assure you she has made a very deep impression, and improved me; for I 'feel my wings budding,'" wrote Canby. In 1885, a year after Higginson's biography, a group of women in Knoxville, Tennessee, formed a literary society called the Ossoli Circle. In 1880, thirty years after she had worked at the *Tribune*, the newspaper's staff still admired Fuller's work. An Extra published in the memory of George Ripley, the literary critic who succeeded Fuller, praised her work.[9]

Two of the most noted people to praise Fuller were Elizabeth Cady Stanton and Eleanor Roosevelt. In 1889 Stanton commented, "Margaret Fuller possessed more influence upon the thought of America, than any woman previous to her time." Roosevelt in 1930 called *Woman in the Nineteenth Century* "an epoch-making book," and observed Fuller's "power to impress her personality and her greatness of soul on those around her." Beginning with Thomas Wentworth Higginson in 1884 and Katharine Anthony in 1920, many scholars have sought to establish Fuller's importance in American literary history, but most of the people who have written positively about Fuller have not had the public stature of her detractors.[10]

History, then, has both praised and censured Fuller. Along with the derogatory Emerson-Miller strand of Fuller literature another viewpoint has always existed. Fuller advocates have had to decide why so many well-known people said so many mean things about her.

Urbanski has argued that the *Memoirs* caused Fuller's dubious position in history, but Urbanski's argument only works if the *Memoirs* were the first public comments to label Fuller silly and egotistical. Many unflattering assertions about Fuller predate the *Memoirs*.

In 1850, two years before publication of the *Memoirs*, George Ripley wrote a rarely quoted obituary of Margaret Fuller. He described his friend in the awkward terms so often applied to Fuller. He said she did not know how to act properly in social situations. In a group of strangers "her manner was often combative, defiant, presumptuous." In 1852 John S. Hart in a book on women writers said the *Memoirs* would soon appear in print, and he went on to call Fuller "more remarkable for strength and vigour of thought, and a certain absolute and almost scornful independence, than for the graces of style and diction."[11] Both Hart's and Ripley's comments predate the publication of the *Memoirs*. This means the denigration of Margaret Fuller began before publication of the *Memoirs*. The editors of the *Memoirs* may have felt intellectually threatened by Fuller, but their book reported ideas about Fuller already in general circulation.

Derogatory comments about Margaret Fuller appeared in print long before the publication of the *Memoirs*. Why? While Marie Urbanski, Ann Douglas, and others have argued that men found Fuller's intellectual strength intimidating, there is another reason for the denigration of Margaret Fuller. She worked in the field of journalism. When Fuller moved to New York she stopped playing intellectual parlor games and began submitting her thoughts for public review and criticism. Most credit her with writing honest, hard-hitting reviews. When a person publishes tough criticism, that person often draws tough criticism in return.

"Grossly Dishonest"

Henry Wadsworth Longfellow did not respond publicly when a Fuller review called his work imitative. However, in his diary he complained of Fuller's "bilious attack" and "furious onslaught upon me." When Fuller reviewed James Russell Lowell harshly, he attacked her in a poem. Although in 1846 Poe had praised Fuller in print, by 1848 he had changed his estimate of her. He called her "grossly dishonest" and complained, "She has omitted all mention of me." In an 1849 letter, Poe became even more vitriolic, calling Fuller a detestable old maid whose poor reviews of Lowell "set him off at a tangent and he has never been quite right since."[12] Poe and Lowell had reason to attack Margaret Fuller. She had either panned or ignored their work. Ripley argued in 1850 that the honesty of Fuller's writing drew fire. Fuller's reviews, he said, lost her "the good opinion of those who saw her in no other aspect, and made enemies for life of many who bore the smart of the wounds that had been inflicted by her hand." After all, Fuller wrote in an era when people sometimes took a violent interest in the content of newspapers. Accounts of shooting matches between newspaper editors and their angry critics litter the pages of nineteenth-century journalism history. In 1842 rioters, angry with the *Tribune*'s depiction of the Irish, threatened to destroy the newspaper office. By comparison, the attacks on Margaret Fuller were genteel.[13]

Fuller, then, drew public disapproval long before publication of the

Memoirs. Many attacks stemmed from what she wrote in the newspaper. Much of the criticism came from people her work had wounded. Many of these angry men did stoop to ad hominem attacks, but this was the norm for journalism in the 1840s. When a writer engages in public discussion, she can expect to draw attacks.

"Something Excellent"

The denigration of Margaret Fuller also occurred because she wrote journalism instead of literature. Historical evaluations of Fuller share the same assumption as literary evaluations of another American genius, James Agee. Paul Ashdown said critics commonly argue Agee might well have produced more quality work if he had spent less time writing for such magazines as *Fortune* and *Time*. Such comments automatically discounted the possibility that Agee's reportage itself rates praise.[14]

Fuller and her contemporaries shared this bias that the writing of essays for newspapers was not creative work. Evaluating Fuller's work in 1855, Parton maintained she understood literature, but argued, "Her understanding was greater than her gift. She could appreciate, not create." Fuller herself commented on the second-class status of journalism as a writer's art. Her old friends, she said, "think I ought to produce something excellent, while I am satisfied to aid in the great work of popular education." By doing journalism, criticizing others' literature, Fuller thought she did valuable work, but not work of the same high quality as poetry or fiction. "I wish I might write something good . . . , but really the paper when I attend to it as much as Mr. Greeley wishes, takes all the time I feel disposed to read or write," she said. While she wrote a great deal, she produced journalism and therefore by definition not quality work, but Fuller was proud of the vast quantity of writing she produced for the newspaper. In the preface to an edition of her *Tribune* essays, she answered "those of my friends, who have often expressed a wish that I 'could find time to write.'" She said she had written enough at the *Tribune* "to make a little library. . . . Should I do no more, I have at least sent my share of paper missives through the world."[15]

Clearly, then, some denigration of Margaret Fuller comes from her occupation. By working for newspapers she automatically opened herself to contentions that her work lacked the quality of fiction or poetry, and even she seemed to accept the truth of these complaints.

In summary, scholars have argued the denigration of Margaret Fuller originated in the *Memoirs* edited by Emerson, Channing, and Clarke; however, others censured her before publication of the *Memoirs*. Besides, detractors were not the only writers on the subject of Margaret Fuller. A continuous strand of literature, dating back to Edgar Allan Poe, praises Fuller. The unkind comments about Fuller stem, in part, from what she wrote. She wrote too honestly for some of her subjects. Scholars should regard much of the denigration, though insultingly ad hominem in form, as the normal course of affairs for one involved in pubic debate. Some denigration stems from the commonly held idea of journalism, compared to fiction, as a second-class occupation.

Much of the derogatory scholarship on Fuller is unforgivable, most particularly Perry Miller's; however, scholars working to repair Miller's damage should take care they do not overprotect Margaret Fuller. Scholars have argued correctly that much of the denigration resulted because her gender made her an anomaly in her day. As an outspoken, intellectual woman ready to defend her ideas, she no doubt disconcerted some of her male adversaries. However, anyone, male or female, who wrote strong criticism in the public press drew attacks, some of them vicious and ad hominem.

Part II.
Margaret Fuller's Journalism:
Forgotten Writings

4
The Rich and the Poor

In these articles a reader meets a strong, opinionated mind. Margaret Fuller used her intellect to attack haughtiness in the rich, bias against the woman who worked outside the home, and stinginess in the operation of institutions that housed criminals, the handicapped, and the insane. Yet Margaret Fuller does challenge the twentieth-century reader. Even in her day, her reputation rested more on what she said than how she said it.

One should read Fuller's work with an understanding that it leans toward the romantic sentimentality that typifies nineteenth-century writing. For example, Fuller's visits to institutions on holidays allowed her to make an ironic contrast between conditions inside and outside the institutions. She often opened her long pieces with a sentimental fiction or with a personal story, but later the conventional opening led to an unconventional idea. The twentieth-century reader longs for Fuller to get to the point, but this sentimentality was an accepted way to write in the nineteenth century. In using the convention she established a link with her equally romantic and sentimental readers.

The modern reader does benefit from this sentimentality. The approach required the recounting of much detail. For instance, in "Our City Charities" (reprinted in Chapter 5), Fuller offered a pathetic report of a dwarf from Holland found abandoned in New York City and taken to Bellevue Alms House. "No one could communicate with her or know her feelings, but she showed what they were by running to the gate whenever it opened." These sentimental descriptions probably inspired a tear of sympathy in the nineteenth-century reader. They sometimes work on the twentieth-century sentiment as well. If nothing else, they benefit the twentieth-century reader by providing descriptive details of life in nineteenth-century New York.

While Fuller obeyed the nineteenth-century conventions of writing, she advocated radical ideas. There was, for instance, Fuller's concern for the welfare of prostitutes. For an upper-middle-class woman in the nineteenth century to acknowledge the existence of prostitution showed mettle. To discuss such a delicate topic and preserve one's social standing took careful attention to word choice. Since Fuller wrote in the vocabulary of a nineteenth-century lady, she avoided using words like *prostitute* and *whore*. Instead, she used the broader term *female convict*. Despite the elliptical word choice, Fuller argued strongly for women who wanted to leave prostitution. In "Asylum for Discharged Female Convicts" (reprinted in Chapter 5), she noted that women become convicts because they "have not been guarded either by social influence or inward strength from that first mistake which the opinion of the world makes irrevocable for women alone." Since society failed to protect these women from their "terrible fall," she urged her readers to at least help the women reform themselves to "that partial restoration which society at present permits."

The language in these passages may seem very polite and veiled and therefore somewhat hard to follow, but Fuller has used this polite language to take a courageous position. She acknowledged that after a woman made that "first mistake," took that "terrible fall" of selling her body for sex, the woman could never again attain complete respectability. She noted, however, that society as a whole must accept some blame for prostitution; therefore, society must help prostitutes who want to reform.

When reading Margaret Fuller's essays, one must remember her audience and adopt a nineteenth-century viewpoint. Fuller's readers found her writing style conventional, but her ideas excited them. These articles of journalism differed from the factual news reports in twentieth-century newspapers because they were essays—advocacy illustrated with on-scene reports. The language and allusions may seem archaic, but many of the problems Fuller described will seem quite familiar to twentieth-century readers. For instance, in "Our City Charities" she wondered why "the human mind which has just invented the magnetic telegraph and Anastatic printing" cannot eliminate the "causes which make the acceptance of public charity necessary." Today's commentator laments that we can put a man on the moon, yet we cannot eliminate unemployment.

Margaret Fuller's most important journalism examined changing conditions in American life. In 1884 her first biographer, Thomas Wentworth Higginson, said more people read Fuller's essays on philanthropic questions than any of her other *Tribune* pieces. One of Horace Greeley's first biographers, Lurton Ingersoll, in 1873 remembered Fuller's social essays as "remarkable for freshness, suggestiveness and wisdom."[1]

A liberal reformer who advocated kinder treatment for inmates of institutions, more rights for women, and freedom for slaves, Margaret Fuller understood her articles would have little effect. "I do not expect to do much, practically, for the suffering; but having such an organ of expression, any suggestions that are well-grounded may be of use," she said. Writing on these topics had a profound personal effect on Fuller. Several scholars have labeled her time in New York a transitional period. In New York her ideas began to change from those of the abstract transcendentalist philosopher who edited the *Dial* to those of the political activist who ran a battlefield hospital during the Italian Revolution of 1848.[2]

The Industrial Revolution

During Andrew Jackson's presidency (1829–37), the United States had evolved from a "pre-industrial society that was slow to accept innovations, to a modern capitalistic state in which people believed that society could be transformed," historian Douglas Miller noted. For two centuries America had been a relatively stable agrarian society, but after 1815 "new technology, new forms of economic organization, growing wealth and geographical expansion presented a challenge to traditional values and ways," said Miller.[3]

The famous textile mill experiment in Lowell, Massachusetts, could be a symbol for the age. The Lowell mills claimed to offer a model program for young farm women who could work under respectable conditions while producing textiles much more efficiently than could individual weavers using hand looms at home. The mills were a regular stop on celebrity tours. Charles Dickens, Davy Crockett, and President Jackson all took guided tours. Crockett found the textile workers "well-dressed, lively and genteel in their appearance, indeed the girls looked as if they were coming from a quilting frolic." The women worked a twelve-hour day, seventy-hour week.[4]

Contemporary observers did notice problems with this new industrial revolution, which brought the production of goods out of individual households and into factories. Herman Melville used a fictional paper mill as the setting for a moving short story. He described the folding room: "At rows of blank-looking counters sat rows of blank-looking girls, with blank, white folders in their blank hands, all blankly folding blank paper."[5] In the mill, "Not a syllable was breathed. Nothing was heard but the low, steady overruling hum of the iron animals. The human voice was banished from the spot. Machinery—that vaunted slave of humanity—here stood menially served by human beings, who served mutely and cringingly as the slave serves the Sultan. The girls did not so much seem accessory wheels to the general machinery as mere cogs to the wheels."[6]

Although industrialization in the 1830s brought many country people and foreign immigrants to New York City seeking jobs running machines, a depression at the end of the decade threw them out of work. By the 1840s, for the first time in American history, cities contained terrible slums. In 1842 novelist Charles Dickens, accompanied by two policemen as bodyguards, toured the infamous Five Points slum. In one dwelling he saw "great mounds of dusty rags upon the ground. . . . Then the mounds of rags are seen to be astir, and rise slowly up, and the floor is covered with heaps of negro women waking from their sleep. . . . Where dogs would howl to lie, women, and men, and boys slink off to sleep, forcing the dislodged rats to move away in quest of better lodgings."[7]

Horace Greeley's *Tribune* joined a general reform movement that arose in the United States to deal with these problems. Historian John Tebbel has called the industrial revolution "a highly painful process full of dislocations, maladjustments, indignities, oppressions, and injustices, along with the normal complement of evil and stupidity. To a man like Greeley, with a highly developed but largely unfocused moral sense, many of these things were intolerable, to be fought with whatever weapon lay at hand."

The reformers hoped that, "removed from society, the needy and deviant could be made whole again," said historian George Tindall.[8] Margaret Fuller lived in New York with the results of this industrial revolution. The differing lives of the rich and the poor struck her, and she wrote a series of columns on these class distinctions. "The Rich Man—An Ideal Sketch" described a businessman who donated generously to reform causes. "He takes care, too, to be personally acquainted with those he employs, regarding them, not as mere tools, of his purpose, but as human beings also."

Fuller argued the goodness of all people. Social circumstances, not innate weakness, caused poverty, she said. As she saw it, the wealthy (and therefore the more fortunate) had an obligation to aid the poor, and this aid should come without condescension. In "Prevalent Idea That Politeness Is Too Great a Luxury to Be Given to the Poor," she pointed out the demeaning nature of much charity and argued against the "insolent rudeness or more insolent affability" of the givers of charity.

One of Fuller's best puns came in "Consecration of Grace Church." Noting the building's fashionable splendor, she observed, Jesus Christ preached to the poor, yet "the poor . . . can have no share in the grace of Grace Church."

She lectured her affluent readers on how they should behave. They should know their employees personally. They should base invitations to their homes on the guests' "intrinsic qualities," not their "wealth and fashion." In a companion piece she said the poor should carry themselves with "dignity and propriety of manner" and not worry about fashionable trappings.

The Rich Man—An Ideal Sketch

In my walks through this City, the sight of spacious and expensive dwelling houses now in process of building, has called up the following reverie.

All benevolent persons, whether deeply thinking on, or only deeply feeling, the woes, difficulties and dangers of our present social system, are agreed either that great improvements are needed, or a thorough reform.

Those who desire the latter, include the majority of thinkers. And we ourselves, both from personal observation and the testimony of others, are convinced that a radical reform is needed. Not a reform that rejects the instruction of the past, or asserts that God and man have made mistakes till now. We believe that all past developments have taken place under natural and necessary laws, and that the Paternal Spirit has at no period forgot his children, but granted to all ages and generations their chances of good to balance inevitable ills.—We prize the Past; we recognize it as our parent, our nurse and our teacher, and we know that for a time the new wine required the old bottles to prevent its being spilled upon the ground.

Still we feel that the time is come which not only permits, but demands, a wider statement, and a nobler action. The aspect of society presents mighty problems, which must be solved by the soul of Man "divinely intending" itself to the task, or all will become worse instead of better, and ere long the social fabric totter to decay.

Yet while the new measures are ripening and the new men educating, there is yet room on the old platform for some worthy action. It is possible for a man of piety, resolution and good sense, to lead a life which, if not expansive, generous, graceful, and pure from suspicion and contempt, is yet not entirely unworthy of his position as the child of God and ruler of a planet.

Let us take then some men just where they find themselves, in a mixed state of society where, in quantity, we are free to say the bad preponderates, though the good, from its superior energy in quality, may finally redeem and efface its plague-spots. Our society is ostensibly under the rule of the precepts of Jesus. We will then suppose a youth sufficiently imbued with these to understand what conveyed under the parables of the unjust steward and the prodigal son, as well as the denunciations of the opulent Jews. He understands that it is needful to preserve purity and teachableness, since of those most like little children is the kingdom of heaven's mercy for the sinner, since there is peculiar joy in Heaven at the salvation of such perpetual care for the unfortunate, since only to the just steward shall his possessions be pardoned. Imbued with such lore the young man joins the commercial world.

His views of his profession are not those which make of the many a herd, not superior, except in the far reach of their selfish instincts, to the animals, mere calculating, money-making machines.

He sees in commerce a representation of most important interests, a grand school that may teach the heart and soul of the civilized world to a willing, thinking mind. He plays his part in the game, but not for himself alone; he sees the interests of all mankind engaged with his, and remembers them while he furthers his own. His intellectual discernment, no less than his moral, thus teaching the undesirableness of lying and stealing, he does not practice or connive at the falsities and meannesses so frequent among his fellows; he suffers many turns of the wheel of Fortune to pass unused, since he cannot avail himself of them and keep clean his hands. What he gains is by superior assiduity, skill in combination and calculation, and quickness of sight. His gains are legitimate so far as the present state of things permits any gains to be.

Nor is this honorable man denied his due rank in the most corrupt state of society. Here, happily, we draw from life, and speak of what we know.—Honesty is, indeed, the best policy, only it is so in the long run, and therefore a policy which a selfish man has not faith and patience to pursue. The influence of the honest man is in the end predominant, and the rogues who sneer because he will not shuffle the cards in *their* way, are forced to bow to it at last.

But, while thus conscientious and mentally progressive, he does not forget to live. The sharp and care-worn faces, the joyless lives that throng his busy street, do not make him forget his need of tender affections, of the practices of bounty and love. His family, his acquaintances, especially those who are struggling with the difficulties of life, are not obliged to wait till he has accumulated a certain sum. He is sunlight and dew to them now, day by day. No less do all in his employment prize and bless the just, the brotherly man. He dares not, would climb to power upon their necks. He requites their toil handsomely always: if his success be unusual, they share the benefit.—Their comfort is cared for in all the arrangements for their work. He takes care, too, to be personally acquainted with those he employs, regarding them, not as mere tools of his purpose, but as human beings also; he keeps them in his eye, and if it be in his power to supply their need of consolation, instruction, or even pleasure, they find they have a friend.

"Nonsense!" exclaims our sharp-eyed, thin-lipped antagonist. "Such a man would never get rich, or even *get along*."

You are mistaken, Mr. Stock-jobber. Thus far many lines are drawn from real life, though for the second part which follows, we want, as yet, a worthy model.

We must imagine, then, our ideal merchant to have grown rich in some forty years of toil passed in the way we have indicated. His hair is touched with white, but his form is vigorous yet. Neither *gormandise* nor the fever of gain have destroyed his complexion, quenched the light of his eye, or substituted sneers for smiles. He is an upright, strong, sagacious, generous looking man, and if his movements be abrupt and his language concise somewhat beyond the standard of beauty, he is still the gentleman mercantile, but a mercantile nobleman.

Our nation is not silly in striving for an aristocracy. Humanity longs for its upper classes. But the silliness consists in making them out of clothes, equipage, and a servile imitation of foreign manners, instead of the genuine elegance and distinction that can only be produced by genuine culture. Shame upon the stupidity which, when all circumstances leave us free for the introduction of a real aristocracy, such as the world never saw, bases its pretensions on, or makes its bow to, the footman behind the coach, instead of the person within it.

But our merchant shall be a real nobleman, whose noble manners spring from a noble mind, whose fashions from a sincere and intelligent love of the Beautiful.

We will also indulge the fancy of giving him a wife and children congenial with himself. Having lived in sympathy with him, they have acquired no taste for luxury; they do not think that the best use of wealth and power is in self indulgence, but, on the contrary, that it is more blessed to give than to receive.

He is now having one of these fine houses built, and, as in other things, proceeds on a few simple principles. It is substantial, for he wishes to give no countenance to the paper buildings that correspond with other worthless paper currency of a credit system. It is thoroughly finished and furnished, for he has a conscience about his house, as about the neatness of his person. All must be of a piece—harmony and a wise utility are consulted without regard to show. Still, as he is a rich man, we allow him reception rooms, lofty, large, adorned with good copies of ancient works of art, and fine specimens of modern.

N.B.—I admit, in this instance, the propriety of my nobleman, often choosing by advice of friends who may have had more leisure and opportunity to acquire a sure appreciation of merit in these walks. His character being simple, he will, no doubt, appreciate a great part of what is truly grand and beautiful. But, also, from imperfect culture, he might often reject what in the end he would have found most valuable to himself and others. For he has not done learning, but only acquired the privilege of helping to open a domestic school in which he will find himself a pupil as well as master. So he may well make use, in furnishing himself with the school apparatus, of the best counsel. The same applies to making his library a good one. Only there must be no sham; no pluming himself on possessions that represent his wealth, but the taste of others. Our nobleman is incapable of pretension, or the airs of connoisseurship; his object is to furnish a home with those testimonies of a higher life in man that may best aid to cultivate the same in himself and those assembled round him.

He shall also have a fine garden and green-houses. But the flowers shall not be used only to decorate his apartments or the hair of his daughters, but shall often bless, by their soft and exquisite eloquence, the poor invalid, or others whose sorrowful hearts find in their society a consolation and a hope which nothing else bestows. For flowers, the highest expression of the bounty of Nature, declare that for all men not merely labor or luxury but gentle, buoyant, ever energetic joy was intended, and bid us hope that we shall not forever be kept back from our inheritance.

All the persons who have aided in building up this domestic temple, from the artist who painted the ceilings to the poorest hodman, shall be well paid and cared for during its erection, for it is a necessary part of the happiness of our nobleman to feel that all concerned in creating his home are the happier for it.

We have said nothing about the architecture of the house, and yet this is only for want of room. We do consider it one grand duty of every person able to build a good house, also to aim at building a beautiful one. We do not want imitations of what was used in other ages, nations and climates, but what is simple, noble and in conformity with the wants of our own. Room enough, simplicity of design, and judicious adjustment of the parts to their uses and to the whole, are the first requisites, the ornaments are merely the finish on these. We hope to see a good style of civic architecture long before any material improvement in the country edifices, for reasons that would be tedious to enumerate here. Suffice it to say that we are far more anxious to see an American architecture, than an American literature, for we are here sure there is already something individual to express.

Well, suppose the house built and equipped with man and horse. You may be sure my nobleman gives his "hired help" good accommodations, both for their sleeping and waking hours,—baths, books, and some leisure to use them. Nay! I assure you, and this assurance also is drawn from life, that it is possible, even in our present social relations, for the man who does common justice in these respects to his fellows, and shows a friendly heart that thoroughly feels service no degradation, but an honor,

> "A man's a man for a' that."
> Honor in the king the wisdom of his service.
> Honor in the serf the fidelity of his service.

can have around him those who do their work in serenity of mind, neither deceiving nor envying those whom circumstances have enabled to command their service. As to the carriage[,] that is used for the purpose of going to and fro in bad weather, or ill health, or haste, or for drives to enjoy the country. But my nobleman and his family are too well born and bred not to prefer using their own feet when possible. And their carriage is much appropriated to the use of poor invalids, even among the abhorred class of poor relations, so that they often have not room in it for themselves, much less for flaunting dames and lazy dandies.

We need hardly add that their attendants wear no liveries. They are aware that, in a society where none of the causes exist that justify this habit abroad, the practice would have no other result than to call up a sneer to the lips of the most complaisant and needy foreign "mi lor" when Mrs. Higginbottom's carriage stops the way with its tawdry, ill-fancied accompaniments. *Will* none of their "governors" tell our cit[izen]s the Æsopean fable of the donkey that tried to imitate the gambols of the little dog?

The wife of my nobleman is so well matched with him that she has no need to be the better half. She is his almoner, his counselor, and the priestess who keeps burning on the domestic hearth a fire from the fuel he collects in his out-door work, whose genial heat and aspiring flame comfort and animate all who come within its range.

His children are his ministers, whose leisure and various qualifications enable them to carry out his good thoughts. They hold all that they possess—time, money, talents, acquirements—on the principle of stewardship. They wake up the seeds of virtue and genius in all the young persons of their acquaintance, but the poorer classes are especially their care. There they seek for those who are threatened with lying mute, inglorious Hampdens and Miltons, but for their scrutiny and care. Of these they become the teachers and patrons to the extent of their power. Such knowledge of the arts, sciences and just principles of action as they have been favored with, they communicate and thereby form novices worthy to fill up the ranks of the true American aristocracy.

And the house—it is a large one, a single family does not fill its chambers. Some of them are devoted to the use of men of genius, who need a serene home, free from care, while they pursue their labors for the good of the world. Thus, as in the palaces of the little princes of Italy in a better day, theses chambers become hallowed by the nativities of great thoughts, and the horoscopes of the human births that may take place there are likely to read the better for it. Suffering virtue sometimes finds herself taken home here, instead of being sent to the almshouse or presented with a half dollar and a ticket for coal, and finds upon my nobleman's mattresses (for the wealth of Croesus would not lure him or his to sleep on down) dreams of angelic protection which enable her to rise refreshed for the struggle of the morrow.

The uses of hospitality are very little understood among us, so that we fear generally there is small chance of entertaining Gods and Angels unawares, as the Greeks and Hebrews did in the generous time of hospitality when every man had a claim on the roof of fellow man. Now, none is received to a bed and breakfast unless he comes as "bearer of despatches" from his Excellency So and So.

But let us not be supposed to advocate the system of all work and no play, or to delight exclusively in the pedagoguish and Goody Two Shoes vein. Reader, if any such accompany me to this scene of my vision, cheer up, I hear the sound of music in full band, and see the banquet prepared. Perhaps even they are dancing the Polka and Redowa in some of those airy, well lighted rooms. In another they find in the acting of extempore dramas, arrangement of tableaux, little concerts or recitations, intermingled with beautiful national or fancy dances, some portion of the enchanting, refining and ennobling influences of the arts. The finest engravings on all subjects attend such as like to employ themselves more quietly, while those who can find a companion or congenial group to converse with, find also plenty of recesses and still rooms with softer light provided for their pleasure.

There is not this side of the Atlantic, we dare our glove upon it, a more devout believer than ourselves in the worship of the Muses and Graces, both for itself and its importance no less to the moral than the intellectual life of a nation. Perhaps there is not one who has *so* deep a feeling or so many suggestions ready, in the fulness of time to be hazarded on the subject.

But in order to such worship what standard is there as to admission to the service? Talents of gold or Delphian talents? fashion or elegance? "standing" or the power to move gracefully from one "position" to any other?

Our nobleman did not hesitate; the handle to his door-bell was not of gold, but mother-of-pearl, pure and prismatic.

If he did not go into the alleys to pick up the poor, they were not excluded, if qualified by intrinsic qualities to adorn the scene. Neither were wealth or fashion a cause of exclusion more than of admission. All depended on the person; yet he did not *seek* his guests among the slaves of Fashion, for he knew that persons highly endowed rarely had patience with the frivolities of that class, but retired and left it to be peopled mostly by weak and plebeian natures. Yet all depended on the person. Was the person fair, noble, wise, brilliant, or even only youthfully innocent and gay, or venerable in a good old age, he or she was welcome. Still, as simplicity of character and some qualification positively good, healthy and natural was requisite for admission, we must say the company was select. Our nobleman and his family had weeded their 'circle' faithfully year by year.

Some valued acquaintances they had made in ball-rooms and boudoirs, and kept; but far more had been made through the daily wants of life, and shoemakers, sempstresses and graziers mingled happily with artists and statesmen, to the benefit of both. (N.B.—None used the poisonous weed in or out of our domestic temple.)

I cannot tell you what infinite good our nobleman and his family were doing by creation of this true social center where the legitimate aristocracy of the land assembled, not to be dazzled by expensive furniture (our nobleman bought what was good in texture and beautiful in form but not *because* it was expensive,) not to be feasted on rare wines and high seasoned dainties, though they found simple refreshments well prepared, (as indeed it was a matter of duty and conscience in that house that the least office should be well fulfilled,) but to enjoy the generous confluence of mind with mind and heart with heart, the pastimes that are not waste-times of taste and inventive fancy, the cordial union of beings from all points and places in noble human sympathy.—New-York was beginning to be truly American or rather Columbian, and money stood for something in the records of history. It had brought opportunity to genius and aid to virtue. But just this moment the jostling showed me that I had reached the corner of Wall-st. I looked earnestly at the omnibuses discharging their eager freight, as if I hoped to see my merchant. Perhaps he has gone to the Post Office to take out letters from his friends in Utopia, thought I. "Please ye give me a penny," screamed a ragged, half-starved little street sweep, and the fancied cradle of the American Utopia receded or rather proceeded fifty years at least into the Future.

✱

[February 6, 1846]

Prevalent Idea That Politeness
Is Too Great a Luxury to Be Given to the Poor

A few days ago, a lady, crossing in one of the ferry boats that ply from this city, saw a young boy, poorly dressed, sitting with an infant in his arms on one of the benches. She observed that the child looked sickly and coughed. This, as the day was raw, made her anxious in its behalf, and she went to the boy and asked whether he was alone there with the baby, and if he did not think the cold breeze dangerous for it. He replied that he was sent out with the child to take care of it, and that his father said the fresh air from the water would do it good.

While he made this simple answer, a number of persons had collected around to listen, and one of them, a well-dressed woman, addressed the boy in a string of such questions and remarks as these:

"What is your name? Where do you live? Are you telling us the truth? It's a shame to have that baby out in such weather; you'll be the death of it. (To the bystanders:) I would go and see his mother and tell her about it, if I was sure he had told us the truth about where he lived. How do you expect to get back? Here, (in the rudest voice,) somebody says you have not told the truth as to where you live."

The child, whose only offence consisted in taking care of the little one in public, and answering when he was spoken to, began to shed tears at the accusations thus grossly preferred against him. The bystanders stared at both; but among them all there was not one with sufficiently clear notions of propriety and moral energy to say to this impudent questioner, "Woman! do you suppose, because you wear a handsome shawl, and that boy a patched jacket, that you have any right to speak to him at all, unless he wishes it, far less to prefer against him those rude accusations? Your vulgarity is unendurable; leave the place or alter your manner."

Many such instances have we seen of insolent rudeness or more insolent affability founded on no apparent grounds, except an apparent difference in pecuniary position, for no one can suppose in such cases the offending party has really enjoyed the benefit of refined education and society, but all present let them pass as matters of course. It was sad to see how the poor would endure—mortifying to see how the purse-proud dared offend. An excellent man who was, in his early years, a missionary to the poor, used to speak afterwards with great shame of the manner in which he had conducted himself towards them.—"When I recollect," said he, "the freedom with which I entered their houses, inquired into all their affairs, commented on their conduct and disputed their statements I wonder I was never horsewhipped and feel that I ought to have been; it would have done me good, for I needed as severe a lesson on the universal obligations of politeness in its only genuine form of respect for man as man, and delicate sympathy with each in his peculiar position."

Charles Lamb, who was indeed worthy to be called a human being from those refined sympathies, said, "You call him a gentleman: does his washerwoman find him so?" We may say, if she did so, she found him a *man,* neither treating her with vulgar abruptness, nor giving himself airs of condescending liveliness, but treating her with that gentle respect which a feeling of equality inspires.

To doubt the veracity of another is an insult which in most *civilized* communities must in the so-called higher classes be atoned for by blood, but, in those same communities, the same men will, with the utmost lightness, doubt the truth of one who wears a ragged coat, and thus do all they can to injure and degrade him by assailing his self-respect and breaking the feeling of personal honor—a wound to which hurts a man as a wound to its bark does a tree.

Then how rudely are favors conferred, just as a bone is thrown to a dog. A gentleman indeed will not do *that* without accompanying signs of sympathy and regard. Just as this woman said, "If you have told the truth I will go and see your mother," are many acts performed on which the actors pride themselves as kind and charitable.

All men might learn from the French in these matters. That people, whatever be their faults, are really well-bred, and many acts might be quoted from their romantic annals, where gifts were given from rich to poor with a graceful courtesy, equally honorable and delightful to the giver and the receiver.

In Catholic countries there is more courtesy, for charity is there a duty, and must be done for God's sake; there is less room for a man to give himself the Pharisaical tone about it. A rich man is not so surprised to find himself in contact with a poor one; nor is the custom of kneeling on the open pavement, the silk robe close to the beggar's rags, without profit. The separation by pews, even on the day when all meet nearest, is as bad for the manners as the soul.

Blessed be he or she who has passed through this world, not only with an open purse and willingness to render the aid of mere outward benefits, but with an open eye and open heart, ready to cheer the downcast, and enlighten the dull by words of comfort and looks of love. The wayside charities are the most valuable both as to sustaining hope and diffusing knowledge, and none can render them who has not an expansive nature, a heart alive to affection, and some true notion, however imperfectly developed, of the nature of human brotherhood.

Such an one can never sauce the given meat with taunts, freeze the bread by a cold glance of doubt, or plunge the man who asked for his hand deeper back into the mud by any kind of rudeness.

In the little instance with which we begun, no help *was* asked, unless by the sight of the timid little boy's old jacket. But the license which this seemed to the well-clothed woman to give to rudeness was so characteristic of a deep fault now existing, that a volume of comments might follow and a host of anecdatos be drawn from almost anyone's experience in exposition of it. These few words, perhaps, may awaken thought in those who have drawn tears from others' eyes through an ignorance brutal, but not hopelessly so, if they are willing to rise above it.

*

[May 31, 1845]

Consecration of Grace Church

Whoever passes up Broadway finds his attention arrested by three fine structures, Trinity Church, that of the Messiah, and Grace Church.

His impressions are, probably, at first of a pleasant character. He looks upon these edifices as expressions, which, however inferior in grandeur to the poems in stone which adorn the older world, surely indicate that man cannot rest content with his short earthly span, but prizes relations to eternity. The house, in which he pays deference to claims which death will not cancel, seems to be no less important in his eyes than those in which the affairs which press nearest are attended to.

So far, so good! That is expressed which gives man his superiority over the other orders of the natural world, that consciousness of spiritual affinities with which we see no unequivocal signs elsewhere.

But, if this be something great when compared with the rest of the animal creation, yet how little seems it when compared with the ideal that has been offered to him, as to the means of signifying such feelings. These temples! how far do they correspond with the idea of that religious sentiment from which they originally sprung?

In the old world the history of such edifices, though not without its shadow, had many bright lines.—Kings and Emperors paid oftentimes for the materials and labor a price of blood and plunder, and many a wretched sinner sought by contributions of stone for their walls! to roll off that he had laid on his conscience. Still the community amid which they rose, knew little of these drawbacks. Pious legends test the purity of feeling associated with each circumstance of their building. Mysterious orders, of which we know only that they were consecrated to brotherly love and the development of mind, produced the genius which animated the architecture, but the casting of the bells and suspending them in the tower was an act in which all orders of the community took part; for when those cathedrals were consecrated it was for the use of all. Rich and poor knelt together upon their marble pavements, and the imperial altar welcomed the obscurest artisan.

This grace our Churches want, the grace which belongs to all religions, but is peculiarly and solemnly enforced upon the followers of Jesus. The poor to whom he came to preach can have no share in the grace of Grace Church. In St. Peter's, if only as an empty form, the soiled feet of travel-worn disciples are washed, but such feet can never intrude on the fane of the holy trinity here in republican America, and the Messiah may be supposed still to give as excuse for delay "The poor you always have with you."

We must confess this circumstance is to us quite destructive of reverence and value for these buildings.

We are told that at the late consecration the claims of the poor were eloquently urged, and that an effort is to be made, by giving a side chapel, to atone for the luxury which shuts them out from the reflection of sunshine through those brilliant windows. It is certainly better that they should be offered the crumbs from the rich man's table than nothing at all. Yet it is surely not *the* way that Jesus would have taught to provide for the poor.

Would you not then have these splendid edifices erected? We certainly feel that the educational influence of good specimens of architecture (and we know no other argument in their favor) is far from being a counterpoise to the abstraction of so much money from purposes that would be more in fulfillment of that Christian idea which these assume to represent.

Were the rich to build such a church, and, dispensing with pews and all exclusive advantages, invite all who would to come in to the banquet, that were, indeed, noble and Christian. And, though we believe more, for our nation and time, in intellectual monuments than those of wood and stone, and, in opposition even to our admired Powers, think that Michael Angelo himself could have advised no more suitable monument to Washington than a house devoted to the instruction of the people, and believe that that great master and the Greeks no less would agree with us if they lived now to survey all the bearings of the subject; yet we would not object to these splendid churches, if the idea of Him they call Master were represented in them. But till it is, they can do no good, for the means are not in harmony with the end. The rich man sits in state while 'near two hundred thousand' Lazaruses linger, unprovided for, without the gate. While this is so, they must not talk much, within, of Jesus of Nazareth, who called to him fishermen, laborers and artisans, for his companions and disciples.

We find some excellent remarks on this subject from Rev. STEPHEN OLIN, President of the Wesleyan University. They are appended as a note to a discourse addressed to Young Men, on the text:

"Put ye on the Lord Jesus Christ, and make not provision for the flesh, to fulfil the lusts thereof."

This discourse, though it discloses formal and external views of religious ties and obligations, is dignified by a fervent, generous love for men, and a more than commonly catholic liberality, and though these remarks are made and meant to bear upon the interests of his own sect, yet they are anti-sectarian in their tendency and worthy the consideration of all anxious to understand the call of duty in these matters. Earnest attention of this sort will better avail than fifteen hundred dollars, or more, paid for a post of exhibition in a fashionable Church, where, if piety be provided with one chance, worldness has twenty to stare it out of countenance.

✻
[March 11, 1846]

The Poor Man—An Ideal Sketch

The sketch of the Rich Man, made some three or four weeks since, seems to require this companion-piece, and we shall make the attempt, though the subject is far more difficult than the former was.

In the first place, we must state what we mean by a poor man, for it is a term of wide range in its relative applications. A pains-taking artisan, trained to self-denial and a strict adaptation, not of his means to his wants, but of his wants to his means, finds himself rich and grateful, if some unexpected fortune enables him to give his wife a new gown, his children cheap holiday joys, and to his starving neighbor a decent meal; while George IV, when heir apparent to the throne of Great Britain, considered himself driven by the pressure of poverty to become a debtor, a beggar, a swindler, and, by the aid of perjury, the husband of two wives at the same time, neither of whom he treated well. Since poverty is made an excuse for such depravity in conduct, it would be well to mark the limits within which self-control and resistance to temptation may be expected.

When he of the olden time prayed, "Give me neither poverty nor riches," we presume he meant that proportion of means to the average wants of a human being which secures freedom from eating cares, freedom of motion, and a moderate enjoyment of the common blessings offered by earth, air, water, the natural relations, and the subjects for thought which every day presents. We shall certainly not look above this point for our poor man.—A Prince may be poor, if he has not means to relieve the sufferings of his subjects, or secure to them needed benefits. Or he may make himself so, just as a well-paid laborer by drinking brings poverty to his roof. So may the Prince, by the mental gin of horse-racing or gambling, grow a beggar. But we shall not consider these cases.

Our subject will be taken between the medium we have spoken of as answer to the wise man's prayer, and that destitution which we must style infamous, either to the individual or to the society whose vices have caused that stage of poverty in which there is no certainty, and often no probability, of work or bread from day to day,—in which cleanness and all the decencies of life are impossible, and the natural human feelings are turned to gall because the man finds himself on this earth in a far worse situation than the brute. In this stage there is no Ideal, and from its abyss, if the unfortunates look up to Heaven, or the state of things as they ought to be, it is with suffocating gasps which demand relief or death. This degree of poverty is common, as we all know, but we who do not share it have no right to address those who do from our own standard, till we have placed their feet on our own level. Accursed is he who does not long to have this so,—to take out at least the physical Hell from this world! Unblest is he who is not seeking either by thought or act to effect this poor degree of amelioration in the circumstances of his race.

We take the subject of our sketch, then, somewhere between the abjectly poor and those in moderate circumstances. What we have to say may apply to either sex and to any grade in this division of the human family, from the hod-man and washerwoman up to the hard-working, poorly paid lawyer, clerk, schoolmaster or scribe.

The advantages of such a position are many. In the first place, you belong, inevitably, to the active and suffering part of the world. You know the ills that try men's souls and bodies. You cannot creep into a safe retreat, arrogantly to judge, or heartlessly to forget, the others. They are always before you; you see the path stained by their bleeding feet; stupid and flinty, indeed, must you be, if you can hastily wound or indolently forbear to aid them. Then, as to yourself, you know what your resources are; what you can do, what bear; there is small chance for you to escape a well-tempered modesty. Then, again, if you find power in yourself to endure the trial, there is reason and reality in some degree of self reliance. The moral advantages of such training can scarcely fail to amount to something, and as to the mental, that most important chapter, how the lives of men are fashioned and transfused by the experience of passion and the development of thought, presents new sections at every turn, such as the distant dilettante's opera-glasses will never detect,—to say nothing of the exercise of mere faculty, which, though insensible in its daily course, leads to results of immense importance.

But the evils, the disadvantages, the dangers, how many, how imminent! True, indeed, they are so.—There is the early bending of the mind to the production of marketable results, which must hinder all this free play of intelligence and deaden the powers that craved instruction. There is the callousness produced by the sight of more misery than it is possible to relieve, the heart, at first so sensitive, taking refuge in a stolid indifference against the pangs of sympathetic pain, it had not force to bear. There is the perverting influence of uncongenial employments, undertaken without or against choice, continued at unfit hours and seasons, till the man loses his natural relations with summer and winter, day and night, and has no sense more for natural beauty and joy. There is the mean providence, the perpetual caution to guard against ill instead of the generous freedom of a mind which expects good to ensue from all good actions. There is the sad doubt whether it will *do* to indulge the kindly impulse, the calculation of dangerous chances and the cost between the loving impulse and its fulfillment. Yes: there is bitter chance of narrowness, meanness and dullness on this path, and it requires great natural force, a wise and large view of life taken at an early age, or fervent trust in God, to evade them.

It is astonishing to see the poor, no less than the rich, the slaves of externals. One would think that, where the rich man once became aware of the worthlessness of the mere trappings of life from the weariness of a spirit that found itself entirely dissatisfied after pomp and self-indulgence, the poor man would learn this a hundred times from the experience how entirely independent of them is all that is intrinsically valuable in our life. But no! The poor man wants dignity, wants elevation of spirit. It is his own servility that forges the fetters that enslave him. Whether he cringe to or rudely defy, the man in the coach and handsome coat, the cause and effect are the same. He is influenced by a costume and a position. He is not firmly rooted in the truth that, only in so far as outward beauty and grandeur are a representative of the mind of the possessor, can they count for anything at all. Oh poor man! you are poor indeed, if you feel yourself so; poor if you do not feel that a soul born of God, a mind capable of scanning the wondrous works of time and space, and a flexible body for its service, are the essential riches of a man, and all he needs to make him the equal of any other man. You are mean, if the possession of money or other external advantages can make you envy or shrink from a being mean enough to value himself upon such. Stand where you may, oh Man, you cannot be noble and rich, if your brow be not broad and steadfast, if your eye beam not with a consciousness of inward worth, of eternal claims and hopes which such trifles cannot at all affect. A man without this majesty is ridiculous amid the flourish and decorations procured by money, pitiable in the faded habiliments of poverty. But a man who is a man, a woman who is a woman, can never feel lessened or embarrassed because others look ignorantly on such matters. If they regret the want of these temporary means of power, it must be solely because it fetters their motions, deprives them of leisure and desired means of improvement, or of benefiting those they love or pity.

I have heard those possessed of rhetoric and imaginative tendency declare that they should have been outwardly great and inwardly free, victorious poets and heroes, if Fate had allowed them a certain quantity of dollars. I have found it impossible to believe them. In early youth penury may have power to freeze the genial current of the soul and prevent it, during one short life, from becoming sensible of its true vocation and destiny. But if it *has* become conscious of these, and yet there is not advance in any and all circumstances, no change would avail.

No! our poor man must begin higher. He must, in the first place, really believe there is a God who ruleth, a fact to which few men vitally bear witness, though most are ready to affirm it with the lips.

2d. He must sincerely believe that rank and wealth—

> —are but the guinea's stamp,
> The man's the gold,

take his stand on his claims as a human being, made in God's own likeness, urge them when the occasion permits, but, at all times, never be so false to them as to feel put down or injured by the want of mere external advantages.

3d. He must accept his lot, while he is in it. If he can change it for the better, let his energies be exerted to do so. But if he cannot, there is none that will not yield an opening to Eden, to the glories of Zion and even to the subterranean enchantments of our strange estate. There is none that may not be used with nobleness.

> "Who sweeps a room, as for Thy sake
> Makes that and th' action clean."

4th. Let him examine the subject enough to be convinced that there is not that vast difference between the employments that is supposed, in the means of expansion and refinement. All depends on the spirit as to the use that is made of an occupation. Mahomet was not a wealthy merchant, and profound philosophers have ripened on the benches, not of the lawyers, but the shoemakers. It did not hurt Milton to be a poor schoolmaster, nor Shak[e]speare to do the errands of a London play house. Yes, the mind is its own place, and if it will keep that place, all doors will be opened from it. Upon this subject we hope to offer some hints at a future day, in speaking of the different trades, professions and modes of labor.

5th. Let him remember that from no man can the chief wealth be kept. On all men the sun and stars shine; for all the oceans swell and rivers flow. All men may be brothers, lovers, fathers, friends; before all lie the mysteries of birth and death. If these wondrous means of wealth and blessing be likely to remain misused or unused, there are quite as many disadvantages in the way of the man of money as of the man who has none. Few who drain the choicest grape know the ecstacy of bliss and knowledge that follows a full draught of the wine of life. That has mostly been reserved for those on whose thoughts society, as a public, makes but a moderate claim. And if bitterness followed on the joy, if your fountain was frozen after its first gush by the cold winds of the world, yet, moneyless men, ye are at least not wholly ignorant of what a human being has force to know. You have not skimmed over surfaces, and been dozing on beds of down during the rare and stealthy visits of Love and the Muses. Remember this, and, looking round on the arrangements of the lottery, see if you did not draw a prize in your turn.

It will be seen that our ideal poor man needs to be religious, wise, dignified and humble, grasping at nothing, claiming all; willing to wait, never willing to give up; servile to none, the servant of all, and esteeming it the glory of a man to serve. The character is rare, but not unattainable. We have, however, found an approach to it more frequent in woman than in man.

Woman, even less than Man, is what she should be, as a whole. She is not that self-centered being, full of profound intuitions, angelic love, and flowing poesy, that she should be. Yet there are circumstances in which the native force and purity of her being teach her how to conquer where the restless impatience of man brings defeat and leaves him crushed and bleeding on the field.

Images rise to mind of calm strength, of gentle wisdom learning from every turn of adverse fate, of youthful tenderness and faith undimmed to the close of life, which redeem humanity and make the heart glow with fresh courage as we write. They are mostly from obscure corners and very private walks; there was nothing shining, nothing of an obvious and sounding heroism to make their conduct doubtful, by tainting their motives with vanity. Unknown they lived, untrumpeted they died. Many hearts were warmed and fed by them, but, perhaps, no mind but our own ever consciously took account of their virtues.

Had Art but the power adequately to tell their simple stories, and to cast upon them the light which, shining through those marked and faded faces, foretold the glories of a second Spring! The tears of holy emotion which fell from those eyes have seemed to us pearls beyond all price, or rather whose price will be paid only when beyond the grave they enter those better spheres in whose faith they felt and acted here.

From this private gallery we will, for the present, bring forward only one picture. That of a Black Nun was wont to fetter the eyes of visitors in the Royal Galleries of France, and my Sister of Mercy too is of that complexion. The old woman was recommended as a laundress by my friend, who had long prized her. I was immediately struck with the dignity and propriety of her manner. In the depth of winter she brought herself the heavy baskets through the slippery streets, and when I asked why she did not employ some younger person to do what was so entirely disproportioned to her strength, simply said, "she lived alone and could not afford to hire an errand-boy." "It was hard for her?" "No! she was fortunate in being able to get work at her age, when others could do it better. Her friends were very good to procure it for her." "Had she a comfortable home?" "Tolerably so; she should not need one long." "Was that a thought of joy to her?" "Yes; for she hoped to see again the husband and children from whom she had long been separated."

Thus much in answer to the questions; but at other times the little she said was on general topics. It was not from her that I learnt how "the great idea of Duty had held her upright" through a life of incessant toil, sorrow, and bereavement, and that not only had she remained upright, but that the character had been constantly progressive. Her latest act had been to take home a poor sick girl, who had no home of her own, and could not bear the idea of dying in a hospital, and maintain and nurse her through the last weeks of her life. "Her eye-sight was failing, and she should not be able to work much longer, but then God would provide. *Somebody* ought to see to the poor motherless girl."

It was not merely the greatness of the act, for one in such circumstances, but the quiet, matter-of-course way in which it was done, that showed the habitual tone of the mind, and made us feel that life could hardly do more for a human being than to make him or her the *somebody* that is daily so deeply needed to represent the right,—to do the plain right thing.

"God will provide." Ay, indeed, it is the poor who feel themselves near to the God of Love.—"Though he slay them, still do they trust him." "I hope," said I to a poor apple-woman who had been drawn on to disclose a tale of distress that almost, in the mere hearing, made me weary of life, "I hope I may yet see you in a happier condition." "With God's help," she replied, with a smile that Raphael would have delighted to transfer to the canvas, a Mozart to his strains of angelic sweetness. All her life she had seemed an outcast child, still she leaned upon her Father's love.

The dignity of a state like this may vary its form in more or less richness and beauty of detail, but here is the focus of what makes life valuable. It is this spirit which makes Poverty the best servant to the Ideal of Human Nature. I am content with this type, and will only quote, in addition, a ballad I found in a foreign periodical translated from Chamisso, and which forcibly recalled my own laundress as an equally admirable sample of the same class, the Ideal Poor, which we need for our consolation so long as there must be real poverty:

THE OLD WASHERWOMAN

>Among yon lines her hands have laden,
>   A laundress with white hair appears,
>Alert as many a youthful maiden,
>   Spite of her five-and-seventy years.
>Bravely she won those white hairs, still
>   Eating the bread hard toil obtained her,
>And laboring truly to fulfil
>   The duties to which God ordained her.
>
>Once she was young and full of gladness,
>   She loved and hoped, was wooed and won;
>Then came the matron's cares, the sadness
>   No loving heart on earth may shun.
>Three babes she bore her mate; she prayed
>   Beside his sick-bed; he was taken;
>She saw him in the church-yard laid,
>   Yet kept her faith and hope unshaken.
>
>The task her little ones of feeding
>   She met unfaltering from that hour;
>She taught them thrift and honest breeding,
>   Her virtues were their worldly dower.
>To seek employment, one by one,
>   Forth with her blessing they departed,
>And she was in the world alone,
>   Alone and old, but still high-hearted.
>
>With frugal forethought, self-denying,
>   She gathered coin, and flax she bought,
>And many a night her spindle plying,
>   Good store of fine-spun thread she wrought.
>The thread was fashioned in the loom;
>   She brought it home, and calmly seated
>To work, with not a thought of gloom,
>   Her decent grave clothes she completed.

The Rich and the Poor
75

> She looks on them with fond elation,
>   They are her wealth, her treasure rare,
> Her age's pride and consolation,
>   Hoarded with all a miser's care.
> She dons the sark each Sabbath day,
>   To hear the Word that faileth never;
> Well pleased she lays it then away,
>   Till she shall sleep in it for ever.
>
> Would that my spirit witness bore me
>   That, like this woman, I had done
> The work my Maker put before me,
>   Duly from morn till set of sun.
> Would that life's cup had been by me
>   Quaffed in such wise and happy measure.
> And that I too might finally
>   Look on my shroud with such meek pleasure.

Such are the noble of the earth. They do not repine; they do not chafe, even in the inmost heart.—They feel that, whatever else may be denied or withdrawn, there remains the better part, which cannot be taken from them. This line exactly expresses the woman I knew:

> "Alone and old, but still high-hearted."

Will any, Poor or Rich, fail to feel that the children of such a parent were rich, when

> "Her virtues were their worldly dower?"

Will any fail to bow the heart in assent to the aspiration—

> "Would that my spirit witness bore me
> That, like this woman, I had done
> The work my Maker put before me,
> Duly from morn till set of sun?"

May not that suffice to any man's ambition?

*

[March 25, 1846]

5
Prison and Asylum Reform

When Margaret Fuller first arrived in New York City, she said one of her first assignments was to "survey" "the Institutions here of a remedial and benevolent kind." She visited these institutions in the company of the Rev. William Henry Channing and wrote a series of articles reprinted here. By describing holidays at these institutions, Fuller tinged her reports with romantic irony. She went to church services at Sing Sing prison on Christmas and Thanksgiving. She visited the Bloomingdale Asylum for the Insane on St. Valentine's Day.[1]

In colonial days local governments kept the insane in jails and poorhouses. The Bloomingdale Asylum, founded by Quakers, was one of the first in the nation. By 1816 it was receiving funds from the New York State Legislature. The large movement to build asylums, though, began in New York and Massachusetts in the 1830s when doctors began to argue that hospitalization would create the perfect setting for curing the insane. Pliny Earle, director at Bloomingdale when Fuller made her visits, advocated the asylum cure for insanity. When he toured European asylums twice, in 1838–39 and 1845, he found the insane warehoused in abandoned convents and castles. Because America designed and built its asylums specifically for the care of the mentally ill, Earle and others hoped the new and comfortable premises would help in the healing process. By the 1840s Bloomingdale housed 150 patients, men and women. Earle trained his attendants and hired one for every seven inmates. Within the walls of the institution, Bloomingdale and other asylums tried to replicate ordinary life as opposed to prison life—no numbers, no special haircuts, no uniforms, no marching from place to place.[2]

In the "Twenty-Fifth Report of the Bloomingdale Asylum for the Insane," Fuller stated her general philosophy on the reform of institutions. She believed that criminals, the insane, or the destitute improved when they received kind treatment, good living conditions, education, and respect. Harsh treatment made them worse, she thought. The late-twentieth-century version of this position turns on issues like air-conditioning for prison cells. In Margaret Fuller's day, the issues were more basic. For instance, in a footnote to her review of the Bloomingdale report, Fuller explained how a strait jacket (referred to here as a camisole) eliminated the cruelty of manacles: "The arms of the patient are carried around the breast, the sleeves are carried around the body and tied behind. There is no pressure on the hands or wrists."

Praising the Bloomingdale Asylum as an enlightened institution, Fuller said she saw no inmates "chained in solitary cells, screaming out their anguish." Instead, inmates attended dances in a hall decorated with Christmas wreaths. This kind treatment, she maintained, would result in well-behaved inmates who acted normally.

In 1848 reformer Dorothea Dix toured Bloomingdale Asylum and described a much harsher place with overcrowded wards and inadequate physical facilities and supervision. Her famous government report damning the institution launched a major reform campaign. Historian David Rothman says asylums like Bloomingdale failed because they became dumping grounds, places of custody for the incurably insane. Because cities preferred to house their indigent insane in common jails, which cost less than the fees charged by Bloomingdale, they committed only hopeless cases to the more expensive asylums.[3]

Fuller's articles on asylum reform aligned with the ideas of the medical profession, but her articles on women prisoners took a more radical view. In the 1840s authorities began jailing women for prostitution and public drunkenness. Once in prison a woman had little hope because institutions made no attempt at rehabilitation. "Instead of sympathy for her plight, . . . most men expressed outright hostility to the fallen woman and blamed her for men's crimes as well," said historian Estelle B. Freedman. Few women reformers came to the aid of women prisoners because reformers wanted to avoid risking their own status as respectable, middle-class ladies, commented Freedman.[4]

One woman, Margaret Fuller, did argue in print for help for women prisoners. "Our City Charities" endorsed a campaign to create a home for discharged women convicts. After the creation of this halfway house, a second column, "Asylum for Female Convicts," called for donations to the home. In these ground-breaking articles, Fuller became one of the first to argue publicly that economic and social forces pushed women into prostitution.[5]

Fuller also discussed her concern for prostitutes in a letter. "I have always felt great interest in those women, who are trampled in the mud to gratify the brute appetites of men, and wished I might be brought, naturally, into contact with them." Noted Horace Greeley, "She had once attended, with other women, a gathering of outcasts of their sex; and, being asked how they appeared to her, replied, 'As women like myself, save that they are victims of wrong and misfortune.'" Greeley also commented, "I have known few women, and scarcely another maiden, who had the heart and the courage to speak with such frank compassion, in mixed circles, of the most degraded and outcast portion of the sex. The contemplation of their treatment, especially by the guilty authors of their ruin, moved her to a calm and mournful indignation, which she did not attempt to suppress or control."[6]

Many of the institutions Fuller visited had much worse conditions than Bloomingdale or the halfway house for released female convicts. At Bellevue Alms House Fuller found people who received decent physical care but sat staring in vacant boredom. She called for books and education to help them find jobs. Conditions at the infamous Tombs prison she found barbarous, "the air in the upper galleries unendurable." Fuller's articles on asylum and prison reform all stressed the same theme: Kind care begets good results. The tale "Caroline" articulates this moral.

In these articles Fuller sided with a group of reformers who hoped that decent treatment would restore mental health to the insane and moral probity to the criminal. In 1844, for example, middle-class professionals organized the New York Prison Association to push for rehabilitation rather than punishment. This group sought the causes of crime. With a known cause, one would also find a cure, they assumed. Reformers like Margaret Fuller and the members of the New York Prison Association fought what prison historian Larry Sullivan called "an era of moral terrorism." In the thirty years before the Civil War, America made the poor and the criminals "scapegoats for what the moralists saw as an increasingly disordered society," said Sullivan.[7]

St. Valentine's Day—
Bloomingdale Asylum for the Insane

This merry season of light jokes and lighter love-tokens in which Cupid presents the feathered end of the dart, as if he meant to tickle before he wounded the captive, has always had a great charm for me: When but a child, I saw Allston's picture of the "Lady reading a Valentine," and the mild womanliness of the picture, so remote from passion no less than vanity, so capable of tenderness, so chastely timid in its self-possession, has given a color to the gayest thoughts connected with the day. From the ruff of Allston's Lady, whose clear starch is made to express all rosebud thoughts of girlish retirement, the soft unfledged hopes which never yet were tempted from the nest, to Sam Weller's Valentine is indeed a broad step, but one which we can take without material change of mood.

But of all the thoughts and pictures associated with the day, none can surpass in interest those furnished by the way in which we celebrated it last week.

The Bloomingdale Asylum for the Insane is conducted on the most wise and liberal plan known at the present day. Its superintendent, Dr. Earle, has had ample opportunity to observe the best modes of managing this class of diseases both here and in Europe, and he is one able, by refined sympathies and intellectual discernment, to apply the best that is known and to discover more.

Under his care the beautifully situated establishment at Bloomingdale loses every sign of the hospital and the prison, not long since thought to be inseparable from such a place. It is a house of refuge where those too deeply wounded or disturbed in body or spirit to keep up that semblance or degree of sanity which the conduct of affairs in the world at large demands may be soothed by gentle care, intelligent sympathy, and a judicious attention to their physical welfare, into health, or, at least, into tranquillity.

Dr. Earle, in addition to modes of turning the attention from causes of morbid irritation, and promoting brighter and juster thoughts, which he uses in common with other institutions, has this winter delivered a course of lectures to the patients. We were present at one of these some weeks since. The subjects touched upon were, often, of a nature to demand as close attention as an audience of regular students (not college students, but real students) can be induced to give. The large assembly present were almost uniformly silent, to appearance interested, and showed a power of decorum and self-government often wanting among those who esteem themselves in healthful mastery of their morals and manners. We saw, with great satisfaction, generous thoughts and solid pursuits offered as well as light amusements for the choice of the sick in mind. For it is our experience that such sickness arises as often from want of concentration as any other cause. One of the noblest youths that ever trod this soil was wont to say "he was never tired, if he could only see far enough." He is now gone where his view may be less bounded, but we, who stay behind, may take the hint that mania, no less than the commonest forms of prejudice, bespeaks a mind which does not see far enough to connect partial impressions. No doubt in many cases, dissipation of thought, after attention is once distorted into some morbid direction, may be the first method of cure, but we are glad to see others provided for those who are ready for them.

St. Valentine's Eve had been appointed for one of the dancing parties at the Institution, and a few friends from "the world's people" invited to be present.

At an early hour the company assembled in the well-lighted hall, still gracefully wreathed with its Christmas evergreens; the music struck up and the company entered.

And these are the people who, half a century ago, would have been chained in solitary cells, screaming out their anguish till silenced by threats or blows, lost, forsaken, hopeless, a blight to earth, a libel upon heaven.

Now they are many of them happy, all interested. Even those who are troublesome and subject to violent excitement in every-day scenes, show here that the power of self-control is not lost, only lessened. Give them an impulse strong enough, favorable circumstances, and they will begin to use it again. They regulate their steps to music; they restrain their impatient impulses from respect to themselves and to others. The power which shall yet shape order from all disorder and turn ashes to beauty, as violets spring up from green graves, hath them also in its keeping.

The party were well-dressed, with care and taste. The dancing was better than usual, because there was less of affectation and ennui. The party was more entertaining, because native traits came out more clear from the disguises of vanity and tact.

There was the blue-stocking lady, a mature belle and bel-esprit. Her condescending graces, her rounded compliments, her girlish, yet "highly intellectual" vivacity, expressed no less in her headdress than her manner, were just that touch above the common with which the illustrator of Dickens has thought fit to highten [*sic*] the charms of Mrs. Leo Hunter.

There was the traveled Englishman, *au fait* to every thing beneath the moon and beyond. With his clipped and glib phrases, his bundle of conventionalities carried so neatly under his arm, and his "My dear sir" in the perfection of cockney dignity, what better could the most select dinner party furnish us in the way of distinguished strangerhood?

There was the hoydenish young girl, and the decorous elegant lady smoothing down "the wild little thing." There was the sarcastic observer on the folly of the rest; in that, the greatest fool of all, unbeloved and unannealed. In contrast to this were characters altogether lovely, full of all sweet affections, whose bells, if jangled out of tune, still retained their true tone.

One of the best things on the evening was a dance improvised by two elderly women. They asked the privilege of the floor, and, a suitable measure being played, performed this dance in a style lively, characteristic, yet moderate enough. It was true dancing, like peasant dancing.

An old man sang comic songs in the style of various nations and characters, with a dramatic expression that would have commanded applause "on any stage."

And all was done decently, and in order; each biding his time. Slight symptoms of impatience here and there were easily soothed by the approach of this, truly a "good physician," the touch of whose hand seemed to possess a talismanic power to soothe. We doubt not that all went to their beds exhilarated, free from irritation, and more attuned to concord than before. Good bishop Valentine? thy feast was well kept, and not without the usual jokes and flings at old bachelors, the exchange of sugar-plums, mottos and repartees.

This is the second festival I have kept with those whom society has placed, not outside her pale, indeed, but outside the hearing of her benison. Christmas I passed in a prison! There too, I saw marks of the miraculous power of Love, when guided by a pure faith in the goodness of its source, and intelligence as to the design of the creative intelligence. I saw enough of its power, impeded as it was by the ignorance of those who, eighteen hundred years after the coming of Christ, still believe more in fear and force. I saw enough, I say, of this power to convince me, if I needed conviction, that it is indeed omnipotent, as he said it was.

A companion, of that delicate nature by which a scar is felt as a wound, was saddened by the sense how very little our partialities, undue emotions, and manias need to be exaggerated to entitle us to rank among madmen. I cannot view it so. Rather let the sense that, with all our faults and follies, there is still a sound spot, a presentiment of eventual health in the inmost nature, embolden us to hope—to *know* it is the same with all. A great thinker has spoken of the Greek, for highest praise as "a self-renovating character." But we are all Greeks, if we will but think so. For the mentally or morally insane, there is no irreparable ill if the principle of life can but be aroused. And it can never be finally benumbed, except by our own will.

One of the famous pictures at Munich is of a mad house. The painter has represented the moral obliquities of society exaggerated into madness; that is to say, self-indulgence has, in each instance, destroyed the power to forbear the ill or to discern the good. A celebrated writer has added a little book, to be used while looking at the picture, and drawn inferences of universal interest.

Such would we draw; such as this! Let no one dare to call another mad who is not himself willing to rank in the same class for every perversion and fault of judgment. Let no one dare aid in punishing another as criminal who is not willing to suffer the penalty due to his own offences.

Yet, while owning that we are all mad, all criminal, let us not despair, but rather believe that the Ruler of all never could permit such wide-spread ill but to good ends. It is permitted to give us a field to redeem it—

> ———"to transmute, bereave
> Of an ill influence and a good receive."

It flows inevitably from the emancipation of our wills, the development of individuality in us. These aims accomplished, all shall yet be well; and it is ours to learn *how* that good time may be hastened.

We know no sign of the times more encouraging than the increasing nobleness and wisdom of view as to the government of asylums for the insane and of prisons. Whatever is learnt as to these forms of society is learnt for all. There is nothing that can be said of such government that must not be said, also, of the government of families, schools, and States. But we have much to say on this subject, and shall revert to it again, and often, though, perhaps, not with so pleasing a theme as this of St. Valentine's Eve.

✱

[Feb. 22, 1845]

*Twenty-fifth Annual Report of the
Bloomingdale Asylum for the Insane
By Pliny Earle, M. D.
Physician to the Asylum.
New-York, 1845*

These reports ought to be circulated extensively and read by every person capable of thought on subjects of every day interest. Unhappily, this *is* a subject of every day interest in this country, where insanity is not only a prevalent form of disease. And the exciting causes also being on the increase, great wisdom as to prevention, no less than cure, is demanded to preserve our people from a permanent condition of semi-mania.

Every one should read on this subject, and we would point the attention of all readers to what is said by Dr. Earle of the great importance of having recourse as soon as possible to scientific treatment. It is too usual to tamper with such cases till the true remedies come too late.

When the insane are placed under proper curative treatment in the early stages of the disease, from 75 to 90 per cent. recover.

"*On the contrary, if they be not put under treatment before the disease has continued a year or more, from 15 to 20 per cent. only are cured.*"

Let all fix in their minds a statement which may become so important to them in the guardianship of those they hold most dear.

The chapter on Moral Treatment is of deep interest, and shows the enlightened mind, gentleness and dignity that have given the physician such power to benefit the objects of his care.

"Burns, in expounding the principles of 'Justice' asserts that 'any man may justify confining and *beating* his friend, being mad.' It might be asked, which of the two, the maniac or his 'friend,' would, under such circumstances, be the most truly mad.

"For centuries, however, this system was pursued in the treatment of the insane, and, even at the present time, is not abolished in some places. In the most enlightened communities, there is still an impression that persons of disordered mind can be governed only through fear. But few ideas are more erroneous than this. It is not intended that fear shall enter, as a principle, into the system of management pursued at this institution, and all measures calculated to inspire the patients with awe, are as far as possible avoided.

"Show the insane man that you feel an interest in his ease, that you really consult his welfare; that you will even submit to some self-denial or self-sacrifice to promote his interests, and, in nineteen cases out of twenty, you have secured a friend who will be the foremost to protect you from injury. There are but very few persons laboring under mental derangement who cannot be approached as a brother would meet a brother. There is no place in all the earth where the infant can be more safely entrusted than in most of the halls of a well-regulated asylum for the insane; and none where the little child is more petted and caressed.

"It is a fact which probably will not be questioned, that, in what point of view soever the subject be considered, the true policy in an institution like this, is to make it, as far as the circumstances and condition of the patients will admit, an agreeable home. Render the insane comfortable and a great point is gained, not only in preserving quiet in the house, but in hastening a cure, if a cure be possible. It is believed to be the honest endeavor, not only of the Committee, but of the officers and others concerned in the management of the Asylum, to effect the object mentioned.

"The apartments of the patients are well furnished, their tables mostly set with cloths and all the furniture used in private families, and well supplied, in both quantity and quality, with a sufficient variety of meats, vegetables, pastry and fruit. They have access to a variety of means of instruction and amusement, a more particular account of some of which may not be devoid of interest."

In reference to what is said of entrusting an infant to the Insane, we must relate a little tale which touched the heart in childhood from the eloquent lips of a mother.

The "minister" of the village had a son of such uncommon powers that the slender means on which the large family lived were strained to the utmost to send him to college. The boy prized the means of study as only those under such circumstances know how to prize them, indeed far beyond their real worth, since by excessive study, prolonged often at the expense of sleep, he made himself insane.

All may conceive the feelings of the family when their star turned to them again shorn of its beams, their pride, their hard earned hope, sunk to a thing so hopeless, so helpless, that there could be none so poor as to do him reverence. But they loved him and did what the ignorance of the time permitted. There was little provision, then, for the treatment of such cases, and what there was of a kind that they shrunk from resorting to, if it could be avoided.—They kept him at home, giving him, during the first months, the freedom of the house, but on his making an attempt to kill his father, and confessing afterwards that his old veneration had, as is so often the case in these affections, reacted morbidly by its opposite, so thus he never saw a once loved parent turn his back without thinking how he could rush upon him and do him an injury, they felt obliged to use harsher measures, and chained him to a post in one room of the house.

There, so restrained, without exercise or proper medicine, the fever of insanity came upon him in its wildest form. He raved, shrieked, struck about him, and tore off all raiment that was put upon him.

One of his sisters, named Lucy, whom he had most loved while well, had now power to soothe him. He would listen to her voice, and give way to a milder mood, while she talked or sang. But this favorite sister married, went to her new home, and the maniac became wilder and more violent than ever.

After two or three years she returned, bringing with her an infant. She went into the room where the naked, blaspheming, raging object was confined. He knew her instantly and felt joy at seeing her.

"But, Lucy," said he suddenly, "is that *your* baby you have in your arms? Give it to me; I want to hold it."

A pang of dread and suspicion shot through the young mother's heart; she turned pale and faint.—Her brother was not so mad that he could not understand her fears.

"Lucy," said he, "do you suppose I would hurt your child?"

His sister had strength of mind and of heart. She could not resist the appeal and hastily placed the baby in his arms. Poor fellow!—he held it awhile, stroked its little face, and melted into tears, the first he had shed since his insanity.

For some time after that he was better, and probably had he been under such intelligent care as may be had at present, the crisis might have been followed up and a favorable direction given to his disease. But the subject was not understood then, and having once fallen mad he was doomed to live and die a madman.

The account of the religious services, school, lectures and amusements provided for the use of the Insane and the effects produced, will be read with delight by every good man. The Committee, by the apparatus provided, have shown a truly wise and generous spirit, and the effects of the Orrery and Magic lantern may be traced in the section of Restraints, which we give entire.

"Restraints.—No subject connected with the management of institutions for the insane, has received more attention, or awakened more discussion, during the last few years, both in Great Britain and the United States, than that of corporeal restraints. Although, in some instances, this may have resulted in an ultraism of sentiment, yet much good has been effected. The important fact has been learned, that the insane can be as easily and better managed with a comparatively rare resort to mechanical appliances for the confinement of the limbs, as by a constant or very frequent use of them; while much is gained on the score of humanity.

"It is now one year and eight months since the 'tranquilizing chairs,' so called, were taken from the halls, and neither of them has since been used. It is more than thirteen months since the muffs, mittens, wristbands, straps, and all other leathern apparatus were removed, and during that period not one of them has been carried into the men's department.

"During the cold weather of last January, one of the men-patients, who was dangerously ill and in the delirium of a typhoid condition, threw off the clothing of his bed, and exposed himself to the air to such an extent that it was thought expedient to confine his hands.—This was accordingly done, for three days, with the camisole.

"Some time in the Summer the hands of another man were similarly restrained, a few hours, while a blister was *'drawing.'* These are the only instances during the afore-mentioned thirteen months in which the limbs of any of the men have been confined by any means whatever. During that period the average number of men has been about sixty five. Of those who have been admitted, no less than five were brought to the Asylum in irons, and several others with their limbs bound with ropes, leathern thongs, or other implements.

"Probably not one in ten of those admitted, has seen, while in the Asylum, any apparatus for confining either the hands or the feet. Many of them have left and whatever other recollections soever they may have of the institution, they certainly have none of the means of corporeal restraint. There is no hesitation in asserting the belief that the patients have been more quiet and orderly, under this general disuse of the means in question, than they could have been with their constant use. Moreover, the amount of damage to clothing, windows and furniture, has not increased.

"In the female department there has not been so general an exemption from restraints, yet their use has been greatly diminished, and the camisole[*] has almost invariably been sufficient."

Who does not see that all observed here applies with the same force to the mode of governing Prisons? Now that the late atrocious offence per-

---

[*] If the sleeve of the ordinary female dress be made of twice the length of the arm, they answer the purpose of the camisole. The arms of the patient being folded across the breast, the sleeves are carried around the body and tied behind. There is thus no pressure upon the hands or wrists.

petrated against humanity in Auburn has brought the subject before the public, we hope that some will think on the above remarks in that relation, and be led to see that the same methods would be effectual with the morally as with the mentally insane.

The important remarks that follow on the subject of Attendants, would also apply to the qualifications for office in the case of the prisoners.

"Attendants.—The character of the persons employed to take the immediate care of the insane has very important influence in determining the extent to which confinement of the limbs is expedient. There is this difference in attendants; that, with a given class of patients, while one would find it necessary to ask a resort to restraints, perhaps daily, and even then be in the midst of continual disorder, another would preserve satisfactory degree of tranquillity without ever having recourse to those means of confinement. The latter would also have an easier task than the former and perform it with generally milder measures. Nature, to some extent, qualifies men for all the departments of duty in life. A peculiar talent and a peculiar tact are requisite to the good government of persons whose reason is disordered.

"It is highly essential that the qualifications of attendants should be such that they will be regarded by the patients as friends and companions. The advantages thus derived are greater than can easily be conceived by one unacquainted with the subject. In reference to this end there has been an endeavor to procure persons of intelligence, education, and disciplined passions. Five of the attendants in the men's department, at the present time, have been successful school-teachers.

"It is to be hoped that the time will come when persons will be specially educated for attendants, as teachers are educated in the Normal schools, or as nurses are taught in France. During the past few years the subject has received much attention in England, and in 1849 a society was formed in London, with the Earl of Shaft[e]sbury at its head, the object of which is—'The advancement of the moral, intellectual and professional education of the immediate attendants on insane patients.'

"The same subject presents an uncultured field to the philanthropists of the United States."

The slightest touch upon this subject suggests far more than we have time to write down, but we shall be satisfied if we turn the attention of some persons to perusal of the Report.

✻

[Feb. 11, 1846]

Our City Charities
Visit To Bellevue Alms House, to the Farm School, the Asylum for the Insane, and Penitentiary on Blackwell's Island

The aspect of Nature was sad; what is worse, it was dull and dubious, when we set forth on these visits. The sky was leaden and lowering, the air unkind and piercing, the little birds sat mute and astonished at the departure of the beautiful days which had lured them to premature song. It was a suitable day for such visits. The pauper establishments that belong to a great city take the place of the skeleton at the banquets of old. They admonish us of stern realities, which must bear the same explanation as the frequent blight of Nature's bloom. They should be looked at by all, if only for their own sakes, that they may not sink listlessly into selfish ease, in a world so full of disease. They should be looked at by all who wish to enlighten themselves as to the means of aiding their fellow-creatures in any way, public or private. For nothing can really be done till the right principles are discovered, and it would seem they still need to be discovered or elucidated, so little is done, with a great deal of desire in the heart of the community to do what is right. Such visits are not yet calculated to encourage and exhilarate, as does the story of the Prodigal Son; they wear a grave aspect and suit the grave mood of a *cold* Spring day.

At the Alms House there is every appearance of kindness in the guardians of the poor, and there was a greater degree of cleanliness and comfort than we had expected. But the want of suitable and sufficient employment is a great evil. The persons who find here either a permanent or temporary refuge have scarcely any occupation provided except to raise vegetables for the establishment, and prepare clothing for themselves. The men especially have the most vagrant, degraded air, and so much indolence must tend to confirm them in every bad habit. We were told that, as they are under no strict discipline, their labor at the various trades could not be made profitable; yet surely the means of such should be provided, even at some expense. Employments of various kinds must be absolutely needed, if only to counteract the bad effects of such a position. Every establishment in aid of the poor should be planned with a view to their education. There should be instruction, both practical and in the use of books, openings to a better intercourse than they can obtain from their miserable homes, correct notions as to cleanliness, diet, and fresh air. A great deal of pains would be lost in their case, as with all other arrangements for the good of the many, but here and there the seed would fall into the right places, and some members of the down-trodden million, rising a little from the mud, would raise the whole body with them.

As we saw old women enjoying their dish of gossip and their dish of tea, and mothers able for a while to take care in peace of their poor little children, we longed and hoped for that genius, who shall teach how to make, of these establishments, places of rest and instruction, not of degradation.

The causes which make the acceptance of public charity so much more injurious to the receiver than that of private are obvious, but surely not such that the human mind which has just invented the magnetic telegraph and Anastatic printing, may not obviate them. A deeper religion at the heart of Society would devise such means. Why should it be that the poor may still feel themselves men; paupers not? The poor man does not feel himself injured but benefitted by the charity of the doctor who gives him back the bill he is unable to pay, because the doctor is acting from intelligent sympathy—from love. Let Society do the same. She might raise the man, who is accepting her bounty, instead of degrading him.

Indeed, it requires great nobleness and faith in human nature, and God's will concerning it, for the officials not to take the tone toward these under their care, which their vices and bad habits prompt, but which must confirm them in the same. Men treated with respect are reminded of self-respect, and if there is a sound spot left in the character, the healthy influence spreads.

We were sorry to see mothers with their newborn infants exposed to the careless scrutiny of male visitors. In the hospital, those who had children scarce a day old were not secure from the gaze of the stranger. This cannot be pleasant to them, and, if they have not refinement to dislike it, those who have should teach it to them. But we suppose there is no woman who has so entirely lost sight of the feelings of girlhood as not to dislike the scrutiny of strangers at a time which is sacred, if any in life is. Women they may like to see, even strangers, if they can approach them with delicacy.

In the yard of the hospital, we saw a little Dutch girl, a dwarf, who would have suggested a thousand poetical images and fictions to the mind of Victor Hugo or Sir Walter Scott. She had been brought here to New-York, as we understood, by some showman and then deserted, so that this place was her only refuge. No one could communicate with her or know her feelings, but she showed what they were, by running to the gate whenever it was opened, though treated with familiar kindness and seeming pleased by it. She had a large head, ragged dark hair, a glowering wizard eye, an uncouth yet pleasant smile, like an old child;—she wore a gold ring, and her complexion was as yellow as gold, if not as bright; altogether she looked like a gnome, more than any attempt we have ever known to embody in Art that fabled inhabitant of the mines and secret caves of earth.

From the Alms House we passed in an open boat to the Farm School. We were unprepared to find this as we did, only a school upon a small farm, instead of one in which study is associated with labor. The children are simply taken care of and taught the common English branches till they are twelve years old, when they are bound out to various kinds of work. We think this plan very injudicious. It is bad enough for the children of rich parents, not likely in after life to bear a hard burden, and who are, at any rate, supplied with those various excitements, required to develop the character in the earliest years; it is bad enough, we say, for these to have no kind of useful labor mingled with their plays and studies. Even these children would expand more, and be more variously called forth, and better prepared for common life, if another course were pursued. But, in schools like this at the farm, where the children, on leaving it, will be at once called on for adroitness and readiness of mind and body, and where the absence of natural ties and the various excitements that rise from them inevitably give to life a mechanical routine calculated to cramp and chill the character, it would be peculiarly desirable to provide various occupations, and such as are calculated to prepare for common life. As to economy of time, there is never time lost, by mingling other pursuits with the studies of children; they have vital energy enough for many things at once, and learn more from books when their attention is quickened by other kinds of culture.

Some of these children were pretty, and they were healthy and well grown, considering the general poverty or vice of the class from which they were taken. That terrible scourge, ophthalmia, disfigured many among them. This disease, from some cause not yet detected, has been prevalent here for many years. We trust it may yield to the change of location next summer. There is not water enough here to give the children decent advantages as to bathing. This, too, will be remedied by the change. The Principal, who has been almost all his life connected with this establishment and that at Bellevue, seemed to feel a lively interest in his charge. He has arranged the dormitories with excellent judgment, both as to ventilation and neatness. This, alone, is a great advantage these children have over those of poor families living at home. They may pass the night in healthy sleep, and have thereby a chance for innocent and active days.

We saw with pleasure the little children engaged in the kind of drill they so much enjoy, of gesticulation regulated by singing. It was also pretty to see the babies sitting in a circle and the nurses in the midst feeding them, alternately, with a spoon. It seemed like a nest full of little birds, each opening its bill as the parent returns from her flight.

Hence we passed to the Asylum for the Insane. Only a part of this building is completed, and it is well known that the space is insufficient. Twice as many are inmates here as can be properly accommodated. A tolerable degree, however, of order and cleanliness is preserved. We could not but observe the vast difference between the appearance of the insane here and at Bloomingdale, or other Institutions where the number of attendants and nature of the arrangements permit them to be the objects of individual treatment; that is, where the wants and difficulties of each patient can be distinctly and carefully attended to. At Bloomingdale, the shades of character and feeling were nicely kept up, decorum of manners preserved, and the insane showed in every way that they felt no violent separation betwixt them and the rest of the world, and might easily return to it. The eye, though bewildered, seemed lively, and the tongue prompt. But *here*, insanity appeared in its more stupid, wild, or despairing forms. They crouched in corners; they had no eye for the stranger, no heart for hope, no habitual expectation of light. Just as at the Farm School, where the children show by their unformed features and mechanical movements that they are treated by wholesale, so do these poor sufferers. It is an evil incident to public establishments, and which only a more intelligent public attention can obviate.

One figure we saw, here also, of high poetical interest. It was a woman seated on the floor, in the corner of her cell, with a shawl wrapped gracefully around her head and chest, like a Nun's veil. Her hair was grey, her face attenuated and very pallid, her eyes large, open, fixed and bright with a still fire. She never moved them nor ceased chanting the service of the Church. She was a Catholic, who became insane while preparing to be a Nun. She is surely a Nun now in her heart; and a figure from which a painter might study for some of the most consecrated subjects.

Passing to the Penitentiary, we entered on one of the gloomiest scenes that deforms this great metropolis. Here are the twelve hundred, who receive the punishment due to the vices of so large a portion of the rest. And under what circumstances! Never was punishment treated more simply as a social convenience, without regard to pure right, or a hope of reformation.

Public attention is now so far awake to the state of the Penitentiary that it cannot be long, we trust, before proper means of classification are devised, a temporary asylum provided for those who leave this purgatory, even now, unwilling to return to the inferno from which it has for a time kept them, and means presented likely to lead some, at least, among the many, who seem hardened, to better views and hopes. It must be that the more righteous feeling which has shown itself in regard to the prisons at Sing Sing and elsewhere, must take some effect as to the Penitentiary also. The present Superintendent enters into the necessity of such improvements, and, should he remain there, will do what he can to carry them into effect.

The want of proper matrons, or any matrons, to take the care so necessary for the bodily or mental improvement or even decent condition of the seven hundred women assembled here, is an offence that cries aloud. It is impossible to take the most cursory survey of this assembly of women; especially it is impossible to see them in the Hospital, where the circumstances are a little more favorable, without seeing how many there are in whom the feelings of innocent childhood are not dead, who need only good influences and steady aid to raise them from the pit of infamy and wo into which they have fallen. And, if there was not one that could be helped, at least Society owes them the insurance of a decent condition while here. We trust that interest on this subject will not slumber.

The recognized principles of all such institutions which have any higher object than the punishment of fault, (and we believe few among us are so ignorant as to avow that as the only object, though they may, from want of thought, act as if it were,) are—Classification as the first step, that the bad may not impede those who wish to do well; 2d. Instruction, practical, oral, and by furnishing books which may open entirely new hopes and thoughts to minds oftener darkened than corrupted; 3d. A good Sanitary system, which promotes self-respect, and, through health and purity of body, the same in mind.

In visiting the Tombs the other day, we found the air in the upper galleries unendurable, and felt great regret that those confined there should be constantly subjected to it. Give the free breath of Heaven to all who are still permitted to breathe.—We cannot, however, wonder at finding this barbarity in a prison, having been subjected to it at the most fashionable places of public resort. Dr. Griscom has sent us his excellent lecture on the health of New-York, which we recommend to all who take a vital interest in the city where they live, and have intellect to discern that a cancer on the body must in time affect the head and heart also. We thought, while reading, that it was not surprising typhus fever and ophthalmia should be bred in the cellars, while the families of those who live in palaces breathe such infected air at public places, and receive their visitors on New Year's day by candle-light. (That was a bad omen for the New Year—did they mean to class themselves among those who love darkness rather than light?)

We hope to see the two thousand poor people, and the poor children, better situated in their new abode, when we visit them again. The Insane Asylum will gain at once by enlargement of accommodations; but more attendance is also necessary, and, for that purpose, the best persons should be selected. We saw, with pleasure, tame pigeons walking about among the most violent of the insane, but we also saw two attendants with faces brutal and stolid. Such a charge is too delicate to be intrusted to any but excellent persons. Of the Penitentiary we shall write again. All criticism, however imperfect, should be welcome. There is no reason why New-York should not become a model for other States in these things. There is wealth enough, intelligence, and good desire enough, and *surely, need enough*. If she be not the best cared for city in the world, she threatens to surpass in corruption London and Paris. Such bane as is constantly poured into her veins demands powerful antidotes.

But nothing effectual can be achieved while both measures and men are made the sport of political changes. It is a most crying and shameful evil, which does not belong to our institutions, but is a careless distortion of them, that the men and measures are changed in these institutions with changes from Whig to Democrat, from Democrat to Whig. Churches, Schools, Colleges, the care of the Insane, and suffering Poor, should be preserved from the uneasy tossings of this delirium. The Country, the State, should look to it that only those fit for such officers should be chosen for such, apart from all considerations of political party. Let this be thought of; for without an absolute change in this respect no permanent good whatever can be effected; and farther, let not economy but utility be the rule of expenditure, for, here, parsimony is the worst prodigality.

✽

[March 19, 1845]

Asylum for Discharged Female Convicts

The ladies of the Prison Association have been, for some time, engaged in the endeavor to procure funds for establishing this asylum. They have met, thus far, with little success; but, touched by the position of several women, who, on receiving their discharge, were anxiously waiting in hope there would be means provided to save them from return to their former suffering and polluted life, they have taken a house and begun their good work in faith that Heaven must take heed that such an enterprise may not fail, and touch the hearts of men to aid it.

They have taken a house and secured the superintendence of an excellent woman. There are already six women under her care. But this house is unprovided with furniture or the means of securing food for body and mind to these unfortunates during the brief novitiate which gives them so much to learn and unlearn.

The object is to lend a helping hand to the many who show a desire of reformation, but have hitherto been inevitably repelled into infamy by the lack of friends to procure them honest employment, and a temporary refuge till it can be procured. Efforts will be made to instruct them how to break up bad habits and begin a healthy course for body and mind.

The house has in it scarcely any thing; it is a true Lazarus establishment, asking for the crumbs that fall from the rich man's table. Old furniture would be acceptable, clothes, books that are no longer needed by their owners.

Such a statement we make in appealing to the poor, though they are, usually, the most generous. Not that they are, originally, better than the rich, but circumstances have fitted them to appreciate the misfortunes, the trials, the wrongs, that beset those a little lower down than themselves. But we have seen too many instances where those who were educated in luxury would cast aside with eagerness the sloth and selfishness that ensue when once awakened to better things, not to hope in appealing to the rich also.

And to all we appeal. To the poor, who will know how to sympathize with those who are not only poor but degraded, diseased, likely to be harried onward to a shameful, hopeless death. To the rich, to equalize the advantages of which they have received more than their share. To men, to atone for the wrongs inflicted by men on that "weaker sex," who should, they say, be soft, confiding, dependent on them for protection. To women, to feel for those who have not been guarded either by social influence or inward strength from that first mistake which the opinion of the world makes irrevocable for women alone. Since their danger is so great, their fall so terrible, let mercies be multiplied when there is a chance of that partial restoration which society at present permits.

In New York we have come little into contact with that class of society who have a surplus of leisure at command; but in other cities we have found in that class many, some men, more women, who wanted only a decided object and clear light to fill the noble office of disinterested educators and guardians to their less fortunate fellows. It has been our happiness, in not a few instances, by merely apprising such persons of what was to be done, to rouse that generous spirit which relieved themselves from ennui, dejection, and a gradual ossification of the whole system, into a thoughtful, sympathetic and beneficent existence. Such no doubt are near us here, if we could but know it. A poet writes thus of the cities:

> "Cities of proud hotels,
>   Houses of rich and great,
> A stack of smoking chimneys,
>   A roof of frozen slate.
> It cannot conquer folly,
>   Time and space conquering steam,
> And the light-outspeeding telegraph
>   Bears nothing on its beam.
>
> "The politics are base,
>   The letters do not cheer,
> And 't is far in the deeps of history
>   The voice that speaketh clear;
> Trade and the streets ensnare us,
>   Our bodies are weak and worn,
> We plot and corrupt each other,
>   And we despoil the unborn.
>
> "Yet there in the parlor sits
>   Some figure of noble guise,
> Our angel in a stranger's form,
>   Or woman's pleading eyes;
> Or only a flashing sunbeam
>   In at the window-pane,
> Or music pours on mortals
>   Its beautiful disdain."

These pleading eyes, these angels in a stranger's form we meet or seem to meet as we pass through the thoroughfares of this great city. We do not know their names or homes. We cannot go to those still and sheltered homes and tell them the tales that would be sure to awaken the heart to a deep and active interest in this matter. But should these words meet their eyes we would say, Have you entertained your leisure hours with the Mysteries of Paris or the pathetic story of Violet Woodville? Then you have some idea how innocence worthy of the brightest planet may be betrayed by want, or by the most generous tenderness; how the energies of a noble reformation may lie hidden beneath the ashes of a long burning, as in the case of La Louve. You must have felt that yourselves are not better, only more protected children of God than those. Do you want to link these fictions, which have made you weep, with facts around you where your pity might be of use? Go to the Penitentiary at Blackwell's Island. You may be repelled by seeing those who are in health, while at work together, keeping up one another's careless spirit and effrontery by bad association. But see them in the hospital where the worn features of the sick show the sad ruins of past loveliness, past gentleness. See in the eyes of the nurses the woman's spirit still, so kindly, so inspiring. See those little girls huddled in a corner, their neglected dress and hair contrasting with some ribbon of cherished finery held fast in a childish hand. Think what "sweet seventeen" was to you, and what it is to them, and see if you do not wish to aid in any enterprise that gives them a chance of better days. We assume no higher claim for this enterprise. The dreadful social malady which creates the need of it is one that imperatively demands deep-searching preventive measures; it is beyond cure. But, here and there, some precious soul may be saved from unwilling sin, unutterable woe. Is not the hope to save, here and there *one,* worthy of great and persistent exertion and sacrifice?

Although Hood's poem, "The Bridge of Sighs," has been inserted once before in this paper, we are anxious to make use of it again, as more touching and forcible than any thing that has been or is likely to be written on this subject. We think that many will be willing to give much time, thought, hope and money to save even one from falling from this.

✻

[June 19, 1845]

Twenty-seventh Annual Report and Documents of the New-York Institution for the Instruction of the Deaf and Dumb to the Legislature of the State of New York for the Year 1845

This interesting pamphlet contains the following statement:

"From the catalogue herewith returned, it will be seen that the present number of pupils is two hundred, being a large increase on the number of any previous year, and with the single exception of the Institution of London, a much larger number of deaf mutes than has ever been collected together in one school. Of these there are supported by the State of New-York one hundred and sixty; by the State of New-Jersey, three; by the Corporation of New-York, thirteen; by their friends, fourteen; and by the institution, ten.

"This large increase is mainly owing to the act, to which the Board refer with high gratification, passed at the last session of the Legislature, making provision for four additional State pupils from each Senate District; thus increasing the number of State beneficiaries from one hundred and twenty-eight to one hundred and sixty."

The "Elementary Lessons for the Deaf and Dumb," prepared by the Principal of the Institution, Mr. Harvey P. Peet, have been adopted as "a textbook for elementary classes in eight of the ten American Institutions for the Deaf and Dumb, and in some of the British Isles. It has even found its way to China, where it is used in the Missionary Schools, for teaching the vocabulary and structure of our language to the youth of the Celestial Empire."

We observe also, with pleasure, that dwelling houses are to be provided for the valued teachers of the School, so that the scene of their labors shall become, in every sense, their home. Whoever understands the workings of the affections on the mental powers will know that this generosity of treatment is essential to securing the best aid in these enterprises. But there is such frequent blindness or insensibility testified in similar cases that an instance to the contrary is pleasant to behold.

Fortunately, the qualifications for teaching in these institutions are something positive. Either a man is well qualified for instructing the deaf mute, or the blind, or he is not; his adaptation to such an office can be judged of with tolerable justice by all men. The agents and arrangements in such institutions are not likely to be affected by changes in politics, fashion, or opinion, as almost every thing else is in our revolutionary country, and therefore something radically, positively, and progressively good may be hoped in these departments.

In Mr. Peet's establishment, the speaking radiance of look in many of the pupils is a sufficient voucher for the benefits of that ministry which has lifted the heavy pall from their young lives, and defeated the worst action of their fate. That they have their share in all the best gifts of this earthly life the following little composition by one of them sufficiently proves:

"The Mind.—What is the Mind, and what does it enable us to do?

"The Mind is the intellectual part of the soul. It is spiritual. It is immaterial. It is immortal. It is invisible. It is intangible. It is without color. It is without form. It is without weight. It is supposed to be situated in the head. It dwells in the brain, on whose throne it sits. It is the king of the whole body. It gains itself knowledge of the external world by means of the five senses of the body. It is very active. It operates daily in acquiring knowledge of all external objects of the world. It is very subtle in its nature. It is much quicker in its movements than lightning. Its operations of thought are fleeter than a flash of electricity. The senses are the attendants of the Mind. The nerves of the brain are its servants. The limbs and all parts of the body are its subjects. They are all obedient to the Mind. They are subservient to it. The Mind possesses the faculty of perception by the five senses. It enables us to think, conceive, imagine, reflect, remember, recognize or recollect, and memorize the knowledge of past events or ideas. It also enables us to reason, distinguish, measure and estimate the values of the worldly goods—to count all things—to compare things, and to determine , &c. &c. We must thank our Creator of the Universe for having kindly bestowed upon us such a noble Mind. It is the most important and the noblest part of our system."

As we range the crowded streets, we meet not many in enjoyment of all the advantages of a complete organization who evince the consciousness of our nobler life and its infinite joys expressed in this little essay. It has been remarked of the Deaf and the Dumb that they have, frequently, a purity and religious fervor of expression, as if they were kept in a better state by remaining ignorant of a large portion of the wicked and mean things that fly from tongue to tongue in common society. No less observable is an uncommon vivacity of eye when the thoughts have once been awakened, which seems to say that the mind only vindicates its powers the more, from being necessarily more introverted than with others.

This fact and the unusual education of the whole person, especially the hands, from the habit of using the language of signs, must ever make the society of the Deaf and Dumb deeply interesting to those who are capable of thought and observation. They present, indeed, the most interesting subject for the study of the metaphysician and philologist, and we are surprised that no more use has been made of it. The single fact that *they think in signs, not words,* opens volumes of speculation.

Their minds come to ours with the freshness of foreigners, while, at the same time, by community of many circumstances in climate, constitution, &c. we may establish an intimate connection with them and win the full benefit of their impressions as we cannot from a foreigner.

"It is to be considered that our language is foreign to them. It is as Chinese to a school-boy. Nor have they the advantage which a hearing foreigner would possess in the study of English, by becoming daily more familiar with the usages of the language from the mouths of all with whom he should become familiar. Nor again are they forced, as a foreigner would be, to make frequent trials of their skill in procuring, by means of English, what they need. All their own conversation is in the sign language. Whatever they learn of English must be learned, until they are able to read for themselves, from a few instructors, who, except in the recitation room, almost necessarily speak to them in their native language."

It is obvious how favorable this state of the Deaf and Dumb must be to the original poetic elements of language, to the use of likenesses or images, and the direct expression of simple feelings. Their style is naturally a ballad style, and reveals secrets that seemed lost with the cradle of humanity. We have never seen any book more significant in this way than a little English collection of prayers by deaf and dumb boys at a private school founded by some lady, who represented to them, as the Saints Theresa, Rosalia and Cecilia do to the Catholic, the ideal of all that is peculiarly lovely and excellent in woman. The description of moods of mind by these boys, the correspondences discerned between their own lives and the forms of nature, the swelling lyric sweetness with which their aspirations are expressed belong to the highest, simplest state of poesy.

It is from considerations like these that we look with deep interest on this important Institution, no less than from joy at goodness and justice manifested toward a portion of our race less favored by nature than the rest. But, indeed, on this side, we cannot be too grateful to see so many relieved from the tortures of suspicion and the phantoms of doubt which beset the uneducated deaf mute.

The Institution propose to make partial use of the European methods for teaching the articulation of words. The following extract upon this subject from the Report of the Committee of Instruction deserves to be read and considered:

"The only other system which has received favor is distinguished, theoretically, by its use of articulation in the place of signs as an instrument of instruction. It is not our purpose to enlarge on the characteristic differences of the two systems and their relative merits.—From the days of Heinicke and De l'Epée, the founders of the German and French schools respectively, each system has had its admirers, and it is therefore no novelty at this day to hear that the Deaf and Dumb can be taught to speak. Indeed it would seem to be most natural for the first attempts in educating a deaf mute, to teach him to use his tongue, and it would be only after the failure of efforts in this way that some other more practicable method would be devised. Hence we find in the history of the deaf-mute instruction that almost invariably the earlier instructors tried to teach their pupils an oral language. Even in the Seventh Century, according to the venerable Bede, (Ecc. Hist. Vol. V. Chap. 2,) John, Bishop of Hagustald, took charge of a deaf mute, and succeeded in teaching him first the sounds of the letters, and then the pronunciation of words and phrases in connected sentences. The first practical treatise on the art of deaf-mute instruction, was published by John Paul Bonet, at Madrid, in 1620. In this work the author gives specific directions upon the manner of teaching a deaf mute to articulate each of the letters of the alphabet and utter words in continuous discourse. Peter Ponce of Spain, who preceded Bonet, also taught articulation. Efforts of the same kind were made by Wallis and Holder in England, Van Helmont and Amman in Holland, Kerger and Arnoldi in Germany, Ernaud and the Abbé Deschamps in France, and many others in later times, especially in Great Britain and Germany. In the countries last mentioned many schools still make use of articulation to a greater or less extent.

"But the attempt to restore speech to the Deaf and Dumb as a class has never been successful. Individuals have received benefit from efforts made to call into exercise their vocal organs. But whenever a substantial gain has resulted to the pupil by such exercises, it will be found either that he was not entirely deaf and dumb, or, if he were, that he had enjoyed better advantages than could be afforded generally to such pupils, or was possessed of superior natural abilities. In the wonderful achievements recorded of some who have been taught to articulate, it has not been stated, as it should have been, that such persons had never lost entirely the use of speech. Their education consisted in improving a faculty which they had never wholly lost. And even when a pupil has ceased to articulate, having in early life begun to use a spoken language, it is a fact well known to those at all familiar with the practice of deaf-mute instruction, that in the acquisition of a written language, the progress of persons of this class is much more rapid than that of one perfectly deaf and dumb.

"We have alluded to a distinction which is not always taken into consideration, and which has an important bearing upon the discussion of questions relative to systems of instruction. It is an established fact, that persons are dumb in consequence of their being deaf.—If the deafness be entire and has been from birth, the individual, without special instruction, will be perfectly dumb. Not being able to hear any sounds, he will not, as other children do, naturally learn to imitate them.—But if the deafness be partial, then in proportion as vocal sounds are distinguished, he will copy them, and utter similar sounds with his own voice. There are five degrees of infirmity of hearing, as distinguished by the celebrated Dr. Itard, formerly Physician to the Royal Institution at Paris, in his able work on the Diseases of the Ear and Hearing, *(des maladies de l'oreille et de l'audition)*:

"1st. That in which articulate sounds are perceptible, when pronounced in an elevated tone of voice.

"2d. That in which analogous articulations are liable to be confounded.

"3d. In which articulation is lost, and intonation is alone distinguishable.

"4th. In which heavy peals, as of artillery or of thunder, only are perceptible, and the human voice no longer produces an impression upon the ear.

"5. Profound deafness.

"An Institution for the Deaf and Dumb properly includes persons in each of these various classes, for they are not able to be taught by the ordinary methods of instruction in schools designed only for children who can hear and speak. They require special instruction. But such a difference of condition as appears in these five classes, would suggest some difference in the mode of instruction. Usually from one-fifth to one-eighth of the pupils of a Deaf and Dumb Institution have some ability to articulate at the time of their first admission. The most of these retain some degree of hearing; the others though entirely deaf, are still able to speak, having learned to use their vocal organs before they lost their hearing.

"Some attention has been given to this class of pupils from time to time since the establishment of our Institution. But the efforts on their behalf have been limited to individuals, and no general classification has been effected so that regular instruction could be given them in distinction from others. The desirableness of such an organization has been often a subject of remark, and has been alluded to with favor in the Annual Reports of the Institution. In the last Report, after referring to the reasons which had appeared to the Board decisive against any attempt to teach articulation to the bulk of our pupils, it is added, p. 15—'The formation of a class, to include those whose attainments, in this accomplishment, were likely to be of some value, still seemed desirable, but in the way of this there were, and still are, many grave obstacles; the principal of which are, the increased expense for the favored class, the hindrance to their mechanical instruction, and the invidiousness of making a selection.' Rev. Mr. Day, in his very able and conclusive Report on the Schools for the Deaf and Dumb in Central and Western Europe, expresses the following opinion:—'That in spite of the peculiar difficulties, even a deaf mute from birth, by unwearied pains, and the expenditure of much time, *might,* to a certain extent, be taught to articulate in English, I have no doubt, and, where parents have the necessary leisure, I would by no means be understood as dissuading them from the attempt; but *as a regular part of a system of public education, its introduction into our Institutions, I am persuaded, would be a serious misfortune to the cause of Deaf and Dumb instruction.*'

"He then adds:—'That there are few, usually reckoned among deaf mutes, consisting of those to whom hearing, or the power of speaking, partially remains, to whom instruction in articulation is desirable, is self-evident. These cases are of a peculiar character, and are to be decided on by themselves.'

"Similar sentiments are expressed by Mr. Weld, the Principal of the American Asylum, in the extended and valuable Report of his visit to the Institutions for the Deaf and Dumb in Europe during the last year. He says:

'I can then recommend no fundamental change in the system pursued in the Institution with which I am connected, or in the other American schools. The most faithful use of all the facilities afforded by our present system, it is our constant duty to make, and to devise and adopt every real improvement in our power. Instead of regretting the original adoption of our system by Mr. Gallaudet, I am truly thankful that he was led to its adoption. But I would by no means exclude improvements. Men are neither perfect in their theories, nor in their practice. We have improved on our original system, and we may yet improve, and ought so to do; certainly in practice—if possible, in theory.

'Though then, I cannot recommend the adoption of the German, or any other system, instead of our own, still I do respectfully recommend as an additional means of usefulness, the giving of instruction in articulation and in labial reading, to certain classes of the pupils of the American Asylum. In this number I would include especially those descriptions of deaf and dumb persons, so called, often mentioned in my accounts of the European schools, who retain in a considerable degree the articulation they acquired before becoming deaf, and those who still have some discriminate hearing. These are, on the whole, the classes of persons principally benefited by attention to articulation in the articulating schools I have visited abroad. There is still another class whom I would not exclude from the benefits of a fair experiment. I mean those, few indeed in number, but yet sometimes found, who, possessed of superior natural powers and in all respects under favorable circumstances, are anxious to undertake the labor, and are found so persevering and successful as to warrant its continuance.'

"In view of the manifest advantages to be derived by a portion of the pupils of our Institution, by affording them facilities for instruction in articulation, and reading upon the lips, the Committee would respectfully recommend that such of the pupils as shall be deemed capable of receiving benefit from the exercise of their organs of speech and practice in labial reading, be provided with the means of regular instruction in these branches. The details of the plan of instruction they would leave for future adjustment."

The following letter from a young deaf and dumb child may be deemed by some too childish for so grave a place as this, but we must give it as an instance of how much pure happiness may be afforded by a little act of thoughtful kindness. We should, for our own part, prefer being the giver of the 'sweet kitten' to almost any office in the gift of the State of New-York. Blest be the charities of daily life! These little flowers have, indeed, a chance to bloom and bless; they lie too low to be destroyed by the sudden blast that cuts sheer off the tops of the loftiest trees. None so poor that he cannot bring cheer to the forsaken, for a rush candle is more cheering even than a star to the benighted wanderer: and none so powerless that he cannot confer on a childish heart a kingly gift of unalloyed felicity such as is portrayed in these lines:

"THE KITTEN.—Some years ago, on Sunday, my brother and sister-in-law and myself went to their friends to visit them. My sister-in-law's favorite parents gave me a pretty kitten. I was very glad. They and myself staid till six o'clock. They and myself came to home in the wagon. I sat on a little bench with the kitten, which slept on my lap in there. At night they and myself arrived at home. I carried my sweet kitten, and I walked through the gate, while I thought that I would be take care good of my kitten. Then I opened my sweet father's door of his house, I entered the door and saw my brother, Samuel came there from the Institution. He told me that the kitten is yours? I answered yes, it is mine. Sometimes I told my sister that she bring me some milk. She brought me some milk in the saucer. I put it on the floor, and the kitten was not come to drink milk, because it was very afraid. I was sorry. The next day I carried the kitten to my brother's house. He took care of my sweet kitten. It is a cat now. She has some young kittens. I have seen them last vacation.   S.T.

We regret much to have missed the opportunity of attending the examinations at Mr. Peet's Institution, in which we have heard others express so much satisfaction.

*

[March 18, 1846]

Prison Discipline

Annual Report of the Inspectors of the Mount Pleasant State Prison to the Legislature of the State of New-York, January 19th, 1846

Second Report of the Prison Association of New-York, 1846

Third Annual Report of the Managers of the State Lunatic Asylum, Made to the Legislature, January 23d, 1846

Report of the Pennsylvania Hospital for the Insane, for the Year 1845

We know no printed pages that convey more encouragement as to the progress and aspirations of the human mind than those of these Reports.

It is no longer only beings distinguished for shining attributes of unmistakable excellence that can inspire their brother men with faith in their possession of immortal souls. It is not only the eye of the poet, or that of private personal love, that can pierce through the thick crusts that have hid and dimmed the jewel, to see in him whom the world has cast off a fellow man, who may be helped, who may be saved,—who may even be aroused to help and save himself. There are symptoms that mankind at large begin to have some sympathy with the divine love of Jesus, who redoubled his encouragements to the prodigal son instead of punishing him for past transgressions, and was not afraid to preach that even at the eleventh hour men might come to work in the vineyard. Harsh bigots may sneer at this spirit of mercy as "sickly sentimentality," but the spark has been struck, and, nothing daunted, the fire glows, grows, rises, and begins to cast a light around.

The Report of the Prison Association and that of the Inspectors of Mount Pleasant—(shade of Bunyan! what a strangely chosen name—or is it perhaps an omen of better times?)—breathe somewhat of that genuine philanthropy which cannot see in a Man merely a social nuisance, because he has ignorantly, weakly or wickedly offended against society. Those who have understood and obeyed the laws are not afraid to look into the causes that have made their brothers outlaws. They are not afraid that sin will seem less hateful or less noxious, because it may be traced back to hereditary taint, bad education or corrupting influences of a half-civilized state. They are not afraid to do all they can to help a fallen brother man to rise, by putting his life under more healthful conditions both of body and mind. If they think themselves better and better situated than others, it is not in the blasphemous temper of "My God! I thank thee that I am not as other men are," but with a desire to make their privileges avail for the guardianship and instruction of those less favored. The God to whom they aspire is not a God of Wrath, "Master, Owner, rightful possessor of wrath—one who claims it as his rightful prerogative," but a God of Love.

Attention is paid to making the prison maintain itself and to maintaining discipline there, not merely for the sake of the rest of the world, but of the prisoners themselves. Yea, sick, brutalized, contaminated though they be, they also shall be esteemed and cared for as men, and all possible chance of self-recovery allowed them, both in the prison and on leaving it.

The suggestions as to supplying the prison with pure water, with instruction, with a library, are all harmonious to our eye, all expressive of that wiser sense of the claims of humanity which redeems our age despite its myriad vices and basenesses.

We regret that the report of the Matron of the Female Department at Sing-Sing is not in a form accessible to the general reader. This lady shows the powers of her large and clear mind no less in statement of her reasons than in the conduct they produce. The simple narrative of the state of things under her government is worth volumes of argument. May she never turn aside from this cause till she has made a mark that cannot be effaced upon its history!

We give some extracts from her report:

"It may be said that this mode of treatment will lessen the terror of punishment, and thereby diminish the restraint which it is intended to impose upon the tendencies to crime. But some experience and much reflection have convinced me that this apprehension is groundless. The character of criminals is for the most part strongly marked by the predominance of propensity over all the better powers. Of the females especially a large majority have been reared and habituated to scenes of violence and depravity, that would themselves be the greatest terror to better constituted minds. Years of such excitement have prepared them to enjoy only scenes like those in which they have previously participated. Thus trained, aggression and resistance are the spontaneous and continued fruits of their minds. They come to the prison therefore, prepared to war against physical measures, and the supremacy of animal courage, and to derive their highest enjoyment from such contest.

"While in this condition, no punishment could be more severe than the unseen, quiet restraints of a moral system, which furnish no excitement to their resisting faculties, offer no provocation to endurance, open no account of injuries to be revenged on some future occasion. The mental inanition of this period, the presence and supremacy of influences with which the mind has no sympathy, the monotonous character of the life, contrasted with the intense excitements which have preceded it, the absence of all stimulus to the physical as well as the mental energies, are circumstances, the combined severity of which seems sufficient to answer the strongest faith in the saving influences of punishment.

"Yet this is the lot which inevitably awaits all whose lives have been thus spent, and the more perfect the moral government of the institution, the more severe is it to those who remain in this condition. An occasional burst of passion and resort to coercion; an occasional scene in which depravity makes itself heard in foul language or deeds of violence, are holidays to them. Something of the old life is again felt in their veins; something of the old spirit is rekindled. The countenance and entire manner indicate the vivifying influences which such scenes have exerted over them.

"But one primary object of our system is to cause this state to be superseded by one of greater activity in the moral and intellectual powers; to kindle purer and more elevated desires in the mind, and thus re-create some capacity in the convict to derive pleasure from the influences with which she is surrounded. The progress to this condition is slow and tedious, and when reached its newly awakened sensibilities are far from being sources of happiness, having nothing in the past and so little in the future on which to feed. Indeed the keenest suffering which the incarcerated ever experienced is that which flows from these sensibilities when the horrors of former years pass in review before the mind and the future threatens equal terrors when they shall find themselves without protection, without sympathy, overwhelmed with disgrace and the consciousness of guilt. But painful though it be, it is the first indication of promise, the first step in the path of reform. It is the price which all who are susceptible of improvement must pay for the comparative tranquillity and sense of comfort which our system furnishes to those who are capable of enjoying them. Thus the gentler features of this system do not become sources of comfort until there is an adaptation to receive them as incentives also, and aids to reformation. When the individual is fairly set out in this path, I permit myself to indulge no doubt as to the character of the treatment most favorable for its sound continuance. The ways of virtue must be made pleasant if we would have the wanderer accept our invitation to walk therein. Comfort, peace, sympathy, commendation and respect, are the natural fruits of integrity and well doing to the free. Can they be less necessary to sustain the feeble who are struggling to deserve them? Are they less justly due to the great efforts which such persons must make than to the conduct which flows from the natural choice of a better constitution."

Under this treatment these are the results:

"The following abstract of violations and punishments, as illustrating these remarks, may not be out of place here.

"In April, 1844, the first month after my connection with the prison, there were:

	violations			punishments	
		35			13
May	"	18	May	"	12
June	"	20	June	"	6
July	"	17	July	"	17
August	"	10	August	"	7
September	"	9	September	"	9
October	"	5	October	"	5
November	"	6	November	"	5
December	"	4	December	"	4
January, 1845	"	4	January, 1845	"	4
February	"	6	February	"	6
March	"	3	March	"	3
April	no violations		April	no punishments	
May	"	1	May	"	1
June	"	3	June	"	3
July	"	11	July	"	11
August	"	1	August	"	1
September	"	2	September	"	2
October	"	2	October	"	2
November	"	7	November	"	7
Total		164	Total		108

"It will be observed that in the early months the number of punishments often fell far short of the number of violations. Many of the offenders were admonished and warned of the consequences that would follow a repetition of their offences. This treatment often secured all that was desired, and where it failed, the second act was promptly followed by the penalty which had been previously promised. Some of the punishments have been very slight, such as the deprivation of a meat; of books; the prohibition of exercise, &c. In a very few cases they have been severe. Such are the long terms of solitary confinement and the cropping of the hair. This last has been resorted to in but one instance, but with excellent effect.

"Thus it will be seen that the whole number of violations for the past year, exceed those of the first month by only ten; a result which is doubly gratifying when the character of the offences is considered.

"An immense majority of those running through the year, was of the lightest description; simple infractions of arbitrary rules, arguing neither depravity nor a rebellious spirit so much as the supremacy of natural law, over those imposed by the unnatural condition of the offender."

The following beneficent plan will commend itself to every unprejudiced mind:

"But it is not to be supposed that a state of feeling so favorable to the growth of better principles can be produced and sustained without the expenditure of much labor and the use of various means chosen for the purpose. Those which I esteem most efficient have been the use of books, the daily chapel reading and personal instruction.

"The State makes no provision for books, other than the Bible. A few old volumes were found in an attic store-room, which were put in requisition on my first coming here, but they were, for the most part, ill adapted to the taste as well as the condition of our readers. Our great need in this respect was made known to a few philanthropic ladies in New-York and Boston, who soon collected several hundred miscellaneous volumes, the private charities of their friends. But these sources are entirely inadequate for any permanent supply of sound reading. And the larger number of persons in the male prison to whom such reading would be still more valuable than to the female convicts, are dependent on the same precarious bounties. In view of these facts, I would beg leave to suggest a plan by which a small fund might be raised for increasing the libraries of both prisons; this is to grant to our better class of female convicts a half holiday at the close of the week, which should be spent in manufacturing various fancy articles to be kept for sale at the prison to visitors and others. The advantages of this plan would be manifold. As an indulgence the holiday would be highly prized; but it would be enjoyed only by those whose conduct had been unexceptionable during the week, and who also had accomplished the largest amount of work required from them. Thus, instead of diminishing the productiveness of their labor for the State, it would rather stimulate them to increased exertion. Beside, many of the females have husbands or friends in the male prison, and there is a strong feeling of sympathy toward the inmates of that institution generally, which would find a very pure and generous gratification in conferring this kind of benefits upon them. It is thought that the adoption of this or some similar plan would enable us to raise a fund sufficient to add to both libraries several volumes each month, an object which, in the absence of all other means of procuring them, would be of no small importance."

We have put under this head reports from the Utica and Pennsylvania Asylums for the Insane, because we do believe that advancement in thought and wisdom of treatment in both these departments are and will be simultaneous. When there is a well-digested system of treatment for the one, that for the other will not be far behind. We have no fear of the consequences. We do not think men will seek the causes of excitement that lead to insanity because the disease becomes, by judicious treatment, more easy of cure. We are sure that the better man is by this means led to understand his own constitution, the more he is likely to avoid these causes. And we believe that an anxiety to call sinners to repentance instead of casting them down to perdition for the first offence, yea and for offences seventy times seven, is just as little likely to promote sin as the angel-like ministry now bent on ameliorating the condition of the deaf and dumb, or so-called idiots, is to enlarge those unfortunate classes.

These reports correspond in the more important features with that of the Bloomingdale Asylum, which we noticed some days ago. Two or three suggestions, however, they bring to us.

It is stated that some patients have left the Asylum even improved in mind, either from the favorable crisis in their health, or the discipline to which they have been subjected. Whichever way this be viewed, the hint may be turned to vast profit.

We see with pleasure the tendency to provide something like a home for incurable cases. We do believe that under a still more intelligent *regime* even the incurables will not pass the years without profit, as well as happiness. Surely their chance is fairer than that of the miser, egotist, or sensual man whom the world does not characterize as insane.

The project (in the Pennsylvania Hospital) of giving the patients an interest in the care of trees, is worthy all attention. Dr. Kirkbridge says:

"We have continued steadily to carry out the system originally adopted, of each year planting a considerable number of trees and shrubs, and already have some of the results of this labor become strikingly conspicuous to every visitor to and resident of the Hospital. The variety on the premises is large, and has been in many cases a matter of much interest to patients fond of studies of this description. It would be easy in a few years to have within our enclosures a specimen of every tree that will live in this climate, and I know of no spot near Philadelphia where a complete *arboretum* could be established with less trouble, or be a subject of greater interest or more utility than upon the 41 acres which compose our pleasure grounds."

He also mentions that animals have been added to the Park.

Whoever has experienced the need of renovation, when the mind has lost its force and serenity, whether from irritation or exhaustion, will find nothing so healthful as the care and companionship of trees and animals. The thousand charms of their spontaneity, of their instinctive life, rouse and feed just those sympathies that are needed to restore the injured nature to its balance. The care of flowers is rather more anxious and too often leads to stooping, therefore is less safe, but their presence has the same balmy, restorative influence.

The name of Amariah Brigham (New-York State Lunatic Asylum) excites to mention of a debt of gratitude. He will be glad to learn that, from writings of his, one, at a dangerous crisis, received admonition that saved the best hopes of life from shipwreck. This person, originally of a mind too ardent and willing for the bodily strength, "fed in youth with the poisonous names" of Julius Caesar and other such worthies, who scarce needed sleep, gave no moment to leisure, or that thoughtless growth, without which, in fact, no genius ever came to flower. This poor young disciple, seized with the fever of thought and study, believed that constant tension was the only fit state for an immortal spirit, and so went on, with daily increasing impetus, an intellectual race that neared the precipice when writings of Dr. Brigham, describing the causes and symptoms of congestion of the brain, arrested attention just in time to save from the worst effects of these mistakes, and ransom for the pupil taught the inevitable reaction of body on mind, many years of joyous and active existence that might else have been passed in the sorrowful twilight of insanity, or been broken into worthless pieces by other forms of disease.

What has been brought out on these subjects during each year, both as to principle and fact, ought to be embodied in pamphlet shape for the use of the people. These reports are little circulated, and every person ought to have full means of information on topics like these.

※

[Feb. 25, 1846]

Condition of the Blind in This Country and Abroad

Report on the Benevolent Institutions of Great Britain and Paris, including the Schools and Asylums for the Blind, Deaf and Dumb, and Insane, Being Supplementary to the Ninth Annual Report of the Ohio Institution for the Education of the Blind By William Chapin, Superintendent. Columbus, 1846

Sixth Annual Report of the Managers of the New-York Institution for the Blind to the Legislature of the State. 1840

We take a great interest in reports on this subject, and only regret that they are not made accessible to the public at large by the common channels of sale. The spread of enlightened views and just regard for those members of the human family, who are inferior to the others in bodily organization, is the redeeming sign of the time, which shows so many of selfishness and baseness. Since men are earnestly desirous to redeem those suffering from bodily infirmity and secure them some share of the dower of human nature, may we not hope that this desire will gradually extend its benefits to all those who are suffering from inferiority of any kind nor rest till it has finally secured to all who wear the form of man the prerogatives of humanity?

The following practical observations will be read with interest. It is pleasant to see Ohio sending out her delegate to make such in the Old World:

I proceed, with as much brevity as the subject will admit, to make some observations of a general nature:

I. It will be perceived that the British Institutions are, with two or three exceptions, almost entirely *manufacturing establishments*. In this respect they are generally successful. Some of them, the Glasgow and Edinburgh asylums in particular, are doing a large business—the sales of the former amounting to about $20,000 a year.

A large portion of work is done by the *adult* blind, who receive wages, the asylums affording shops, tools, &c. and disposing of the work to the best advantage, without loss to themselves.

In our own country, very little has yet been attempted by way of employing the blind after they have learned trades, or even of receiving the adult blind to acquire an occupation. The Massachusetts Asylum has done more in this respect than any other, and designs to incorporate this feature in their plan as far as practicable. But the main object of the American Institutions, thus far, has been to *teach* rather than to *employ* the blind. Nor are we prepared to say this is not the best principle on which to conduct *educational* establishments. I think this is clearly so, without a change in their domestic arrangements.

A system which professes to employ all the older blind who are able to work, in connection with the education of the younger children, would be liable to very serious objection. The habits of the different classes are so dissimilar that they could not lodge in the same house, and form the same general family, with profit to the children. There could be very little harmony in such an association, if much extended.

These remarks, however, do not go to exclude entirely the employment of pupils in our schools, after they have acquired a business and passed through the usual term. On the contrary, with proper discretion and, under judicious limits, the benefits of the Institution should be extended to such persons as far as possible.

But when we contemplate the extension of the plan, in the mechanical departments like those in Great Britain, as some think advisable, it imposes a different and very important view of the subject. The elements of such a broad and extended system being incongruous, it would be vain to look for entire success. One part of it—either the intellectual or the mechanical—would soon fall into entire subordination to the other, and, as in foreign Institutions, the probability is, the department of mental instruction would sink into comparative insignificance.

Asylums for the Industrious Blind.—II. If the above views be correct, they lead to a conclusion which I believe is entertained in all the Institutions in the United States, namely—the expediency, if not necessity, at a period not very distant, of *separate asylums* for the industrious blind, yet united under the direction of the same Board of Trustees.

Such asylums would rescue from idleness, dependence, and want, a large number of meritorious blind persons, now rejected by existing Institutions on account of their age, and give profitable employment to an increasing number of those who have acquired trades—affording them materials at the lowest wholesale prices, and finding the best market for their work. A house of so congenial a nature for the older blind, of regular industrious habits, would confirm to them all the great advantages which the present Institutions afford, and realize every benevolent hope in their future happiness.

It is certainly a favorable consideration, that a department confined to industry exclusively, could be conducted at a comparatively small expense. With a fair demand for its manufactures, it might indeed be made well nigh to support itself.

In whatever view the British Asylums may be taken, they certainly give an encouraging example to our own, of what may be done by the blind, both in *extent* and *variety* of manufacturing. The are several new branches of work, for both sexes, which we propose to introduce here as early as possible, which, it is hoped, will contribute to the economy and profit of the Institution, as well as the blind themselves.

General Instruction.—III. With the exception of the Paris, York, and one of the London schools, very little attention is given to mental improvement. In this respect they present to us a *negative* example. Their Superintendents are selected with reference to their *business* talents—as general overseers, or stewards—and without any particular regard to education—they having nothing to do with teaching.

The effect of this general neglect of intellectual improvement is quite visible in the deportment of the pupils. They have not the bright and animated appearance of the blind in our own schools.

While in Great Britain eight and even ten hours a day are devoted to labor, only three or four are so employed here. The rest of the time is given to mental improvement and music, particularly the former. It is thought there, that very little education is necessary for a blind person who must depend upon his labor for subsistence. It is believed here that a good education, especially in useful knowledge, is a very important element of success in life, and particularly to the blind, who otherwise labor under such great disadvantages. It is true, also, as a general rule, that a well-informed person will make a better and more successful mechanic.

The British Institutions, however, may in this only conform to their pecuniary circumstances, which do not admit of the additional expenses required for school instruction. They seldom have more than one teacher, of moderate abilities, and for a portion of the day only.

But whatever particular views may be entertained on this subject, an enlightened public sentiment in this country requires that the blind, as well as other children, shall receive a good practical education.

There are, moreover, many blind persons of a high order of talent, capable of becoming instructors. That system which overlooked such claims would be imperfect if not unjust.

Support.—IV. Some of the Asylums are largely endowed by legacies and bequests. But they depend mainly upon annual subscriptions, and a small pay from each pupil. The donations and subscriptions are of course precarious and uncertain, and require constant effort to meet the necessary expenditures. Several of them appear to be declining for want of means.

Except in Paris, Government contributes nothing to their support. The opinion prevails in Great Britain that charitable institutions should depend upon the contributions of the benevolent. It is supposed this creates a closer sympathy between them and the public, and also leads to their better management.

A different and it is thought a better policy governs the American Institutions. Here they are sustained directly by each State, in whole or in part. There is no exception to this—though the Massachusetts, New-York and Pennsylvania Institutions do receive contributions, and they are not governed in their management by their State Legislatures. All the schools that have been established since these, are regarded exclusively as State foundations, and directly dependent upon Legislative support from year to year.

The Massachusetts Institution received a munificent donation from T. K. Perkins, Esq. of a valuable building in the City of Boston, which was subsequently exchanged for their present splendid edifice in South Boston. They have received, also, other liberal donations.

The New-York Institution is authorized to receive, at the expense of the State, upward of one hundred pupils. They also received large grants from the Legislature, from time to time, toward the erection of their beautiful building. These grants were made upon condition of other large sums being raised by private subscriptions.

The Pennsylvania Institution has been endowed by a large legacy from Wm. Y. Birch, valued, at the time, at $180,000. Its actual value, at this time, is estimated at $100,000, or less. The income of this being insufficient, they receive, annually, an appropriation of several thousand dollars from the State.

The other institutions in the country, in the order of their dates, are the Ohio, Virginia, Kentucky, and Tennessee. Each of those, as remarked, is directly founded by the State. There is a prospect of another in Indiana, on the same plan.

It appears to be a well settled opinion, that these and the kindred benevolent asylums, should be exclusively State works. It is believed they are as economically conducted, and much more efficient than they could be under the very uncertain resources of individual subscriptions.

The blind, and deaf and dumb, and insane being few in number compared with the whole population, there is no danger of the generous humanity of the State ever leading to excess and abuse.

The single serious objection at first entertained by many, that Institutions under the direct control of successive Legislatures, would be liable to frequent political changes, to their great detriment, has in no instance, we believe, been realized. As a proof of this, few asylums of any description in the United States, have exhibited the uniformity and the eminence of those under the control of the State of Ohio.

Buildings.—These, with two or three exceptions, are not equal to those in the United States. Some of them are houses [that] were formerly used as dwellings, and are not well adapted to their purposes—nor can they accommodate many boarders. The Manchester and one [of the] London schools, are exceptions to this. The Bel[mont] and Bristol schools, also, are said to occupy fine buildings. The institutions for the blind, and deaf and dumb in Paris, are splendid and costly edifices—built at the expense of Government.

The buildings of the benevolent institutions generally, throughout Great Britain, are *not so high* as ours, and cover more ground. In respect to convenience, this is decidedly preferable to our lofty structures, though less imposing, perhaps, according to architectural taste.

When we consider the amount of daily labor constantly repeated in such large establishments, it is of great importance to the comfort and economy of the house, that this labor should be abridged in every possible way. Where there is sufficient building room, it is a perpetual evil to sacrifice the convenience of a building for its particular purposes, to external show.

The report of the New-York Institution gives a promising view of the position of their affairs. In the history of its growth, it was very pleasant to see how large a tree had grown from the kernel no bigger than a mustard seed, dropped by Samuel Wood in 1830. It should encourage every one to attend carefully to every benevolent suggestion, however slight, that rises in the mind.

It is probable, therefore, and as will appear when we come to notice the efforts of the philanthropic in behalf of the blind, that the scheme originated in various minds about the same time. Mr. Samuel Wood, an aged and respectable member of the Society of Friends, who is now no more, and to whose efforts, united with those of Dr. Samuel Akerly, this institution mainly owes its origin, seems first to have conceived the idea of such an establishment in the years 1827 or '28. He was at that time, and for several years subsequently, a trustee and frequent visitor of the school for the orphan and other indigent children of the New-York Alms House. Several of the children, whom, in his visitations he frequently saw about the school, had recently been deprived of sight by an ophthalmic disease, and thus kindled in his bosom a lively interest for that afflicted class now the objects of our care. As he witnessed their eagerness to acquire knowledge, their activity and apparent intelligence, the idea occurred to him, "cannot something be done for these unfortunate children?" In one of his visits to the school about this time, after noticing in the book usually kept for the purpose, (and which is fortunately still preserved) the general condition of the school, he says:

"The pen with which this was written, was made by one of the six boys who lost his sight by the sore-eye distemper lately prevalent here. *Query.* Ought not some exertion to be made to help these unfortunate children to be more comfortable and useful to themselves and society in the long stage of darkness (all their lives) which must be their lot?"

Signed, SAMUEL WOOD."

11th mo. 4th, 1830."

To this question, put so gently only fifteen years ago, the New-York Institution makes an imposing reply. Would that the question "ought not" were always as fully and as promptly answered by "there ought and there shall."

We observe with regret that "the reluctance of parents to give information as to the causes of blindness" is mentioned as an obstacle to obtaining exact knowledge on the subject. When will people learn the importance of supplying the true statement of a case, precisely and thoroughly, in order to [take] those preventive and remedial measures imperatively required by the curses ever threatening their race? The worst fact may contribute to a divine good if told in the spirit [of truth].

We find here this remark, whose justice we doubt and should like to hear farther about it.

"It is observed that there is less energy of character, both physical and mental, in those who have been born blind than in those who have been made so by accident or disease. The absence of such energy is, however, only another result of that general disorganization of the constitution of which congenital blindness is but a single feature. In addition it may be sold that instruction is more readily imparted, and ideas more correctly formed when the individual possesses the advantage of having once seen."

The latter clause may be true, but as to "general disorganization," it seems, in other cases, that Nature strives hard to effect a compensation, bestowing on those she has suffered to be mutilated in one way more growth and energy in some other department to make up for it.

Defective organizations afford the best hints for study of the law of perfection, as we are constantly excited to look at causes, and the correspondence between one part of the system and the other. When we find an average health, the attention is easily satisfied and the mind is not excited to the labor of reconstruction which would teach it so much.

✻

[April 18, 1846]

Floral Fete for the Children of the Farm Schools on the Fourth July

We would again call the attention of our citizens to this truly kind plan for casting a gleam of light over the dull and mechanical existence of these poor little beings. Poor children! Severed from all those endearments and daily enlivenments of which the worst home offers some to rouse the faculties and cheer the hearts of young human beings! If they are in one sense better off than in sordid or vicious homes—if shelter, food, clothing and some instruction be provided for many who would otherwise have none at all—yet, how far this is from being enough, their forlorn and lack-lustre looks declare. Here is a chance to give them some of the feelings awakened in the hearts of other children by visits and affectionate, disinterested attentions from relatives which form so valuable and so well remembered a part in the schooling of young years.—We hope a multitude will go, buy the bouquets, and take with them "something nice" for the picknick. We have never heard of an occasion when that "something nice" would hold so honorable a place as on this.

[July 4, 1846]

Caroline

The other evening I heard a gentle voice reading aloud the story of Maurice, a boy who, deprived of the use of his limbs by paralysis, was sustained in comfort, and, almost, in cheerfulness, by the exertions of his twin sister. Left with him in orphanage, her affections were centered upon him, and, amid the difficulties his misfortunes brought upon them, grew to a fire intense and pure enough to animate her with angelic impulses and powers. As he could not move about, she drew him everywhere in a little cart, and, when at last they heard that sea-bathing might accomplish his cure, conveyed him, in this way, hundreds of miles to the seashore. Her pious devotion and faith were rewarded by his cure, and (a French story would be entirely incomplete otherwise) with money, plaudits, and garlands from the bystanders.

Though the story ends in this vulgar manner, it is, in its conduct, extremely sweet and touching, not only as to the beautiful qualities developed by these trials in the brother and sister, but in the purifying and softening influence exerted by the sight of his helplessness and her goodness on all around them.

Those who are the victims of some natural blight, often fulfil this important office, and bless those within their sphere more, by awakening feelings of holy tenderness and compassion, than a man, healthy and strong, can do by the utmost exertion of his good will and energies. Thus, in the East, men hold sacred those in whom they find a distortion or alienation, of the mind, which makes them unable to provide for themselves. The well and sane feel themselves the ministers of Providence to carry out a mysterious purpose while taking care of those who are thus left incapable of taking care of themselves, and, while fulfilling this ministry, find themselves refined and made better.

The Swiss have similar feelings as to those of their families whom cretinism has reduced to idiocy. They are attended to, fed, dressed clean, and provided with a pleasant place for the day, before doing any thing else, even by very busy and poor people.

We have seen a similar instance in this country of voluntary care of an idiot, and the mental benefits that ensued. This idiot, like most that are called so, was not without a glimmer of mind. His teacher was able to give him some notions both of spiritual and mental facts, at least she thought she had given him the idea of a God; and though it appeared by his gestures that to him the moon was the representative of that idea! yet he certainly did conceive of something above him, and which inspired him with reverence and delight. He knew the names of two or three persons who had done him kindness, and, when they were mentioned, would point upwards as he did to the moon, showing himself susceptible, in his degree, of Mr. Carlyle's grand method of education—hero-worship. She had awakened in him a love of music, so that he could be soothed in his most violent moods by her gentle singing. It was a most touching sight to see him sitting opposite to her at those times, his wondering and lacklustre eyes filled with childish pleasure, while in hers gleamed the same pure joy that we may suppose to animate the looks of an angel appointed by Heaven to restore a ruined world.

We knew another instance in which a young girl became to her village a far more valuable influence than any patron saint who looks down from his stone niche, while his votaries recall the legend of his goodness in days long past. Caroline lived in a little quiet country village, quiet as no village can now remain, since the railroad strikes its spear through the peace of country life. She lived alone with a widowed mother, for whom, as well as for herself, her needle won bread, while the mother's strength and skill sufficed to the simple duties of their household. They lived content and hopeful, till, whether from sitting still too much, or some other cause, Caroline became ill, and soon the physician pronounced her spine to be affected, and to such a degree that she was incurable.

This news was a thunderbolt to the poor little cottage. The mother, who had lost her elasticity of mind, wept in despair, but the young girl who found so early all the hopes and joys of life taken from her, and that she was left seemingly without any shelter from the storm, had, even at first, the faith and strength to bow her head in gentleness and say, God will provide. She sustained and cheered her mother.

And God did provide. With simultaneous vibration the hearts of all their circle acknowledged the divine obligation of love and mutual aid between human beings. Food, clothing, medicine, service, were all offered freely to the widow and her daughter.

Caroline grew worse, and was at last in such a state that she could only be moved upon a sheet and by the aid of two persons. In this toilsome service, and every other that she needed for years, her mother never needed to ask assistance. The neighbors took turns in doing all that was required, and the young girls, as they were growing up, counted it among their regular employments to work for or read to Caroline.

Not without immediate reward was their service of love. The mind of the girl, originally bright and pure, was quickened and wrought up to the finest susceptibility by the nervous exaltation that often comes upon affection of the spine. The soul, which had taken an upward impulse from its first act of resignation, grew daily more and more into communion with the higher regions of life permanent and pure. Perhaps she was instructed by spirits which, having passed through a similar trial of pain and loneliness, had risen to see the reason why. However that may be, she grew in nobleness of view and purity of sentiment, and, as she received more instruction from books also, than any other person in her circle, had from many visitors abundant information as to the events which were pending around her and leisure to reflect on them with a disinterested desire for truth, she became so much wiser than her companions as to be, at last, their preceptress and best friend, and her brief, gentle comments and counsels were listened to as oracles from one enfranchised from the films which selfishness and passion cast over the eyes of the multitude.

The twofold blessing conferred by her presence, both in awakening none but good feelings in the hearts of others, and in the instruction she became able to confer was such that, at the end of five years, no member of that society would have been so generally lamented as Caroline if Death had called her away.

But the Messenger, who so often seems capricious in his summons, took first the aged mother, and the poor girl found that life had yet the power to bring her grief, unexpected and severe.

And now the neighbors met in council. Caroline could not be left quite alone in the house. Should they take turns and stay with her by night as well as by day?

"Not so," said the blacksmith's wife. "The house will never seem like home to her now, poor thing, and 't would be kind of dreary for her to change about her "nurses" so. I'll tell you what; all my children but one are married and gone off; we have property enough. I will have a good room fixed for her and she shall live with us. My husband wants her to as much as me."

The Council acquiesced in this truly humane arrangement, and Caroline lives there still; and we are assured that none of her numerous friends dread her departure so much as the blacksmith's wife.

"'T ant no trouble at all to have her," she says; "and if it was, I should'n't care; she is so good and still, and talks so pretty. It 's as good to be with her as goin' to meetin'."

De Maistre relates some similar passages as to a sick girl in St. Petersburg, though his mind dwelt more on the spiritual beauty, evinced in her remarks, than on the good she had done to those around her. Indeed, none bless more than those who only stand and wait. Even if their passivity be enforced by fate, it will become a spiritual activity, if accepted in a faith higher above fate than the Greek Gods were supposed to sit enthroned above misfortune.

*

[April 9, 1846]

6
Equality for Women and African Americans

Readers of Horace Greeley's *New York Tribune* in the 1840s nicknamed the newspaper "The Great Moral Organ" because it endorsed so many nineteenth-century reform movements. Greeley favored Fourieristic socialism, abolitionism, trade unionism, vegetarianism, and spiritualism plus land reform, woman's rights, temperance, protective tariffs, and improved farming methods. All of these interests led people to comment on the *Tribune's* fondness for "isms." Greeley addressed a general public belief in progress. "Most individuals, whether participating reformers or not, shared the faith in human betterment and believed that perfection itself could be achieved in the foreseeable future," said historian Douglas Miller. Although many of the paper's isms may seem credible to a modern reader, some have lost their luster in 150 years. For instance, both Fuller and Greeley believed in phrenology, the idea that the shape of a person's skull determined character.[1]

Greeley advocated a form of socialism proposed by Charles Fourier, who believed in the natural goodness of man. The new industrial society, Fourier argued, had perverted this goodness. Fourier proposed to reorganize society into small social units called phalanxes with 1,620 people in each group. Each phalanx would hold property communally. Greeley helped found the first phalanx, Sylvania, in Pennsylvania, but the social experiment lasted only one year and lost him five thousand dollars.[2]

Personal reform was also on the agenda for the age. Sylvester Graham, inventor of the graham cracker, started in 1830 as a temperance speaker and became an advocate of "proper habits of dress, hygiene, sex and mind," said historian George Brown Tindall. By the 1840s Graham health clubs, camps, and sanitariums all advocated the Graham dietary philosophy. Graham encouraged people to eat grains, vegetables, and fruits, but to avoid alcohol, coffee, tea, and tobacco. Greeley was dedicated to Graham's ideas. In fact, Greeley first met his wife, Molly, at Graham's boardinghouse in New York, according to biographer Francis Nicoll Zabriskie.[3]

Fuller generally agreed with Greeley on reform, but Robert Hudspeth has pointed out a difference between their views. While Greeley addressed national political issues, Fuller looked at local social problems. "While

Greeley regularly damned the administration, especially after the outbreak of the [Mexican] war, Fuller concentrated on New York City," Hudspeth said.[4] Although articles on prisons and institutions dominated Margaret Fuller's reform writing, she took up other causes as well.

Fuller's fame comes from *Woman in the Nineteenth Century,* her landmark statement on woman's rights. The book grew out of an essay, "The Great Lawsuit," which first appeared in the *Dial.* In both pieces she argued that women should have the same rights and opportunities as men because women had minds of an intellectual capacity equal to men. She also said women could do physically demanding labor, as demonstrated by washerwomen, who stood at tubs, scrubbed laundry all day, and then carried loads home.[5]

Widely reviewed, the book became an instant topic of discussion. Robert Browning, Thomas Carlyle, and George Sand all commented on the book in their letters. Scholar Joseph Deiss said many readers saw the book as "scandalous, hysterical, revolutionary. To many Americans the idea of equal rights for women was simply preposterous. Yet the first edition was sold out within a week." Charles F. Briggs, reviewing *Woman in the Nineteenth Century* for the *Broadway Journal,* called Fuller a "thinking, right judging person" but disagreed with her woman's rights theme: "The only way in which any good can be rendered to society, is by making woman more womanly and man more manly." Edgar Allan Poe called the book "nervous, forcible, thoughtful, suggestive, brilliant, and to a certain extent scholar-like." Scholar Marie Urbanski has called *Woman in the Nineteenth Century* the catalyst for the Seneca Falls Convention on Woman's Rights in 1848. This first conference on woman's rights came three years after the book's publication; unfortunately, Margaret Fuller was in Europe and could not attend.[6]

Given her importance at the birth of the woman's rights movement, Fuller wrote surprisingly few newspaper columns on the issue. One of her strongest pieces, though, "The Wrongs of American Women. The Duties of American Women," made a moving economic argument for an expansion of the types of jobs available to women. She noted that "destiny" did not automatically provide every woman with "the shelter of a parent's or a guardian's roof till she married." A woman could not be "sure of finding immediate protection" with a brother or husband. Since some women needed work, she argued, society should allow them to work as nurses and teachers.

Fuller also discussed intellectual education for women, a new concept in the 1840s. Most women, if they received any education, only learned painting, music, and the alphabet. In the "School of Misses Sedgwick," Fuller attacked this approach. She argued that women's education should produce the "graceful manners which result from an elegant mind" instead of the "clumsy and tasteless mimicry of foreign airs and graces."

A horror of slavery recurred in Fuller's work. She found Frederick Douglass's autobiography "an excellent piece of writing" that should "be prized as a specimen of the powers of the Black Race, which Prejudice persists in disputing." In the "First of August, 1845," she commemorated the anniversary of the emancipation of slaves in the British West Indies. She listed the sins of the British, "the plundered Hindoo, the wronged Irish," but said America had sinned more. A nation founded on the principles of freedom allowed slavery. "We have surpassed them all in trampling under foot the principles that had been assumed as the basis of our national existence." When reviewing a book about Russian serfdom, Fuller noted, "The barbarisms are exactly the same as occur in our own country under different circumstances." "What Fits a Man to Be a Voter?" was an example of a nineteenth-century sentimental allegory directed to a very serious purpose, the argument that skin color makes no difference between people. In "Lyceum of New-Bedford, Mass.," she protested the banning of African Americans from an audience.

Fuller's attack on capital punishment drew Horace Greeley's ire because it took Fuller so long to write the essay.[7] This article drew an attack from a rival newspaper, which argued that a proper lady should avoid discussing such distasteful topics in print. In her response, Fuller made a cogent case for a woman's right to think and debate independently. In an intellectual discussion, she said, a woman's mind had the same power as a man's. Therefore, a woman had the intellectual capacity to take on any topic.

The Wrongs of American Women
The Duty of American Women

The same day brought us a copy of Mr. Burdett's little book, in which the sufferings and difficulties that beset the large class of women who must earn their subsistence in a city like New-York are delineated with so much simplicity, feeling and exact adherence to the facts—and a printed circular containing proposals for immediate practical adoption of the plan more fully described in a book published some weeks since under the title "The Duty of American Women to their Country," which was ascribed alternately to Mrs. Stowe and Miss Catherine Beecher, but of which we understand both those ladies decline the responsibility. The two matters seemed linked with one another by natural piety. Full acquaintance with the wrong must call forth all manner of inventions for its redress.

The Circular, in showing the vast want that already exists of good means for instructing the children of this nation, especially in the West, states also the belief among women, as being less immersed in other cares and toils, from the preparation it gives for their task as mothers, and from the necessity in which a great proportion stand of earning a subsistence somehow, at least during the years which precede marriage, if they *do* marry, must the number of teachers wanted be found, which is estimated already at *sixty thousand.*

We cordially sympathize with these views.

Much has been written about Woman's keeping within her sphere, which is defined as the domestic sphere. As a little girl she is to learn the lighter family duties, while she acquires that limited acquaintance with the realm of literature and science that will enable her to superintend the instruction of children in their earliest years. It is not generally proposed that she should be sufficiently instructed and developed to understand the pursuits or aims of her future husband; she is not to be a helpmeet to him, in the way of companionship or counsel, except in the care of his house and children. Her youth is to be passed partly in learning to keep house and the use of the needle, partly in the social circle where her manners may be formed, ornamental accomplishments perfected and displayed, and the husband found who shall give her the domestic sphere for which exclusively she is to be prepared.

Were the destiny of Woman thus exactly marked out, did she invariably retain the shelter of a parent's or a guardian's roof till she married, did marriage give her a sure home and protector, were she never liable to be made a widow, or, if so, sure of finding immediate protection from a brother or new husband, so that she might never be forced to stand alone one moment, and were her mind given for this world only, with no faculties capable of eternal growth and infinite improvement, we would still demand for her a far wider and more generous culture than is proposed by those who so anxiously define her sphere. We would demand it that she might not ignorantly or frivolously thwart the designs of her husband, that she might be the respected friend of her sons no less than her daughters, that she might give more refinement, elevation and attraction to the society which is needed to give the characters of *men* polish and plasticity—no less so than to save them from vicious and sensual habits. But the most fastidious critic on the departure of Woman from her sphere, can scarcely fail to see at present that a vast proportion of the sex, if not the better half, do not, CANNOT, have this domestic sphere. Thousands and scores of thousands in this country no less than in Europe are obliged to maintain themselves alone. Far greater numbers divide with their husbands the care of earning a support for the family. In England, now, the progress of society has reached so admirable a pitch that the position of the sexes is frequently reversed, and the husband is obliged to stay at home and "mind the house and bairns" while the wife goes forth to the employment she alone can secure.

We readily admit that the picture of this is most painful—that Nature made entirely an opposite distribution of functions between the sexes. We believe the natural order to be the best, and that, if it could be followed in an enlightened spirit, it would bring to Woman all she wants, no less for her immortal than her mortal destiny. We are not surprised that men, who do not look deeply or carefully at causes or tendencies, should be led by disgust at the hardened, hackneyed characters which the present state of things too often produces in women to such conclusions as they are. We, no more than they, delight in the picture of the poor woman digging in the mines in her husband's clothes. We, no more than they, delight to hear their voices shrilly raised in the market-place, whether of apples or celebrity. But we see that at present they must do as they do for bread. Hundreds and thousands must step out of that hallowed domestic sphere, with no choice but to work or steal, or belong to men, not as wives, but as the wretched slaves of sensuality.

And this transition state, with all its revolting features, indicates, we do believe, the approach of a nobler era than the world has yet known.

We trust that by the stress and emergencies of the present and coming time, the minds of women will be formed to more reflection and higher purposes than heretofore—their latent powers developed, their characters strengthened and eventually beautified and harmonized. Should the state of society then be such that each may remain, a[s] Nature seems to have intended, the tutelary genius of a home, while men manage the out-door business of life, both may be done with a wisdom, a mutual understanding and respect unknown at present. Men will be no less the gainers by this than women, finding in pure and more religious marriages the joys of friendship and love combined—in their mothers and daughters better instruction, sweeter and nobler companionship, and in society at large an excitement to their finer powers and feelings unknown at present except in the region of the fine arts.

Blest be the generous, the wise among them who seek to forward hopes like these, instead of struggling against the fiat of Providence and the march of Fate to bind down rushing Life to the standard of the Past. Such efforts are vain, but those who make them are unhappy and unwise.

It is not, however, to such that we address ourselves, but to those who seek to make the best of things as they are, while they also strive to make them better. Such persons will have seen enough of the state of things in London, Paris, New-York, and manufacturing regions every where, to feel that there is an imperative necessity for opening more avenues of employment to women, and fitting them better to enter them, rather than keeping them back. Women have invaded many of the trades and some of the professions. Sewing, to the present killing extent, they cannot long bear. Factories seem likely to afford them permanent employment. In the culture of fruit, flowers and vegetables, even in the sale of them, we rejoice to see them engaged. In domestic service they will be aided, but can never be supplanted, by machinery. As much room as there is here for woman's mind and woman's labor will always be filled. A few have usurped the martial province, but these must always be few; the nature of woman is opposed to war. It is natural enough to see "Female Physicians," and we believe that the lace cap and work-bag are as much at home here as the wig and gold-beaded cane. In the priesthood they have from all time shared more or less—in many eras more than at the present. We believe there has been no female lawyer, and probably will be none. The pen, many of the fine arts they have made their own, and, in the more refined countries of the world, as writers, as musicians, as painters, as actors, women occupy as advantageous ground as men. Writing and music may be esteemed professions for them more than any other.

But there are two others where the demand must invariably be immense, and for which they are naturally better fitted than men, for which we should like to see them better prepared and better rewarded than they are. These are the profession of nurse to the sick and of teacher. The first of these professions we have warmly desired to see dignified. It is a noble one, now most unjustly regarded in the light of menial service. It is one which no menial, no servile nature can fitly occupy. We were rejoiced when an intelligent lady of Massachusetts made the refined heroine of a little romance select that calling. This lady (Mrs. George Lee) has looked on society with unusual largeness of spirit and healthiness of temper. She is well acquainted with the world of conventions, but sees beneath it the world of nature, She is a generous writer and unpretending, as the generous are wont to be. We do not recall the name of the tale, but the circumstance above mentioned marks its temper. We hope to see the time when the refined and cultivated will choose this profession and learn it, not only through experience under the direction of the doctor, but by acquainting themselves with the laws of matter and of mind, so that all they do shall be intelligently done, and afford them the means of developing intelligence as well as the nobler, tenderer feelings of humanity; for even the last part of the benefit they cannot receive if their work be done in a selfish or mercenary spirit.

The other profession is that of teacher, for which women are peculiarly adapted by their nature, superiority in tact, quickness of sympathy, gentleness, patience, and a clear and animated manner in narration or description. To form a good teacher should be added to this sincere modesty combined with firmness, liberal views with a power and will to liberalize them still further, a good method and habits of exact and thorough investigation. In the two last requisites women are generally deficient, but there are now many shining examples to prove that if they are immethodical and superficial as teachers it is because it is the custom so to teach them, and that when aware of these faults they can and will correct them.

The profession is of itself an excellent one for the improvement of the teacher during that interim between youth and maturity when the mind needs testing, tempering, and to review and rearrange the knowledge it has acquired. The natural method of doing this for one's self is to attempt teaching others; those years also are the best of the practical teacher. The teacher should be near the pupil both in years and feelings—no oracle, but the elder brother or sister of the pupil. More experience and years form the lecturer and the director of studies, but injure the powers as to familiar teaching.

These are just the years of leisure in the lives even of those women who are to enter the domestic sphere, and this calling most of all compatible with a constant progress as to qualifications for that.

Viewing the matter thus it may well be seen that we should hail with joy the assurance that sixty thousand *female* teachers are wanted, and more likely to be, and that a plan is projected which looks wise, liberal and generous, to afford the means of those whose hearts answer to this high calling obeying their dictates.

The plan is to have Cincinnati for a central point, where teachers shall be for a short time received, examined and prepared for their duties. By mutual agreement and cooperation of the various sects funds are to be raised and teachers provided according to the wants and tendencies of the various locations now destitute. What is to be done for them centrally, is for suitable persons to examine into their various kinds of fitness, communicate some general views whose value has been tested, and counsel adapted to the difficulties and advantages of their new positions. The Central Committee are to have the charge of raising funds and finding teachers and places where teachers are wanted.

The passage of thoughts, teachers and funds will be from East to West, the course of sunlight upon this earth.

The plan is offered as the most extensive and pliant means of doing a good and preventing ill to this nation, by means of a national education, whose normal school shall have an invariable object in the search after truth and the diffusion of the means of knowledge, while its form shall be plastic according to the wants of the time. This normal school promises to have good effects, for it proposes worthy aims through simple means, and the motive for its formation and support seems to be disinterested philanthropy.

It promises to eschew the bitter spirit of sectarianism and proselytism, else we, for one party, could have nothing to do with it. Men, no doubt, have been oftentimes kept from absolute famine by the wheat with which such tares are mingled; but we believe the time is come when a purer and more generous food is to be offered to the people at large. We believe the aim of all education to be to rouse the mind to action, show it the means of discipline and of information; then leave it free, with God, Conscience, and the love of Truth for its guardians and teachers. Wo be to those who sacrifice these aims of universal and eternal value to the propagation of a set of opinions. But on this subject we can accept such doctrine as is offered by Rev. Calvin Stowe, one of the committee, in the following passage:

"In judicious practice, I am persuaded there will seldom be any very great difficulty, especially if there be excited in the community anything like a whole-hearted honesty and enlightened sincerity in the cause of public instruction.

"It is all right for people to suit their own taste and convictions in respect to sect; and by fair means and at proper times to teach their children and those under their influence to prefer the denominations which they prefer; but farther than this no one has any right to go. It is all wrong to hazard the well being of the soul, to jeopardize great public interests for the sake of advancing the interests of a sect. People must learn to practise some self-denial, on Christian principles, in respect to their denominational preferences, as well as in respect to other things, before pure Religion can ever gain a complete victory over every form of human selfishness."

The persons who propose themselves to the examination and instruction of the teachers at Cincinnati, till the plan shall be sufficiently under weigh to provide regularly for the office, are Mrs. Stowe and Miss Catherine Beecher, ladies well known to fame, as possessing unusual qualifications for the task.

As to finding abundance of teachers, who that reads this little book of Mr. Burdett's, or the account of the compensation of female labor in New-York, and the hopeless, comfortless, useless, pernicious lives those who have even the advantage of getting work must live with the sufferings and almost inevitable degradation to which those who cannot are exposed, but must long to match such as are capable of this better profession, and among the multitude there must be many who are or could be made so, from their present toils and make them free and the means of freedom and growth to others.

To many books on such subjects, among others to "Woman in the Nineteenth Century," the objection has been made that they exhibit ills without specifying any practical means for their remedy. The writer of the last named essay does indeed think that it contains one great rule which, if laid to heart, would prove a practical remedy for many ills, and of such daily and hourly efficacy in the conduct of life that any extensive observance of it for a single year would perceptibly raise the tone of thought, feeling and conduct throughout the civilized world. But to those who ask not only such a principle, but an external method for immediate use, we say, here is one proposed that looks noble and promising, the proposers offer themselves to the work with heart and hand, with time and purse: Go ye and do likewise.

Those who wish details as to this plan, will find them in the "Duty of American Woman to their Country," published by Harper & Brothers, Cliff-st. The publishers may, probably, be able to furnish also the Circular to which we have referred. At a leisure day we shall offer some suggestions and remarks as to the methods and objects there proposed.

✻

[September 30, 1845]

School of the Misses Sedgwick
42 West Washington Place

A friend having placed in our hands the Circular which intimates the plan of this school, we are struck by the simplicity, intelligent appreciation of, and devotion to, the honorable work undertaken that it evinces. Inquiry has confirmed these impressions.

There doubtless are parents in New York, and among the multitude there must be many, though a small majority compared with the whole, to whom the show of an establishment, the array of masters, and the contagion of factitious life are not so desirable for their children as a sincere culture and harmonious development of their powers. There must be some who do not wish for their daughters the premature airs of the woman, and who prefer the graceful manners which result from an elegant mind to a clumsy and tasteless mimicry of foreign airs and graces. There must be some who regard the school education of their children as a serious preparation for the school of life; some who seek in the teacher a wise friend for the child, rather than the upholsterer who is to hide by gay draperies the nakedness of its mind's chambers. To such we would recommend an examination into the pretensions of this school; they are not pompously set forth, and are the more likely to be well founded. A promise is likely to be kept that is made with so much of heart and soul.

This is a boarding as well as a day school, and to parents in the country who wish for a time to exchange its far more favorable influences for those of the city, in view of the better instruction in various accomplishments that may there be found, this might be recommended as a safe place; where they will not suddenly be deprived of all the advantages of home. They will not, for the sake of improving in French and music, be deprived, for many months, of all better things, will not be left to trick the assistant or gossip about street acquaintance, and window flirtations, in absence of all other pleasure, except on regular *reception evenings,* but constitute to share the little daily duties and pleasures of domestic life. The name of Sedgwick alone is a recommendation to the school: It is associated with candor, benevolence and knowledge of the physical and moral laws, and we believe it is rarely in vain that one of a name should show such excellence; it kindles aspiration and imparts light to others who bear it.

*

[August 25, 1845]

Narrative of the Life of
Frederick Douglass, an American Slave,
Written by Himself
Boston: Published at the Anti-Slavery Office,
No. 25 Cornhill. 1845

Frederick Douglass has been for some time a prominent member of the Abolition party. He is said to be an excellent speaker—can speak from a thorough personal experience—and has upon the audience, beside, the influence of a strong character and uncommon talents. In the book before us he has put into the story of his life the thoughts, the feelings and the adventures that have been so affecting through the living voice; nor are they less so from the printed page. He has had the courage to name the persons, times and places, thus exposing himself to obvious danger, and setting the seal on his deep convictions as to the religious need of speaking the whole truth. Considered merely as a narrative, we have never read one more simple, true, coherent, and warm with genuine feeling. It is an excellent piece of writing, and on that score to be prized as a specimen of the powers of the Black Race, which Prejudice persists in disputing. We prize highly all evidence of this kind, and it is becoming more abundant. The Cross of the Legion of Honor has just been conferred in France on Dumas and Souliè, both celebrated in the paths of light literature. Dumas, whose father was a General in the French Army, is a Mulatto; Souliè, a Quadroon. He went from New-Orleans, where, though to the eye a white man, yet, as known to have African blood in his veins, he could never have enjoyed the privileges due to a human being. Leaving the Land of Freedom, he found himself free to develop the powers that God had given.

Two wise and candid thinkers,—the Scotchman, Kinment, prematurely lost to this country, of which he was so faithful and generous a student, and the late Dr. Channing,—both thought that the African Race had in them a peculiar element, which, if it could be assimilated with those imported among us from Europe, would give to genius a development, and to the energies of character a balance and harmony beyond what has been seen heretofore in the history of the world. Such an element is indicated in their lowest estate by a talent for melody, a ready skill at imitation and adaptation, an almost indestructible elasticity of nature. It is to be remarked in the writings both of Souliè and Dumas, full of faults but glowing with plastic life and fertile in invention. The same torrid energy and saccharine fulness may be felt in the writings of this Douglass, though his life being one of action or resistance, was less favorable to *such* powers than one of a more joyous flow might have been.

The book is prefaced by two communications,—one from Garrison, and one from Wendell Phillips. That from the former is in his usual over-emphatic style. His motives and his course have been noble and generous. We look upon him with high respect, but he has indulged in violent invective and denunciation till he has spoiled the temper of his mind. Like a man who has been in the habit of screaming himself hoarse to make the deaf hear, he can no longer pitch his voice on a key agreeable to common ears. Mr. Phillips's remarks are equally decided, without this exaggeration in the tone. Douglass himself seems very just and temperate. We feel that his view, even of those who have injured him most, may be relied upon. He knows how to allow for motives and influences. Upon the subject of Religion, he speaks with great force, and not more than our own sympathies can respond to. The inconsistencies of Slaveholding professors of religion cry to Heaven. We are not disposed to detest or refuse communion with them. Their blindness is but one form of that prevalent fallacy which substitutes a creed for a faith, a ritual for a life. We have seen too much of this system of atonement not to know that those who adopt it often began with good intentions, and are, at any rate, in their mistakes worthy of the deepest pity. But that is no reason why the truth should not be uttered, trumpet-tongued, about the thing. "Bring no more vain oblations"; sermons must daily be preached anew on that text. Kings, five hundred years ago, built Churches with the spoils of War; Clergymen to-day command Slaves to obey a Gospel which they will not allow them to read, and call themselves Christians amid the curses of their fellow men.—The world ought to get on a little faster than that, if there be really any principle of improvement in it. The Kingdom of Heaven may not at the beginning have dropped seed larger than a mustard-seed, but even from that we had a right to expect a fuller growth than can be believed to exist, when we read such a book as this of Douglass. Unspeakably affecting is the fact that he never saw his mother at all by day-light.

"I do not recollect of ever seeing my mother by the light of day. She was with me in the night. She would lie down with me, and get me to sleep, but long before I waked she was gone."

The following extract presents a suitable answer to the hacknied [*sic*] argument drawn by the defender of Slavery from the songs of the Slave, and is also a good specimen of the powers of observation and manly heart of the writer. We wish that every one may read his book and see what a mind might have been stifled in bondage,—what a man may be subjected to the insults of spendthrift dandies, or the blows of mercenary brutes, in whom there is no whiteness except of the skin, no humanity except in the outward form, and of whom the Avenger will not fail yet to demand—"Where is thy brother?"

*

[June 10, 1845]

First of August, 1845

Among the holidays of the year, some portion of our people borrow one from another land. They borrow what they fain would own, since their doing so would increase, not lessen, the joy and prosperity of the present owner. It is a holiday, not to be celebrated, as others are, with boast, and shout, and gay procession, but solemnly, yet hopefully, in humiliation and prayer for much ill now existing—in faith that the God of good will not permit such ill to exist always—in aspirations to become His instruments for its removal.

We borrow this holiday from England. We know not that she could lend us another such. Her career has been one of selfish aggrandizement. To carry her flag every where where the waters flow, to leave a strong mark of her foot-print on every shore that she might return and claim its spoils, to maintain in every way her own advantage, is and has been her object as much as that of any nation on earth. The plundered Hindoo, the wronged Irish—for ourselves we must add the outraged Chinese (for we look on all that has been written as to the right of that war as mere sophistry), no less than Napoleon, walking up and down in his 'tarred green coat' in the unwholesome lodge at St. Helena,—all can tell whether she be righteous or generous in her conquests. Nay! let myriads of her own children say whether she will abstain from sacrificing, mercilessly, human freedom, happiness, and the education of immortal souls, for the sake of gains in money! We speak of Napoleon, for we must ever despise, with most profound contempt, the paltry use she made of her power on that occasion.—She had been the chief means of liberating Europe from his tyranny, and, though it was for her own sake, we must commend and admire her conduct and resolution thus far. But the unhandsome, base treatment of her captive has never been enough contemned. Any private gentleman, in chaining up the foe that had put himself in his power, would at least have given him lodging, food and clothes to his liking, and a civil turnkey—and a great nation could fail in this! Oh, it was shameful, if only for the vulgarity of feeling evinced! All this we say because we are sometimes impatient of England's brag on the subject of Slavery. Freedom! Because she has done one good act, is she entitled to the angelic privilege of being the Champion of Freedom!

And yet it is true that once, once she nobly awoke to a sense of what was right and wise. It is true that she also acted out that sense; acted fully, decidedly. She was willing to make sacrifices even of the loved money.

She has not let go the truth she then laid to heart, and continues the resolute foe of man's traffic in men. We must bend low to her as we borrow this holy day, the anniversary of the Emancipation of Slaves in the West Indies. We do not feel that the extent of her practice justifies the *extent* of her preaching, yet we must feel her to be, in this matter, an elder sister, entitled to cry Shame to us. And, if her feelings be those of a sister indeed, how must she mourn to see her next of kin pushing back as far as in her lies the advance of this good cause, binding those whom the old world had awakened from its sins enough to loose! But courage, sister. All is not yet lost. There is here a faithful band determined to expiate the crimes that have been committed in the name of Liberty. On this day they meet and vow themselves to the service, and, as they look in one another's glowing eyes, they read there assurance that the end is not yet, and that they, forced as they are

> "To keep in company with Pain
> And Fear and Falsehood, miserable train,"

may

> "Turn that necessity to glorious gain,"

may

> "Transmute them and subdue."

Indeed we do not see that they 'bate a jot of heart or hope, and it is because they feel that the power of the Great Spirit and its peculiar workings in the spirit of this age are with them. There is action and reaction all the time, and though the main current is obvious, there are many little eddies and counter-currents. Mrs. Norton writes a poem on the sufferings of the poor, and in it she, as episode, tunefully laments the sufferings of the Emperor of all the Russias for the death of a beloved daughter. And it *was* a deep grief, yet it did not soften his heart, or make it feel for man. The first signs of his recovered spirits are in new efforts to crush out the heart of Poland, and to make the Jews lay aside the hereditary marks of their national existence, to them a sacrifice far worse than death. But then—Count Apraxin is burnt alive by his infuriate serfs, and the life of a serf is far more dog-like or rather machine-like than that of *our* slaves. Still the serf can rise in vengeance, can admonish the Autocrat that humanity will yet turn again and rend him.

So with us. The most shameful deed has been done that ever disgraced a nation; because the most contrary to consciousness of right. Other nations have done wickedly, but we have surpassed them all in trampling under foot the principles that had been assumed as the basis of our national existence and our willingness to forfeit our honor in the face of the world.

The following stanzas, written by a friend some time since, on the Fourth of July, exhibit these contrasts so forcibly, that we cannot do better than insert them here:

> Loud peal of bells and beat of drums
>   Salute approaching dawn,
> And the deep cannons' fearful bursts
>   Announce a Nation's Morn.
>
> Imposing ranks of freemen stand
>   And claim their proud birthright,
> Impostors! rather, thus to brand
>   A name they hold so bright.
>
> Let the day see the pageant show!
>   Float, banners, to the breeze!
> Shout Liberty's great name throughout
>   Columbia's lands and seas!
>
> Give open sunlight to the Free!
>   But for Truth's equal sake,
> When Night sinks down upon the land,
>   Proclaim dead Freedom's Wake!
>
> Beat, muffled drums—toll, funeral bell!
>   Nail every flag half-mast!
> For, though we fought the battle well,
>   We're traitors at the last.
>
> Let the whole nation join in one
>   Procession to appear,
> We and our sons lead on the front,
>   Our slaves bring up the rear.
>
> America is rocked within
>   Thy cradle, Liberty,
> By Africa's poor palsied hand,
>   Strange inconsistency!

> We've dug one grave, as deep as Death,
>   For Tyranny's black sin,
> And dug another at its side
>   To thrust our brother in.
>
> We challenge all the world aloud,
>   "Lo! Tyranny's deep grave!"
> And all the world points back and cries—
>   "Thou fool!—behold thy Slave!"
>
> "Yes, rally, brave America,
>   Thy noble hearts and free,
> Around the Eagle, as he soars
>   Upward in majesty.
>
> "One half thy emblem is the bird,
>   Out-facing thus the day;
> But, wouldst thou make him wholly thine,
>   Give him *a helpless prey.*"

This should be sung in Charleston at 9 o'clock in the evening, when the drums are heard proclaiming "dead Freedom's Wake," as they summon to their homes, or to the custody of the police, every human being with a black skin who is found walking without a pass from the white. Or it might have been sung to advantage the night after Charleston had shown her independence and care of domestic institutions by expulsion of the venerable envoy of Massachusetts! Its expression would seem even more forcible than now, when sung so near the facts, when the eagle soars so close above his prey.

How deep the shadow, yet cleft by light! There is a counter-current that sets toward the deep. We are inclined to weigh as of almost equal weight with all we have had to trouble us as to the prolongation of slavery, the hopes that may be gathered from the course taken by such a man as Cassius Clay. A man open to none of the accusations brought to diminish the influence of Abolitionists in general, for he has eaten the bread wrought from slavery, and has shared the education that excuses the blindness of the slaveholder. He speaks as one having authority; no one can deny that he knows where he is. In the prime of manhood, of talent, and the energy of a fine enthusiasm, he comes forward with deed and word to do his devoir in this cause, never to leave the field till he can take with him the wronged wretches rescued by his devotion.

Now he has made this last sacrifice of the prejudices of "Southern chivalry," more than ever will be ready to join the herald's cry, "God speed the right." And we cannot but believe his noble example will be followed by many young men in the slave-holding ranks, brothers in a new sacred band vowed to the duty not merely of defending, but far more sacred, of purifying their homes.

The event of which this day is the anniversary, affords a sufficient guaranty of the safety and practicability of strong measures for this purification. Various accounts are given to the public of the state of the British West Indies, and the foes of emancipation are of course constantly on the alert to detect any unfavorable result which may aid them in opposing the good work elsewhere. But through all statements these facts shine clear as the Sun at noonday, that the measure was there carried into effect with an ease and success, and has shown in the African race a degree of goodness, docility, capacity for industry and self-culture, entirely beyond or opposed to the predictions which darkened so many minds with fears. Those fears can never again be entertained or uttered with the same excuse. One great example of the *safety of doing right* exists; true, there is but one of the sort, but volumes may be preached from such a text.

We, however, preach not; there are too many preachers already in the field, abler, more deeply devoted to the cause. Endless are the sermons of these modern crusaders, those ardent "sons of thunder," who have pledged themselves never to stop or falter till this one black spot be purged away from the land which gave them birth. They cry aloud and spare not; they spare not others, but then, neither do they spare themselves, and such are ever the harbingers of a new advent of the Holy Spirit. Our venerated friend, Dr. Channing, sainted in more memories than any man who has left us in this nineteenth century, uttered the last of his tones of soft, solemn, persuasive, convincing eloquence on this day and on this occasion. The hills of Lenox laughed and were glad as they heard him who showed in that last address, an address not only to the men of Lenox, but to all men, for he was in the highest sense the Friend of Man, the unsullied purity of infancy, the indignation of youth at vice and wrong, informed and tempered by the mild wisdom of age. It is a beautiful fact, that this should have been the last public occasion of his life.

Last year a noble address was delivered by R. W. Emerson, in which he broadly showed the *juste milieu* views upon this subject in the holy light of a high ideal day. The truest man grew more true as he listened, for the speech, though it had the force of fact and the lustre of thought, was chiefly remarkable as sharing the penetrating quality of the "still, small voice," most often heard when no man speaks. Now it spoke *through* a man, and no personalities, or prejudices, or passions, could be perceived to veil or disturb its silver sound.

These speeches are on record, little can be said that is not contained in them. But we can add evermore our aspirations for thee, O our Country, that thou mayest not long need to borrow a *holy* day, not long have all thy festivals blackened by falsehood, tyranny, and a crime for which neither man below nor God above can much longer pardon thee. For ignorance may excuse error, but thine, it is vain to deny it, is conscious wrong and vows thee to the Mammon whose wages are endless torment or final death.

✻

[August 1, 1845]

The White Slave; or, the Russian Peasant-Girl By the author of "Revelations of Russia," No. 60 of the Library of Select Novels, published by Harper & Brothers, Cliff-st. N.Y. 1845

This is a deeply interesting book. The objects of the author are best stated in his own words:

"The author of the White Slave, anxious to popularize some knowledge of the condition of the Russian serf among a people who sacrificed twenty millions sterling to the enfranchisement of its own colonial blacks, has been desirous of rendering his work amusing, as the readiest means towards effecting this object.

"The personages whom he has called into life in this story, have been introduced, not to aid the writer in effecting a conquest in the domain of fiction, but as the types of classes, and as the vehicles for conveying to the world an impression of a state of things which nothing will tend so much to alter eventually as the public indignation, however slow the remedy.

"He has only used the privilege of the novelist so far as the chronological arrangement of his matter was concerned, and in shifting the scene as well as the period of real events—such as the anachronism of the death of the great Russian poet, or the execution of the sectarian, or making a tavern near St. Petersburg the theatre of violence, which, in reality, took place in the neighborhood of Warsaw.

"At the same time he begs it to be distinctly understood that he has taken no farther liberty with the anecdotes relating to any of the personages named, and that every incident interwoven in his tale is founded on reality, every imaginary character compounded from real characters; that, whilst endeavoring to sketch, as vividly as his powers of description and his personal reminiscences would allow, a few of the most prominent classes of the Russian people, the author has never ventured to quit the regions of probability, unless when he was adhering to a literal though startling truth."

The character of the book is one of living reality. There is none of the productive power of genius—no re-presentation; it is the journal of a kind and generous man, with an eye for character, a keen sense for its higher manifestations, but without wonder at its lower, for he knows how to allow for influences and circumstances. We have seen either these or exactly similar passages given of the conduct of the Grand Duke Constantine in the foreign journals, minus the relentings, the gleams of human nature, through the outrages of the brute. We have never before seen these traced to their causes, nor understood why, if more cruelly mad than his father, he was not likewise arrested in his course. Yet we have always felt an instinctive preference of him to the Emperor Nicholas, who if not so glaringly violent, is more unrelenting in cruelty.—The two characters are well portrayed though with few marks, and the truth of portraiture none can doubt. Nicholas is, as a private man, the slave-master of twenty millions of men, as a public of sixty; never for a moment untrue to the character his position demands. Constantine was a mad bull, that trampled to death many victims, yet was capable sometimes of being turned aside by a gentle hand. Beautiful is the account of his duchess, beautiful even her love for a monster; it was that of a protecting angel for "one whom in the wide world there was none else to love, perhaps to save." This loveliness, this Heaven-inspired motherly love, is seen in the conduct of women every where, but here it shines from the hight [*sic*] with the diamond lustre of a star. The Peasant Girl is also full of a noble, simple inspiration, and seems, no less than the duchess, painted from the life.

The barbarians are exactly the same as occur in our own country under different circumstances.—This book combines foreign with domestic interest.

✽

[September 10, 1845]

What Fits a Man to Be a Voter?
Is It to Be White within, or White Without?

The country had been denuded of its forests, and men cried—"Come! we must plant anew, or there will be no shade for the homes of our children, or fuel for their hearths. Let us find the best kernels for a new growth."

And a basket of butternuts was offered.

But the planters rejected it with disgust. "What a black, rough coat it has," said they; "it is entirely unfit for the dishes on a nobleman's table, nor have we ever seen it in such places. It must have a greasy, offensive kernel; nor can fine trees grow up from such a nut."

"Friends," said one of the planters, "this decision may be rash. The chestnut has not a handsome outside; it is long encased in troublesome burrs, and, when disengaged, is almost as black as these nuts you despise. Yet from it grow trees of lofty stature, graceful form and long life. Its kernel is white and has furnished food to the most poetic and splendid nations of the older world."

"Do n't tell me," says another, "brown is entirely different from black. I like brown very well; there is Oriental precedent for its respectability. Perhaps we will use some of your chestnuts, if we can get fine samples. But for the present I think we should use only English walnuts, such as our forefathers delighted to honor. Here are many basketsfull of them, quite enough for the present. We will plant them with a sprinkling between of the chestnut and acorn." "But," rejoined the other, "many butternuts are beneath the sod, and you cannot help a mixture of them being in your wood at any rate."

"Well! we will grub them up and cut them down wherever we find them. We can use the young shrubs for kindlings."

At that moment entered the council two persons of a darker complexion than most of those present, as if born beneath the glow of a more scorching sun. First came a Woman, beautiful in the mild, pure grandeur of her look; in whose large dark eye a prophetic intelligence was mingled with infinite sweetness. She looked at the assembly with an air of surprise, as if its aspect was strange to her. She threw quite back her veil, and stepping aside made room for her companion. His form was youthful, about the age of one we have seen in many a picture, produced by the thought of eighteen centuries, as of one "instructing the Doctors." I need not describe the features; all minds have their own impressions of such an image,

"Severe in youthful beauty."

In his hand he bore a little white banner on which was embroidered PEACE AND GOOD WILL TO MEN. And the words seemed to glitter and give out sparks, as he paused in the assembly.

"I came hither," said he, "an uninvited guest, because I read sculptured above the door—'All men born Free and Equal,' and in this dwelling hoped to find myself a home. What is the matter in dispute?"

Then they whispered one to another, and murmurs were heard—"He is a mere boy; young people are always foolish and extravagant;" or "He looks like a fanatic." But others said, "He looks like one whom we have been taught to honor. It will be best to tell him the matter in dispute."

When he heard it, he smiled and said, "It will be needful first to ascertain which of the nuts is soundest *within.*" And with a hammer he broke one, two, and more of the English walnuts, and they were mouldy.

Then he tried the other nuts, but found most of them fresh within and *white,* for they were fresh from the bosom of the earth, while the others had been kept in a damp cellar.

And he said, "You had better plant them together, lest none or few of the walnuts be sound. And why are you so reluctant? Has not Heaven permitted them both to grow on the same soil? and does not that show what is intended about it?"

And they said, "But they are black and ugly to look upon." He replied, "They do not seem so to me. What my Father has fashioned in such guise offends not mine eye."

And they said, "But from one of these trees flew a bird of prey who has done great wrong. We meant, therefore, to suffer no such tree among us."

And he replied, "Amid the band of my countrymen and friends there was one guilty of the blackest crime, that of selling for a price the life of his dearest friend, yet all the others of his blood were not put under ban because of his guilt."

Then they said, "But in the Holy Book our teachers tell us, we are bid to keep in exile or distress whatsoever is black and unseemly in our eyes."

Then he put his hand to his brow and cried in a voice of the most penetrating pathos, "Have I been so long among ye and ye have not known me?"—And the Woman turned from them, the majestic hope of her glance, and both forms suddenly vanished, but the banner was left trailing in the dust.

The men stood gazing at one another. After which one mounted on high and said:

"Perhaps, my friends, we carry too far this aversion to objects merely because they are black. I heard, the other day, a wise man say that black was the color of evil—marked as such by God, and that whenever a white man struck a black man he did an act of worship to God.[*] I could not quite believe him. I hope, in what I am about to add, I shall not be misunderstood. I am no Abolitionist. I respect above all things, divine or human, the Constitution framed by our forefathers, and the peculiar institutions hallowed by the usage of their sons. I have no sympathy with the black race in this country. I wish it to be understood that I feel toward negroes the purest personal antipathy. It is a family trait with us. My little son, scarce able to speak, will cry out 'Nigger! Nigger!' whenever he sees one, and try to throw things at them. He made a whole omnibus load laugh the other day by his cunning way of doing this.[†] The child of my political antagonist, on the other hand, says 'he likes *tullared* children the best.'[‡] You see he is tainted in his cradle by the loose principles of his parents, even before he can say nigger or pronounce the more refined appellation. But that is no matter. I merely mention this by the way: not to prejudice you against Mr.———-, but that you may appreciate the very different state of things in my family, and not misinterpret what I have to say. I was lately in one of our prisons where a somewhat injudicious indulgence had extended to one of the condemned felons, a lost and wretched outcast from society, the use of materials for painting, that having been his profession. He had completed at his leisure, a picture of the Lord's Supper. Most of the figures were well enough, but Judas he had represented as a black.[§]—Now, gentlemen, I am of opinion that this is an unwarrantable liberty taken with the Holy Scriptures and shows *too much* prejudice in the community. It is my wish to be moderate and fair, and preserve a medium, neither, on the one hand, yielding the wholesome antipathies planted in our breasts as a safeguard against degradation, and our consti-

---

[*] Fact, that this is affirmed.
[†] Fact.
[‡] Fact.
[§] Fact.

tutional obligations, which, as I have before observed, are, with me, more binding than any other; nor on the other hand forgetting that liberality and wisdom which are the prerogative of every citizen of this free Commonwealth. I agree then with our young visitor. I hardly know, indeed, why a stranger and one so young was permitted to mingle in this council, but it was certainly thoughtful in him to crack and examine the nuts. I agree that it may be well to plant some of the black nuts among the others, so that, if many of the walnuts fail, we may make use of this inferior tree."

At this moment arose a hubbub, and such a clamor of "dangerous innovation," "political capital," "low-minded demagogue," "infidel who denies the Bible," "lower link in the chain of creation," &c. that it is impossible to say what was the decision.

✳

[March 31, 1846]

Lyceum of New-Bedford, Mass.

Our readers may have noticed the act of exclusion by which the citizens of New-Bedford have shown the illiberal prejudice against people of color with an unblushing openness unusual even where it exists in its most unchristian form. The black population were denied, even in the case of the most respectable persons, the privilege of membership, and only allowed to hear lectures if they would confine themselves to a particular part of the house.—A minority protested in the strongest terms, but the majority persisted in the act of proscription. We rejoice to hear that, in consequence of these measures, R. W. Emerson and Charles Sumner, who were engaged as lecturers, have declined addressing an audience whose test of merit, or right to the privileges of a citizen consists not in intelligence or good character, but the color of the skin.

✻

[December 13, 1845]

"Darkness Visible" {1}

A Defence of Capital Punishment; by Rev. George B. Cheever, D.D.; and an Essay on the Ground and Reason of Punishment, with Special Reference to the Penalty of Death; by Tayler Lewis, Esq. et cetera

We have had this book before us for several weeks, but the task of reading it has been so repulsive that we have been obliged to get through it by short stages with long intervals of rest and refreshment between, and have only just reached the end. We believe, however, we are now possessed of its substance, so far as it is possible to admit into any mind matter wholly uncongenial with its structure, its faith and its hope.

Meanwhile others have shown themselves more energetic in the task, and notices have appeared that express, in part, our own views. Among others an able critic has thus summed up his impressions:

"Of the whole we will say briefly, that its premises are monstrous, its reasoning sophistical, its conclusions absurd, and its spirit diabolic."

We know not that we can find a better scheme of arrangement for what we have to say than by dividing it into sections under these four heads:

1st. The premises are monstrous. Here we must add the qualification, they are monstrous *to us*. The God of these writers is not the God we recognize; the views they have of human nature are antipodal to ours. We believe in a Creative Spirit, the essence of whose being is Love. He has created men in the spirit of love, intending to develop them to perfect harmony with himself. He has permitted the temporary existence of evil as a condition necessary to bring out in them free agency and individuality of character. Punishment is the necessary result of a bad choice in them; it is not meant by him as vengeance, but as an admonition to choose better. Man is not born totally evil; he is born capable both of good and evil, and the Holy Spirit in working on him only quickens the soul already there to know its Father. To one who takes such views the address of Jesus becomes intelligible:

"Be ye therefore merciful, as your Father also is merciful." "For with the same measure that ye mete withal, it shall be measured to you again."

Those who take these views of the relation between God and man must naturally tend to have punishment consist as much as possible in the inward spiritual results of faults, rather than a violent outward enforcement of penalty. They must, so far as possible, seek to revere God by showing themselves brotherly to man; and if they wish to obey Christ, will not forget that he came especially to call *sinners* to repentance.

The views of Messrs. Lewis and Cheever are the opposite of all this. We need not state them; they are sufficiently indicated in each page of their own. Their conclusions are the natural result of such premises. We could say nothing about either except to express dissent from beginning to end. Yet would it be sweet and noble, and worthy of this late period of human progress, if this might be done in a spirit of religious, of manly courtesy; if they had the soul to say—"We differ from you, but we know that so wide and full a stream of thought and emotion as you are engaged in could not, under the providential rule in which we believe, have arisen in vain. The object of every such manifestation of life must be to bring out truth; come, let us seek it together. Let us show you our view, compare it with yours, and let us see which is the better. If, as we think, the truth lie with us, what joy will it be for us to cast the clear light on the object of your aspirations!"

Of this degree of liberality we have known some, even, who served the same creed as these writers to be capable. There is, indeed, a higher form which, believing all forms of opinion which we hold in the present stage of our growth can be but approximations to truth, and that God has permitted to the multitude of men a multitude of ways by which they may approach our common goal, looks with reverence on all modes of faith sincerely held and acted upon, and while it rejoices in those who have reached the higher stages of spiritual growth, has no despair as to those who still grope in a narrow path and by a glimmering light. Such liberality is, of course, out of the question with such writers as the present. Their creed binds them to believe that they have absolute truth, and that all who do not believe as they do are wretched heretics. Those whose creed is of narrower scope are to them hateful bigots, but also those with whom it is of wider are latitudinarians or infidels. The spot of earth on which they stand is the only one safe from the conflagration, and only through spectacles and spy-glasses such as are used by them can the sun and stars be seen. Yet, as we said before, some such, though incapacitated for an intellectual, are not so for a spiritual tolerance. With them the heart, more Christ-like than the creed, urges to a spirit of love and reverence even toward convictions opposed to their own. The sincere man is always respectable in their eyes, and they cannot help feeling that wherever there is a desire for truth, there is the spirit of God, and His true priests will approach with gentleness and do their ministry with holy care. Unhappily, it is very different with the persons before us.

We let go the first two counts of the indictment. Their premises are, as we have said, such as we totally dissent from, and their conclusions such as naturally flow from those premises. Yet they are those of a large body of men, and there must, no doubt, be temporary good in this state of things or it would not be permitted. When these writers say that to them moral and penal are coincident terms, they display a state of mind which prefers basing virtue on the fear of punishment rather than the love of right. If this be sincerely their state, if the idea of morality is with them entirely dependent on the retributions upon vice rather than the loveliness and joys of goodness, it is impossible for those who are in a different state of mind to say what they *do* need. It may seem to us, indeed, that, if the strait jacket was taken off, they might recover the natural energy of their frames, and do far better without it; or that, if no longer hurried along the road by the impending lash behind, they might uplift their eyes and find sufficient cause for speed in the glory visible before, though at a distance; however, it is not for us to say what their wants are. Let them choose their own principles of action, and if they lead to purity of life and benevolence and humanity of heart, we will not say a word against them.

But in the instance before us they do not produce these good fruits but the contrary, and therefore we have something to say on the other part of the criticism, to wit: that "the reasoning is sophistical and the spirit diabolic;" for indeed, in the sense of pride by which the angels fell, arrogance of judgment, malice and all uncharitableness, we have never looked on printed pages more deeply sinful.

We wish, however, to make all due allowance for incapacity in these writers to do better, and their disqualifications for their task, apart from a form of belief which inclines them rather to cling to the past, than to seek progress for the future, seem to be many.

From Mr. Lewis's hand we have read but little before these pages, but sufficient to show the quality of his mind. It seems to be what is vulgarly considered the mind of a lawyer, though, in fact, a great lawyer can no more have such an one than a great statesman; but a good advocate may, and the habit of pleading all of one side and seeking to carry a special object, rather than to elicit truth, is likely to give such a cast. It is a mind active, acute upon details, capable of scholarship, but incapable of broad views, or thorough reasoning, and in the last degree unspiritual,—that is to say, blind to the working of principles either in the main stream of life or in the mind of the individual. He has a sense only for rules and precedents and their application to special cases.

Mr. or Dr. Cheever has a mind of better quality and more real life, but that life all tainted by the heat and bitterness of his spirit. He had by nature some congeniality with the noble poetic spirit, but it is soured and checked by the excess of petty and local feelings. It is mournful to see him amid the sublime beauties of Switzerland, fretting himself into a polemical fever against the Roman Catholic Church, or full of anxiety lest he shall forget God, if he cannot put all the emotions such sights inspire into the form of a sermon. It is pitiful to see him in his preface to a work (Vestiges of Creation) which attempts to give a philosophical view of the facts of science, so wholly benighted by his fears as to the spirit and scope of what he treats of, and though, we believe, with a good intention, using the most unfair as well as ridiculous means to provide an antidote against a fancied bane.

The history of this preface is so amusing a specimen of the steps to which the arrogant notions held by some shepherds as to their duties in the care of men's souls may lead, that we must give it here, only premising that we give it, not as one having authority from the publishers or the prefatorial D.D. himself, but as the received version of the affair. If it be not true let it be corrected; if it be, let it figure in the annals of an age when, if Truth be still alive and bold, it is not the fault of Cant.

The book of the Vestiges was no sooner published in Great Britain than those reverend men and women who, with all their professions of honor to God, evince an amazing skepticism as to his power of upholding truth against the invasions of error, stood up, each in his or her place, to hurl their anathema against the dangerous man who tried to show that God works by law. 'If he can only make out his case, cried they, he will get the helm of the Universe so completely in his hand, that he may perhaps steer it quite away from God. He professes indeed, a reverence for God, and that he seeks to prove it by attempting to show the harmony which regulates the world. But that is very unlikely; it is too different from our way of going on. We have been contented to know that God made the world, without caring to know the *how*. Such inquiries are dangerous—who knows whither they may lead? Is it not a horrible thought that men might even be *developed* to the life of angels, instead of being transported into it in an instant by the hand of Death?—Who can tell where this development is to stop? it might even substitute the study of laws and causes for regular attendance on Church service, perhaps! We'll none of it!'

Thus cried they, but each from his or her place. The Author of the Vestiges stood in his place and they in theirs and said their say. They made their critiques and he has answered them according to his judgment and ability in the "Explanations."

Of course a work which had caused so much mental excitement passed over to this country and was published here. It was published, as a matter of business, because it was written and because people wanted to read it. No sooner was it out than our self-elected censors of the press, who, in their vigilance and jealous care, vie with any officials of foreign governments, declare that the book is most shocking, "blasphemous, atheistical," and, if suffered to go abroad will ruin our nation, root and branch, with its insidious canker.

"But what is to be done?" replies the publisher. "The book is in the world, and people choose to read it. Some one would publish it, if I gave up."

The answer was found in a commission to Rev. Dr. Cheever to prepare a short prelude, which, being every where played before the piece itself, should put the ear into such a state as to repel all dangerous intoxication. A device borrowed from the wise man of old, who stopped the ears of his mariners with wax when they were exposed to the perilous song of the Syrens. This preface is, in itself, at once one of the weakest and most unfair productions on which we ever glanced. Like the productions before us (on Capital Punishment) it depends for its stress on appeals to passion and prejudice as to themes, where, if ever, they should be silent. Like these, it shows a want of that power without which no argument can ever be either honorable or cogent—the power of comprehending the other side. The assault is principally made by talking of the author groping amid dead matter and similar remarks. The chief reliance as to prejudicing the reader against the work he is about to read is upon addresses to the author as *thou fool,* or a use of the term "dead" which shows either an utter ignorance and misconception of the work or a willing perversion of truth.

But what we would wish to lay emphasis upon as illustrative of the state of this person's mind, is the indelicacy, impertinence and arrogance of the position he assumes. Suppose a self-constituted master of ceremonies thus to introduce to a circle an *invited* guest, "Mr.——is here; you have invited him and I cannot help his entering the room. But I wish first to give you the correct view of him, which you must be careful not to lay aside for any other. *I know* that he is a wicked, unprincipled man, in fact an Atheist. If he says any thing that seems to imply the contrary, you are to infer that he adds the vice of hypocrisy to all his others. If you find that, in spite of what I say, his conversation and manners make a favorable impression on you, then, indeed, is your danger dreadful and imminent. Do not trust yourself to examine farther, but think of my words, turn in all haste and flee from the wrath to come."

Such is the position assumed by the Rev. Mr. Cheever in regard to this work; a position not unworthy the worst days of the class he most detests, the framers of golden bulls and expurgatory indexes. So inconsistent is man, and so sadly needful is it that he should, day by day, recall the precept, "Judge not that ye be not judged."

We know of no parallel yet to offer to the future D'Israeli of our literary history except the preface by another such self-elected guardian to Sir Humphrey Davy's Consolations in Travel, who charges the reader to attach no importance to the heretical views advanced in the book, as there is every reason to believe that the author recanted them and died a Christian.

The Public, we suppose, have in the present case rejected the guardianship of Mr. Cheever, as the preface is dropt from the third edition, and we found it almost impossible now to procure a copy for the refreshment of our memory.

This position is more legitimately occupied in the book on Capital Punishment, but in the same spirit. We love an honest lover, but next best we, with Dr. Johnson, know how to respect an honest hater. But even he would scarce endure so bitter and ardent a hater as Mr. Cheever, and with so many and inconsistent objects of hatred—one who hates Catholics and thorough Protestants, hates materialists and hates spiritualists. His list is really too large for *human* sympathy.

Messrs. Lewis and Cheever profess to occupy the position of defence; surely never was one sustained so in the spirit of offence.

The "reasoning is sophistical," and it would need the patience of a Socrates to ravel the weary web and convince these sophists against their will that they are exactly in the opposite region to what they suppose. For the task we have not space, skill or patience, but we can give some hints by which readers may be led to examine whether it is so or not.

1st. Mr. Lewis appeals either to the natural or regenerate man as suits his purpose. Sometimes all traditions and their literal interpretations are right; sometimes it is impossible to interpret them aright unless according to some peculiar doctrine, and the natural inference of the common mind would be an error.

2d. He strains, but vainly, to show the New Testament no improvement on the Old, and himself in harmonious relations to both. On this subject we would confidently leave the arbitration to a mind, could such an one be found, sufficiently disciplined to examine the subject, and new both to the New Testament and his essay, as that of Rammohun Roy might have been, whether his views are not of the same strain that Jesus sought to correct and enlighten among the Jews, and whether he does not treat the teachings of the new dispensation most unfairly in his desire to wrest them into the service of the old.

3d. Wherever there is a weak place in the argument, it is filled up by abuse of the opposite party. The words 'absurd,' 'infidel,' 'blasphemous,' 'shallow philosophy,' 'sickly sentimentalism,' and the like, are among the favorite missiles of these *defenders* of the truth. They are of a sort whose frequent use is generally supposed to argue a want of a shield of reason and a heart of faith.

And this brings us to a more close consideration of the *spirit* of this book, characterized by our contemporary as 'diabolic.' And we, also, cannot excuse ourselves from marking it as, in this respect, one of the worst books we have ever seen.

It is not merely bitter intolerance, arrogance and want of spiritual perception which we have to condemn in these writers. It is a want of fairness and honor, of which we think they must be conscious. We fear they are of those who hold the opinion that the end sanctifies the means, and who, by pretending to serve the God of Truth by other means than strict truth, have drawn upon the 'professors of religion' the frequent obloquy of 'priestcraft.' How else are we to construe that artful use of the words 'dishonest' and 'infidel' wherever they are likely to awaken the fears and prejudices of the ignorant? How the studied introduction and coupling together of the names of Paine and Parker, and the relation in which they stand? *Does* the writer here sincerely express any conviction of his mind? If he does *not,* while daring to accuse others of dishonesty, the words moral and penal should, indeed, be associated for him!

Of as bad a stamp as any is the part of the book headed "Spurious Public Opinion." Here, as in the insinuations against Charles Burleigh, we are unable to believe the writers to be sincere. Where we think they are, however poor and narrow we may esteem their statement, we can respect it, but here we cannot.

Who can believe that such passages as the following stand for any thing real in the mind of the writer?

"Indeed there is nothing that can possibly check the spirit of murder, but the fear of death! That was all that Cain feared; he did not say, people will put me in prison, but, they will put me to death; *and how many other murders he may have committed when released from that fear, the sacred writer does not tell us!!"*

Why does not the writer draw the inference and accuse God of mistake, as he says His opponents accuse Him, whenever they attempt to get beyond the Jewish ideas of vengeance. He plainly thinks death was the only safe penalty in this case of Cain!

"The reasoning from these drivelings of depravity in malefactors is to the last degree wretched and absurd.—Hard pushed indeed must he be in argument, who can consent to dive down into the polluted heart of a Newgate criminal, in order to fish up, from the confessions of his monstrous, unnatural obduracy, an argument in that very obduracy against the fit punishment of his own crimes."

We can only wish for such a man that the vicissitudes of life may break through the crust of theological arrogance and Phariseeism and force him to "dive down" into the depths of his own nature.—We should see afterward whether he would be so forward to throw stones at malefactors, so eager to hurry souls to what he regards as a final account.

But we have said enough as to the spirit and tendency of this book. We shall only add a few words as to the unworthy use of the word "infidel" in the attempt to fix a stigma upon opponents. We feel still more contempt than indignation at the desire to work in this way on the unthinking and ignorant.

We ourselves are of the number stigmatized by these persons as sharing an infidel tendency, as are all not enlisted under their own sectarian banner. They, on their side, seem to us unbelievers in all that is most pure and holy, and in the saving grace of love. They do not believe in God, as we believe; they seem to us utterly deficient in the spirit of Christ, and to be of the number of those who are always calling 'Lord, Lord,' yet never have known him. We find throughout these pages the temper of "Lord, I thank thee that I am not as other men are," hatred of those whom they deem Gentiles, and a merciless spirit toward the sinner, yet we do not take upon ourselves to give them the name of Infidels, and we solemnly call them to trial before the bar of the Only Wise and Pure, the Searcher of hearts, to render an account of this daring assumption. We ask them in that presence if they are not of the class threatened with "retribution" for saying to their brother "Thou fool," and that not merely in the heat of anger, but coolly, pertinaciously and in a thousand ways.

We call to sit in council the spirits of our Puritan fathers, and ask if such was the right of individual judgment, of private conscience, they came here to vindicate. And we solicit the verdict of posterity as to whether the spirit of mercy or of vengeance be the more divine, and whether the denunciatory and personal mode chosen by these writers for carrying on this inquiry be the true one.

We wish most sincerely the book had been a wise and noble book. To ascertain just principles, it is necessary that the discussion should be full and fair and both sides ably argued. After this has been done, the sense of the world can decide. It would be a happiness for which it might seem that man at this time of day is ripe, that the opposing parties should meet in open lists as brothers, believing each that the other desired only that the truth should triumph, and able to clasp hands as men of different structure and ways of thinking, but fellow students of the Divine will. O had we but found such an adversary, above the use of artful abuse, or the feints of sophistry, able to believe in the noble intention of a foe as of a friend, how cheerily would the trumpets ring out while the assembled world echoed the signal words, "GOD SPEED THE RIGHT!" The tide of Progress rolls onward, swelling more and more with the lives of those who would fain see all men called to repentance. It must be a strong arm, indeed, that can build a dam to stay it even for a moment. None such do we see yet, but we should rejoice in a noble and strong opponent, putting forth all his power for conscience' sake.—God speed the Right!

*

[March 4, 1846]

"Darkness Visible" {2}

We see with pleasure that an article under this head in last Wednesday's Tribune is to become the means of instruction to the public, through the columns of the Courier & Enquirer, as to the precise meaning attached by the writers who were the subject of that article to their favorite stigma of 'infidelity,' The public will, in future, know exactly what they mean by the use of the term, and if excited to horror and aversion toward those to whom it is applied, it will not be in ignorance or mistake. A series of articles is to be published which may easily be read, as in length they will generally 'not exceed a column.' There is promise of clear and straightforward statements, such as may be met in a 'chivalrous' spirit; this is all that can be desired.

Suitable opponents are challenged, and, indeed, are no longer to be permitted "to skulk behind a female, who, however personal and abusive she might be, could not, especially on such questions as these, be treated as a proper and legitimate adversary."

We were not aware that the Bible, or the welfare of human beings were subjects improper for the consideration of 'females,' whether *'fair'* or otherwise. We had also supposed that, in the field of literature, the meeting was not between man and woman, but between mind and mind. Personal allusions to private life should, indeed, be excluded from this field, whether man meets man, or man meets woman. On occasions where the theme is purely intellectual we had supposed that, in all civilized communities, the question was, Is the mode of treating the subject noble, the statement commanding, the thought just? or the reverse? and that, in either case, it mattered not whether the mind from which such statement originated was placed here on earth, as man or as woman. Even among the Hebrews—the only sufficient authority, we believe, with T.L.—we find numerous instances in which all such considerations were set made as not to the purpose on such an occasion. Though, however, we are now informed that there are minds so penetrated with the spirit of chivalry that they cannot regard a woman as an adversary, we should not advise the band of "heroic philanthropists" censured in the Courier & Enquirer for seeking to protect themselves behind the veil and parasol of this mistaken Clorinda, to regard them as secure panoply, the impossibility of assailing a female writer being expressed in the following passage:

"Of course, no reply will be made to that very modest lady who so foolishly, and with so much vanity, suffered herself to be thrust forward in an argument for which she herself admits, 'she has neither skill nor patience.' Indeed, although this most amiable representative of the school of 'love and philanthropy' and of the 'spiritual insight' seems quite at home in such very common language as 'monstrous,' 'detestable,' 'horrible,' 'demoniac,' 'diabolical,' &c. yet she should know that the proper discussion of the question so rashly ventured upon, requires something more than this; and that it is indeed quite a different matter from doing up the slop literature of The Tribune, or writing unmeaning rhapsodies on the unutterable ideas of Ole Bull, or repeating the cant and drivel of the Harbinger about Dante and Beethoven, or praising the chaste 'creations' of that most chaste and 'spiritual' creature, George Sand."

Here we find our old acquaintance, the word "drivel" in a no less impressive connection than when the "drivelings of depravity in malefactors" were denounced.

We await with interest the future developments of T.L. as to the nature and precise limits of infidelity. The tax of reading will no longer be too much for our "patience" as the articles are not to exceed a column in length, and, if feminine incapacity prevent some readers from doing justice to the thoughts, we trust they will still be able to appreciate the dignity and temper with which they may be expressed, and to transfer a portion of the value received into "slop literature" addressed to the use of the common reader.

*

[March 10, 1846]

7
The Irish

Despite her avowal of abolitionism, woman's rights, and prison reform, Margaret Fuller had one liberal blind spot. In common with many others in nineteenth-century America, she looked down upon the Irish. The following three columns have astonished twentieth-century readers, especially given Fuller's general views on equality, slavery, and poverty. Using stereotypes, Fuller described the Irish as foolishly romantic, musically gifted, extremely ignorant, blindly devoted to the church, pliant in the hands of demagogues, lazy, and ungrateful. She then condescendingly suggested ways to reform them. In "The Irish Character," she argued, "steadfast patience and love" could teach Irish servants not to lie, but she advised readers never to expect gratitude. Instead, people should aid the Irish "for God's sake and as a debt to humanity."

Margaret Fuller wrote these three columns in the summer of 1845, at an important moment of transition for the Irish. As these columns went to press, the great tragedy of Irish history, the Potato Famine, had just begun in the homeland. For six years, from 1845 to 1851, a fungus destroyed the potato crop, the major source of food in the Irish diet. In the early 1880s Ireland had a population of 8 million, but fifty years after the famine, the population of Ireland was only 3 million. Between 1845 and 1855 1.8 million Irish emigrated to the United States.[1]

Since the Potato Famine was barely underway when these columns appeared, Fuller here addressed the anti-Irish sentiment that already existed in the United States. While the huge emigration of Irish to the United States resulted from the Potato Famine, an earlier wave had already brought many Irish to the country. In all but two years between 1820 and 1854, more Irish emigrated to the United States than any other ethnic group. Emigrants in the early 1840s were "comparatively poor Catholic subtenants, farmers' sons, and laborers from the three southern provinces," said historian Kerby Miller.[2]

The dominant American culture saw these immigrants through a negative stereotype. The Irish were derisively called "Paddy" and "Bridget." In a content analysis of American publications between 1820 and 1844, researcher Dale Knobel found the stereotype did not focus "on Irish religious affinities or political loyalties or economic condition but on interpersonal style, fundamental morality and intelligence." American language in the period ascribed to Paddy and Bridget impudence, ingratitude, ignorance, foolishness, wickedness, and contrivance, said Knobel.[3]

By the 1840s this anti-Irish stereotype had coalesced in the birth of the nativist Know-Nothing Party. The Know-Nothings wanted only native-born Americans to hold public office and argued that a person should live in the United States for twenty-five years before receiving citizenship. *Awful Disclosures*, a book by Maria Monk, heightened anti-Catholic attitudes. This supposedly "eyewitness" account described licentiousness in convents. The book alleged that nuns and priests had sex, baptized the resulting children, and then murdered them. *Awful Disclosures* sold three hundred thousand copies and became the *Uncle Tom's Cabin* of the Know-Nothing movement. Despite the anti-Catholic arguments made by the Protestant Know-Nothings, religion was not the root of prejudice against the Irish. Historian William Shannon argued the Irish "threatened the patterns of job and trade competition, the old values, the homogeneity of the once-small cities."[4]

Anti-Irish sentiment was more than a political party platform. The first violence came in 1831 with the burning of a convent in Charlestown, Massachusetts, near Boston. In Philadelphia, nativists and Irish fought in the streets. On May 6, 1844, nativists invaded the Irish neighborhood of Kensington, burning down blocks of houses and two Catholic churches. On July 5, 1844, when a mob threatened to storm St. Philip de Neri Church in Southwark, another Irish section of Philadelphia, the governor called out the militia and used cannon to battle Protestant rioters and protect the church. This rioting caused a backlash among middle- and upper-middle-class Americans, who turned against the nativists, said Shannon.[5]

Although Margaret Fuller's three columns discuss the Irish in stereotypical terms, in the context of their times the columns read as an anti-nativist plea for tolerance. Fuller's contemporary, James Parton, saw the columns as a "defense of the Irish Character" and called them "very touching and just."[6] When a "J O'C." attacked Fuller for the prejudice in her first two Irish columns, she wrote a third piece defending herself, but this piece reads like a rationalization when contrasted with the strong defense she made of her capital punishment piece. Fuller claimed she was writing about all servants and not just the Irish.

The Irish columns illustrated the virulence of the prejudice against the Irish in nineteenth-century America. In the face of powerful anti-Irish sentiment, the mild tone of these columns became a defense of the Irish. Interestingly, Fuller did not discuss African Americans in the same stereotypical terms she used for the Irish. Andrew Greeley has pointed out that antebellum abolitionists often made unfavorable comparisons between the Irish and African Americans. While they saw African Americans as ennobled by the martyrdom of slavery, they saw the Irish as a lesser race.[7]

The Irish Character {1}

In one of the eloquent passages quoted in The Tribune of Wednesday under the head 'Spirit of the Irish Press,' we find these words:

"Domestic love, almost morbid from external suffering, prevents him [the Irishman] from becoming a fanatic and a misanthrope, and reconciles him to life."

This recalled to our mind the many touching instances known to us of such traits among the Irish we have seen here. We have seen instances of morbidness like this. A girl sent "home," after she was well established herself, for a young brother of whom she was particularly fond. He came, and, shortly after, died. She was so overcome by his loss, that she took poison and died. The great poet of serious England says, and we believe it to be his serious thought though laughingly said, "Men have died and worms have eaten them, but not for love." Whether or no[t] death may follow from the loss of a lover or a child, we believe that among no people but the Irish would it upon loss of a young brother.

Another poor young woman, in the flower of her youth, denied herself, not only every pleasure, but almost the necessaries of life, to save the sum she thought ought to be hers before sending to Ireland for a widowed mother. Just as she was on the point of doing so, she heard that her mother had died fifteen months before. The keenness and persistence of her grief defy description. With a delicacy of feeling which shewed the native poetry of the Irish mind she dwelt, most of all, upon the thought that while she was working and pinching and dreaming of happiness with her mother, it was, indeed, but a dream, and that cherished parent lay still and cold in the ground. She felt fully the cruel cheat of fate. "Och, and she was dead all those times I was a thinking on her!" was the deepest note of her lament.

They are able, however, to make the sacrifice even of these intense family affections in a worthy cause. We knew a woman who postponed sending for her only child, whom she had left in Ireland, for years, while she maintained a sick friend who had none else to help her.

The poetry of which I have spoken shows itself even here, where they are separated from old romantic associations, and begin the new life in the new world by doing all its drudgery. We know flights of poetry repeated to us by those present at their wakes—passages of natural eloquence from the lamentations for the dead, more beautiful than those recorded in the annals of Brit[t]any or Roumelia.

It is the same genius, so exquisitely mournful, tender, and glowing too with the finest enthusiasm, that makes their national music, in these respects, the finest in the world. It is the music of the harp; its tones are deep and thrilling. It is the harp so beautifully described in "The harp of Tara's halls," a song whose simple pathos is unsurpassed. A feeling was never more adequately embodied.

It is the genius which will enable Emmett's appeal to draw tears from the remotest generations, however much they may be strangers to the circumstances which called it forth. It is the genius which beamed in chivalrous loveliness through each act of Lord Edward Fitzgerald,—the genius which, ripened by English culture, favored by suitable occasions, has shed such glory on the land which has done all it could to quench it on the parent hearth.

When we consider all the fire which glows so untameably in Irish veins, the character of her people, considering the circumstances—almost miraculous in its goodness—we cannot forbear, notwithstanding all the temporary ills they aid in here, to give them all a welcome to our shores. Those ills we need not enumerate; they are known to all, and we rank among them what others would not, that by their ready service to do all the hard work they make it easier for the rest of the population to grow effeminate and help the country to grow too fast. But that is her destiny, to grow too fast; it is useless talking against it. Their extreme ignorance, their blind devotion to a priesthood, their pliancy in the hands of demagogues threaten continuance of these ills; yet, on the other hand, we must regard them as a most valuable element in the new race. They are looked upon with contempt for their want of aptitude at learning new things, their ready and ingenious lying, their shady eye service. These are the faults of an oppressed race which must require the aid of better circumstances through two or three generations to eradicate. Their virtues are their own;—they are many, genuine, and deeply rooted. Can an impartial observer fail to admire their truth to domestic ties, their power of generous bounty and more generous gratitude, their indefatigable good humor, (for ages of wrong, which have driven them to so many acts of desperation, could never sour their blood at its source) their ready wit, their elasticity of nature. They are at bottom one of the best nations of the world.—Would they were welcomed here, not to work merely, but to intelligent sympathy and efforts, both patient and ardent for the education of their children. No sympathy could be better deserved, no efforts wiselier timed. Future Burkes and Currans would know how to give thanks for them, and Fitzgeralds rise upon the soil, which boasts the magnolia with its kingly stature and majestical white blossoms, to the same lofty and pure beauty. Will you not believe it, merely because that bog-bred youth you solaced in the mud-hole tells you lies and drinks to cheer him in those endless diggings? You are short-sighted, my friend; you do not look to the future, you will not turn your head to see what may have been the influences of the past; you have not examined your own breast to see whether the monitor there had not commanded you to do your part to counteract these influences, and yet the Irishman appeals to you eye to eye. He is very personal himself; he expects a personal interest from you. Nothing has been able to destroy this hope, which is the fruit of his nature. We were much touched by O'Connell's direct address to the Queen as "Lady," but she did not listen, and we fear few ladies and gentlemen will, till the prayers of destiny compels them.

*

[June 28, 1845]

The Irish Character {2}

Since the publication of a short notice under this head in The Tribune, several persons have expressed to us that their feelings were awakened on the subject, especially as to their intercourse with the lower Irish. Most persons have an opportunity of becoming acquainted, if they will, with the lower class of Irish, as they are so much employed among us in domestic service, and other kinds of labor.

We feel, say these persons, the justice of what has been said as to the duty and importance of improving these people. We have sometimes tried, but the want of real gratitude which, in them, is associated with such warm and wordy professions of regard, with their incorrigible habits of falsehood and evasion, have baffled and discouraged us. You say their children ought to be educated, but how can this be effected, when the all but omnipotent sway of the Catholic religion and the example of parents are both opposed to the formation of such views and habits as we think desirable to the citizen of the new world?

We answer first, with regard to whose who have grown up in another land and who, soon after arriving here, are engaged in our service.

First, as to ingratitude. We cannot but sadly smile at the remarks we hear so often on this subject. Just Heaven, and to us how liberal! who has given those who speak thus an unfettered existence, free from religious or political oppression, who has given them the education of intellectual and refined intercourse with men to develop those talents which make them rich in thoughts and enjoyment, perhaps in money too, certainly rich in comparison with the poor emigrants they employ, what is thought in Thy clear light of those who expect in exchange for a few shillings spent in presents or medicine, a few kind words, a little casual thought or care, such a mighty payment of *gratitude?* Gratitude!—Under the weight of old feudalism, their minds were padlocked by habits against the light; they might be grateful then, for they thought their lords were as gods, of another frame and spirit than theirs, and that they had no right to have the same hopes and wants, hardly to suffer from the same maladies with those creatures of silk and velvet and cloth of gold. Then, the crumbs that fell from the rich man's table might be received with gratitude, and, if any but the dogs came to tend the beggar's sores, such might be received as angels. But the institutions which sustained such ideas have fallen to pieces; it is understood, even in Europe, that

"The rank is but the guinea stamp,
The man's the gowd for a' that."
"A man's a man for a' that."

And being such, has a claim on this earth for something better than the nettles of which the French peasantry made their soup, and with which the persecuted Irish, "under hiding," turned to green the lips white before with famine.

And, if this begins to be understood in Europe, can you suppose it is not by those who, hearing that America opens a mother's arms with the cry "All men born free and equal," rush to her bosom to be consoled for centuries of woe, for their ignorance, their hereditary degradation, their long memories of black bread and stripes? However little else they may understand, believe they understand well *this much*. Such inequality of privileges among men all born of one blood should not exist. They darkly feel that those to whom much has been given owe to the Master an account of stewardship. They know now that your gift is but a small portion of their right.

And you, O giver! *how* did you give? With religious joy, as one who knows that he who loves God cannot fail to love his neighbor as *himself?* With joy and freedom, as one who feels that it is the highest happiness of gift to us that we have something to give again? Didst thou put thyself into the position of the poor man, and do for him what thou wouldst have had one able do for thee? Or, with affability, and condescending sweetness made easy by internal delight at thine own wondrous virtue, didst thou give five dollars to balance five hundred spent on thyself? Did you say, "James, I shall expect you to do right in every thing and attend to my concerns as I should myself, and, at the end of the quarter, I will give you my old clothes and a new pocket handkerchief, beside seeing that your mother is provided with fuel against Christmas"?

Line upon line and precept upon precept the tender parent expects from the teacher to whom he confides his child, vigilance unwearied, day and night, throughout long years. But he expects the raw Irish girl, or boy, to correct at a single exhortation the habit of deceiving those above them which the expectation of being tyrannized over has rooted in their race for ages. If we look fairly into the history of their people and the circumstances under which their own youth was trained, they cannot expect that any thing short of the most steadfast patience and love can enlighten them as to the beauty and value of implicit truth, and having done so, fortify and refine them in the practice of it.

This we admit at the outset. 1st. You must be prepared for a religious and patient treatment of those people, not merely uneducated but ill-educated, a treatment far more religious and patient than is demanded by your own children, if they were born and bred under circumstances at all favorable.

2d. Dismiss from your minds all thought of gratitude. Do what you do for them for God's sake and as a debt to humanity, interest to the common creditor upon principal left in your care. Then insensibility, forgetfulness or relapse will not discourage you, and you will welcome proofs of genuine attachment to yourself chiefly as being tokens that your charge has risen into a higher state of thought and feeling, so as to be enabled to value the benefits conferred through you. Could we begin so, there would be hope of our really becoming the instructors and guardians of this swarm of souls which come from their regions of torment to us, hoping, at least, the benefits of purgatory.

The influence of the Catholic Priesthood must continue very great till there is a complete transfusion of character in the minds of their charge. But as the Irishman or any other foreigner becomes Americanized, he will demand a new form of religion to suit his new wants. The priest, too, will have to learn the duties of an American citizen; he will live less and less for the Church and more for the People, till, at last, if there be Catholicism still, it will be under Protestant influences, as begins to be the case in Germany. It will be, not Roman, but American Catholicism—a form of worship which relies much, perhaps, on external means and the authority of the clergy, for such will always be the case with religion while there are crowds of men still living an external life, and who have not learned to make full use of their own faculties, but where a belief in the benefits of confession and the power of the Church, as Church, to bind and loose, atone for, or decide upon sin, with similar corruptions, must vanish in the free and searching air of a new era.

At present, the Catholic priesthood are the best friends of these poor people, and, if they do them harm, do them also great good. All that is desirable is that they should also have other friends as sympathizing, as well acquainted with their wants and weaknesses, and who view their situation from another point. Thus they would have the benefit of various aids and means.

Between employer and employed there is not sufficient pains taken on the part of the former to establish a mutual understanding. People meet in the relations of master and servant who have lived in two different worlds. In this respect we are much worse situated than the same parties have been in Europe. There is less previous acquaintance between the upper and lower classes. (We must, though unwillingly, use these terms to designate the state of things as at present existing.) Meals are taken separately, work is seldom shared, there is very little to bring the parties together, except sometimes the farmer works with his hired Irish laborer in the field, or the mother keeps the nurse-maid of her baby in the room with her.

In this state of things the chances for instruction, which come every day of themselves where parties share a common life instead of its results merely, do not occur. Neither is there opportunity to administer instruction in the best manner nor to understand when and where it is needed.

The farmer who works with his men in the field—the farmer's wife who attends with her women to the churn and the oven, may, with ease, be true father and mother to all who are in their employ, and enjoy health of conscience in the relation, secure that, if they find cause for blame, it is not from faults induced by their own negligence. The merchant who is from home all day, the lady receiving visiters or working slippers in her nicely furnished parlor, cannot be quite so sure that their demands, or the duties involved in them, are clearly understood, nor estimate the temptations to prevarication.

It is shocking to think to what falsehoods human beings like ourselves will resort to excuse a love of amusement, or hide ill-health, while they see us indulging freely in the one, yielding lightly to the other; and yet we have, or ought to have, far more resources in either temptation than they. For us it is hard to resist, to give up going to the places where we should meet our most interesting companions, or do our work with an aching brow. But we have not people over us whose careless hasty anger drives us to seek excuses for our failures; if so, perhaps—perhaps, who knows? we, the better educated, rigidly, immaculately true as we are at present, *might* tell falsehoods. Perhaps we might, if things were given us to do which we never had seen done, if we were surrounded by new arrangements in the nature of which none instructed us. All this we must think over before we can be of much use.

We have spoken of the nursery-maid as *the* hired domestic with whom her mistress, or even the master, is most likely to be acquainted. But, only a day or two since, we saw, what we see so often, a nursery-maid, with the family to which she belonged, in a public conveyance. They were having a pleasant time, but in it she had no part, except to hold a hot, heavy baby and receive frequent admonitions to keep *it* comfortable. No inquiry was made as to *her* comfort—no entertaining remark, no information as to the places of interest we passed was addressed to her. Had she been in that way with that family ten years, she might have known *them* well enough for their characters lay only too bare to a careless scrutiny; but her joys, her sorrows, her few thoughts, her almost buried capacities, would have been as unknown to them and they as little likely to benefit her, as the Emperor of China.

Let the employer place the employed first in good physical circumstances, so as to promote the formation of different habits from those of the Irish hovel and illicit still-house. Having thus induced feelings of self-respect, he has opened the door for a new set of notions. Then let him become acquainted with the family circumstances and history of his new pupil. He has now got some ground on which to stand for intercourse. Let instruction follow for the mind, not merely by having the youngest daughter set, now and then, copies in the writing-book, or hear read aloud a few verses in the Bible, but by putting good books in their way if able to read, and by intelligent conversation when there is a chance, the master with the man who is driving him, the lady with the woman who is making her bed; explain to them the relations of objects round them; teach them, too, *why* it is better. Thus will the mind be prepared by development for a moral reformation; there will be some soil fitted to receive the seed.

When the time is come,—and will you think a poor, uneducated person in whose mind the sense of right and wrong is confused, the sense of honor blunted, easier of access than one refined and thoughtful? Surely you will not, if you yourself are refined and thoughtful, but rather that the case requires far more care in choice of a favorable opportunity.—When then the good time is come, perhaps it will be best to do what you do in a way to make a permanent impression. Show the Irishman that a vice not indigenous to his nation (for the rich and noble who are not so tempted are chivalrous to an uncommon degree in their openness, bold sincerity, and adherence to their word) has crept over and become deeply rooted in the poorer people from the long oppressions they have undergone. Show them what efforts and care will be needed to wash out the taint. Offer your aid, as a faithful friend, to watch their lapses and refine their sense of truth. You will not speak in vain. If they never mind, if habit is too powerful, still their nobler nature will not have been addressed in vain. They will not forget the counsels they have not strength to follow, and the benefits will be seen in their children or children's children.

Many say—"Well, suppose we do all this, what then?—They are so fond of change they will leave us." What then? Why, let them go to carry the good seed elsewhere. Will you be as selfish and short-sighted as those who will never plant trees to shade a hired house lest some one else should be blest by their shade?

It is a simple duty we ask you to engage in; it is also a great patriotic work. You are asked to engage in the great work of mutual education, which must be for this country the system of mutual insurance.

We have some hints upon this subject, drawn from the experience of the wise and good—some encouragement to offer from that experience, that the fruits of a wise planting sometimes ripen sooner than we could dare to expect. But this must be for another day.

One word as to this love of change. We hear people blaming it on their servants, who can and do go to Niagara, to the South, to the Springs, to Europe, to the sea-side; in short, who are always on the move whenever they feel the need of variety to reanimate mind, health, or spirits. Change of place, as to family employment, is the only way domestics have of "seeing life." The only way immigrants have of getting thoroughly acquainted with the new society into which they have entered; how natural that they should incline to it? Once more, put yourself in their places, and then judge them gently from your own, if you would be just to them, if you would be of any use.

✻

[July 15, 1845]

The Irish Character {3}

In answer to remarks by J. O'C. in yesterday's Tribune, we would say it was never intended to speak of *ingratitude* as a trait peculiar, or peculiarly ascribed to, the Irish. The writer had in mind remarks such as are made by the employer about the employed generally. It did not seem to us that in attempting to show the groundlessness of such objections to plans of improvement, we took part in casting the imputation on any class of persons. It is our belief that under associative principles, New Jerusalem principles, Christian principles or any other that assert the right of every man to justice, and even to a charitable examination into the motives that have influenced his conduct and the circumstances that have made him what he is, the charge of ingratitude would almost wholly disappear. This charge is generally made by inconsiderate and selfish persons, who overrate the trifling benefits they confer, because they are not capable of doing as they would be done by—a rule transcendental in most men's eyes, and yet proposed by the head of the European and American Church as the only safe practical one for all men.

This is in substance what the writer meant to express in the communication referred to by J. O'C. We have never heard Irish domestics or laborers especially spoken of as ungrateful, but have heard this reproach cast upon all laborers, who being tolerably well treated, or instructed with some care, did not improve, were willing to change their place, deceived their employer, or in any way disappointed hopes and claims we consider unreasonable and unjust. We have a great deal of personal acquaintance with the lower Irish, and have found them unusually affectionate and unduly grateful for trifling kindnesses. Like all uncultivated men, their impulses are often superficial; this is because in a soil that has not been opened to the sun and air, new roots do not so easily strike deep but again we know several instances where the native strength of the soil reared the generous growth, without need of culture. We hope we have now made our meaning clear. Since we did not before, as must often be the case in rapidly written articles for a daily paper, where the form and space permit only to seize on salient points of large themes, we cannot fail to thank those who give an opportunity to correct false impressions. Especially in this case, it would have grieved us to be supposed to injure those we were anxious to serve.

✱

[July 24, 1845]

8
A Miscellany

The pieces in this last section show the breadth of topics Fuller addressed. She wrote an essay endorsing the creation of Thanksgiving as an official holiday. The governor of New York proclaimed it a state holiday in the 1830s; Abraham Lincoln declared the fourth Thursday in November a national holiday in 1865. Many of Fuller's contemporaries, including John Greenleaf Whittier, Lydia Maria Child, Nathaniel Hawthorne, Harriet Beecher Stowe, and Ralph Waldo Emerson, also wrote essays or short stories advocating the creation of the new Thanksgiving holiday.[1]

Since many of Fuller's reviews of American literature have appeared elsewhere, none appear here. Still Fuller reviewed not only literature but all the arts. She analyzed a painting in "Peale's Court of Death" and music in "The Grand Festival Concert at Castle Garden" and "Leopold de Meyer."

In "Physical Education and the Preservation of Health," she addressed the nineteenth-century enthusiasm for health fads.

Fuller spoke French and German. "The Beethoven Monument," "Study of the German Language," and "Instruction in the French Language" illustrated her strong advocacy of Continental, as opposed to British, culture.

Of course, Margaret Fuller did not always write memorable work. "Discoveries" tritely celebrated her century's idea of childhood. However, she sincerely held these views. Many scholars have discussed Fuller's affection for Greeley's young son and the grief she and Greeley shared when the child died suddenly.

In the last piece, "Farewell," Fuller explained the impact newspaper work had on her and how much she looked forward to the trip to Europe from which she never returned.

Thanksgiving

> Canst thou give thanks for aught that has been given
> Except by making earth more worthy heaven?
> Just stewardship the master hoped from thee;
> Harvests from Time to bless Eternity.

Thanksgiving is peculiarly the festival day of New-England. Elsewhere, other celebrations rival its attractions, but in that region where the Puritans first returned thanks that some among them had been sustained by a great hope and earnest resolve amid the perils of the ocean, wild beasts and famine, the old spirit which hallowed the day still lingers, and forbids that it should be entirely devoted to play and plum-pudding.

And yet, as there is always this tendency; as the twelfth-night cake is baked by many a hostess who would be puzzled if you asked her, "Twelfth night after or before what?" and the Christmas cake by many who know no other Christmas service, so it requires very serious assertion and proof from the minister to convince his parishioners that the turkey and plum-pudding, which are presently to occupy his place in their attention, should not be the chief objects of the way.

And, in other regions, where the occasion is observed, it is still more as one for a meeting of families and friends to the enjoyment of a good dinner, than for any higher purpose.

This, indeed, is one which we want not to depreciate. If this manner of keeping the day be likely to persuade the juniors of the party that the celebrated Jack Horner is the prime model for brave boys, and that grandparents are chiefly to be respected as the givers of grand feasts, yet a meeting in the spirit of kindness, however dull and blind, is not wholly without use in healing differences and promoting good intentions. The instinct of family love, intended by Heaven to make those of one blood the various and harmonious organs of one mind, is never wholly without good influence. Family love, I say, for family pride is never without bad influence, and it too often takes the place of its mild and healthy sister.

Yet where society is at all simple, it is cheering to see the family circle thus assembled, if only because its patriarchal form is in itself so excellent. The presence of the children animates the old people, while the respect and attention they demand refines the gaiety of the young. Yes, it is cheering to see, in some large room, the elders talking near the bright fire, while the cousins of all ages are amusing themselves in knots. Here is almost all the good, and very little of the ill, that can be found in society, got together merely for amusement.

Yet how much nobler, more exhilarating and purer would be the atmosphere of that circle if the design of its pious founders were remembered by those who partake [in] this festival! If they dared not attend the public jubilee till private retrospect of the past year had been taken in the spirit of the old rhyme, which we all bear in mind if not in heart—

> "What hast thou done that 's worth the doing,
> And what pursued that 's worth pursuing?
> What sought thou knew'st that thou shouldst shun,
> What done thou shouldst have left undone?"

and a crusade been vowed into the wild places of the bosom, which should take for its device, "Lord, cleanse thou me from secret faults"—"Keep back thy servant also from presumptuous sins"—would not that circle be happy as if music, from invisible agents, floated through it—if each member of it considered every other member as a bequest from heaven—if he supposed that the appointed nearness in blood or lot was a sign to him that he must exercise his gifts of every kind as given peculiarly in their behalf—that if richer in temper, in talents, in knowledge, or in worldly goods, here was the innermost circle of his poor—that he must clothe these naked, whether in body or mind, soothing the perverse, casting light into the narrow chamber, or, most welcome task of all! extending a hand at the right moment to one uncertain of his way. It is this spirit that makes the old man to be revered as a Nestor, rather than put aside like a worn-out garment. It is such a spirit that sometimes has given to the young child a ministry as of a parent in the house.

But, if charity begin at home, it must not end there; and while purifying the innermost circle, let us not forget that it depends upon the great circle, and that again on it; that no home can be healthful in which are not cherished seeds of good for the world at large. Thy child, thy brother are given to thee only as an example of what is due from thee to all men. It is true that, if you, in anger, call your brother fool, no deeds of so-called philanthropy shall save you from the punishment; for your philanthropy must be from the love of excitement, not the love of man, or of goodness. But then you must visit the Gentiles also, and take time for knowing what aid the woman of Samaria may need.

A noble Catholic writer, in the true sense as well as by name a Catholic, describes a tailor as giving a dinner on an occasion which had brought honor to his house, which, though humble, was not a poor house. In his glee, the tailor was boasting a little of the favors and blessings of his lot, when suddenly a thought stung him. He stopped, and cutting away half the fowl that lay before him, sent it in a dish with the best knives, bread, and napkin, and a brotherly message that was better still, to a widow near, who must, he knew, be sitting in sadness and poverty among her children. His little daughter was the messenger. If parents followed up the indulgences heaped upon their children at Thanksgiving dinners with similar messages, there would not be danger that children should think enjoyment of sensual pleasures the only occasion that demands Thanksgiving.

And suppose while the children were absent on their errands of justice, as they could not fail to think them, if they compared the hovels they must visit with their own comfortable homes, their elders, touched by a sense of right, should be led from discussion of the rivalries of trade or fashion to whether they could not impart of all that was theirs, not merely one poor dinner once a year, but all their mental and material wealth for the benefit of all men. If they do not sell it *all* at once, as the rich young man was bid to do as a test of his sincerity, they may find some way in which it could be invested so as to show enough obedience to the Law and the Prophets to love our neighbor as ourselves.

And he who once gives himself to such thoughts will find it is not merely moral gain for which he shall return thanks another year with the return of this day. In the present complex state of human affairs, you cannot be kind unless you are wise. Thoughts of amaranthine bloom will spring up in the fields plowed to give food to suffering men. It would, indeed, seem to be a simple matter at first glance. "Lovest thou me?"—"Feed my lambs." But now we have not only to find pasture, but to detect the lambs under the disguise of wolves, and restore them by a spell, like that the Shepherd used, to their natural form and whiteness.

And for this present day appointed for Thanksgiving, we may say that if we know of so many wrongs, woes, and errors in the world yet unredressed; if in this nation recent decisions have shown a want of moral discrimination on important subjects, that make us pause and doubt whether we can join in the formal congratulations that we are still bodily alive, unassailed by the ruder modes of warfare, and enriched with the fatness of the land; yet on the other side, we know of causes not so loudly proclaimed why we should give thanks. Abundantly and humbly we must render them for the movement, now sensible in the heart of the civilized world, although it has not pervaded the entire frame. For that movement of contrition and love which forbids men of earnest thought to eat, drink, or be merry, while other men are steeped in ignorance, corruption and wo; which calls the King from his throne of gold, and the Poet from his throne of Mind to lie with the beggar in the kennel, or raise him from it; which says to the Poet, "You must reform rather than create a world," and to him of the golden crown, "You cannot long remain a King unless you are also a Man."

Wherever this impulse of social or political reform darts up its rill through the crusts of selfishness, scoff and dread arise and hang like a heavy mist above it. But the voice of the rill penetrates far enough for those who have ears to hear. And, sometimes, it is the case that 'those who came to scoff remain to pray.' In two articles of reviews, one foreign and one domestic, which have come under our eye within the last fortnight, the writers who began by jeering at the visionaries, seemed as they wrote to be touched by a sense that without a high and pure faith none can have the only true vision of the intention of God as to the Destiny of Man.

We recognized as a happy omen that there is cause for thanksgiving and that our people may be better than they seem, the meeting last week to organize an Association for the benefit of Prisoners. We shall not, then, be wholly Pharisees. We shall not ask the blessing of this day in the mood of "Lord, I thank thee that I, and my son, and my brother, are not as other men are,—not as these publicans imprisoned there," while the still, small voice cannot make us hear its evidence that, but for instruction, example, and the "preventing God," every sin that can be named might riot in our hearts. The prisoner, too, may become a man. Neither his open nor our secret faults, must utterly dismay us. We will treat him as if he had a soul. We will not dare to hunt him into a beast of prey, or trample him into a serpent. We will give him some crumbs from the table which grace from above and parent love below have spread for us, and, perhaps, he will recover from these ghastly ulcers that deform him now.

We were much pleased with the spirit of the meeting. It was simple, business-like, in a serious, affectionate temper. The speakers did not make phrases or compliments; did not slur over the truth. The audience showed a ready vibration to the touch of just and tender feeling. The time was evidently ripe for this movement. We doubt not that many now darkened souls will give thanks for the ray of light that will have been let in by this time next year. It is but a grain of mustard seed, but the promised tree will grow swiftly if tended in a pure spirit; and the influence of good measures in any one place will be immediate in this province, as has been the case with every attempt in behalf of the insane.

While reading a notice of a successful attempt to have musical performances carried through in concert by the insane at Rouen, we were forcibly reminded of a similar performance we heard a few weeks ago at Sing Sing. There the female prisoners joined in singing a hymn, or rather choral, which describes the last thoughts of a spirit about to be enfranchised from the body; each stanza of which ends with the words, "All is well"; and they sang it— those suffering, degraded children of society—with as gentle and resigned an expression as if they were sure of going to sleep in the arms of a pure mother. The good spirit that dwelt in the music made them its own. And shall not the good spirit of religious sympathy make them its own also, and more permanently? We shall see. Should the morally insane, by wise and gentle care, be won back to health, as the wretched bedlamites have been, will not the angels themselves give thanks? And will any man dare take the risk of opposing plans that afford even a chance of such a result?

Apart, then, from good that is public and many-voiced, do not each of us know, in private experience, much to be thankful for? Not only the innocent and daily pleasures that we have prized according to our wisdom; of the sun and starry skies, the fields of green, or snow scarcely less beautiful, the loaf eaten with an appetite, the glow of labor, the gentle signs of common affection. But have not some, have not many of us cause to be thankful for enfranchisement from error or infatuation; a growth in knowledge of outward things, and instruction within the soul from a higher source. Have we not acquired a sense of more refined enjoyments; clear convictions; sometimes a serenity in which, as in the first days of June, all things grow, and the blossom gives place to fruit? Have we not been weaned from what was unfit for us, or unworthy our care? and have not those ties been drawn more close, and are not those objects seen more distinctly, which shall for ever be worthy the purest desires of our souls? Have we learned to do any thing, the humblest, in the service and by the spirit of the power which meaneth all things well? If so we may give thanks, and, perhaps, venture to offer our solicitations in behalf of those as yet less favored by circumstances. When even a few shall dare do so with the whole heart—for only a pure heart can "avail much" in such prayers—then ALL shall soon be well.

✼

[December 12, 1844]

Wonders Have Not Ceased in Our Times

A new gush of lava is seen from Vesuvius; that is a brilliant show, but no wonder, because seen so often that it ceases to move the gazer with a sense of mystery. But manna is now falling once more from Heaven, and we have only to regret that it is not to further the great designs of a Moses.

Translated from the Schnellpost

"A remarkable phenomenon is announced by the gazettes of Constantinople, which all agree in the report—i.e.—that in Asia Minor, in the District of Jenischehir and those of Siwrihissar, Eski Schehir and Seicli Gazi, manna has fallen from Heaven. The *Courrier of Constantinople* contains this notice:—'Letters from Jenischehir inform us that, for some time back, manna has been falling from Heaven, and has supplied the inhabitants with nourishment. They grind it to flour and bake it in the same way as bread, nor is it inferior to what we usually eat.'

"The *Journal de Constantinople* says:—'The same phenomenon which was observed at Ban in 1841 is now repeated in the District of Jenischehir, with similar and no less extraordinary circumstances. It appears, from the testimony of persons of all modes of religious faith, that after a season of partial famine the same marvel that happened in behalf of the people of Israel has occurred again. A shower has fallen from Heaven of substances about the size of hail-stones, not unlike the tear-form manna, and pleasant to the taste. It fell in such quantity as to lie three or four inches thick on the ground, and served the people as food for many days.'"

*

[April 24, 1846]

Peale's Court of Death

This picture, famous in the annals of American art, may now be seen to very good advantage at the Society Library Rooms, either in the brighter hours of the day or by gas-light.

Much stress is laid, in the advertisements, upon the *moral* purpose or influence of the picture.—With regard to this we must observe that moral influence is not the legitimate object of works of art. It may naturally flow from them, in so far as beauty is identical with health and virtue, but the object of the Fine Arts is simply to express thoughts in forms more perfect than the common course of nature furnishes. As all objects in a high way beautiful and perfect are intrinsically pure and noble, the mind of him who contemplates them is by that means elevated and expanded, but it is not their province directly to preach of vice or virtue—sin and its retributions. Where religion has afforded the best of all subjects, it has been because it presented types of what is universal. The Madonna represents a high and grand form of maternal tenderness, the sight of which may teach innumerable lessons, but it must be incidentally. Christ reproving Peter affords a subject for moral instruction, but when the true Artist takes hold of it, all petty details and inferences are subordinated to, or lost in, the sense of a being so raised above the region of doubt, speculation, and special precept by a thorough intelligence of the divine will that He and the Father are one.

We have dwelt for a moment upon this, because the method of advertising Mr. Peale's picture seems as if a work of Art needed some pretext or object beyond its natural one of representing what is most excellent in thought, most clear in imagination, and by so doing to confirm impressions already common enough, which prevent our people from looking at such works from the true point of view.

Let us take, then, the picture in our own way, and inquire, first, as to the object of the artist; second, his mode of treatment; third, the degree of his success.

As to the first, we are informed the object of the artist is two-fold, the moral one of giving juster ideas of death, than are usual, and the other, which seems to us the true poetic or artistic object of the picture, to express in an original way, his own feelings about death.

Death is represented, not in the usual forms of a skeleton, or an old man mowing down lives, as the reaper the ears of corn, but as a Power and a Fate. This conception, quite as open to objection, in a philosophical point of view, as the others, since Death is not positive but negative, being not, in fact, a power, but only the absence of power—that is, of life, is yet poetical, as corresponding to a set of feelings which rise in the mind when we see souls cease to sustain the bodies which had been their temporary abode, and is well expressed by a stately form of old Egyptian calmness and grandeur, which, seated with its foot upon the dead body of a man cut off in the fullness of his strength, makes the centre to the picture.

The statuesque stillness of this figure and its drapery, the shadows that fall around it, the coldness and rigidity of the corpse, form a centre of cold and dark, which bring out into very bold relief the forms and colors of the groups on either side, thus giving to the picture great effect, but one calculated, in our opinion, to produce emotions of solemnity and awe, if not of deep sadness, rather than to give that more serene view of Death which Mr. Peale says was his object. We have never seen any pictures, such as the Descent from the Cross, or Allston's touching of the Dead Man's Bones, where the centre was cold and dark in which this was not the case, while in such as the Nativity, where the light proceeds from the body of the child, or from a central group of warm, living figures, the emotions induced are those of peace, or hope, or joy. How can it be otherwise? The centre always is winning the eye to itself, and gives character to the whole picture.

The leading figures on either side the corpse, Virtue sustaining Old Age, and Pleasure alluring Youth with her charmed cup, are finely conceived and colored. Here the view of the artist seems to have been truly catholic, for he has so done that the gazer may attach an allegorical or a human interest to the figures, according to his turn of mind. Lesser fancies or *concetti* such as that of the smoke from Pleasure's cup hiding the presence of Death from her victim, or of the head of the corpse resting in the stream of oblivion, with which the painter has pleased himself are equally left optional to be seen or not according to the quality of mental sight.

As is usually the case when the contrast is attempted, Pleasure is made far more beautiful than Virtue. But in her train are many shapes of woe, which fill one side of the picture with dark shadows of darker realities.

The group on the other side, representing a warrior accompanied by fire, pestilence and famine, and passing over the dead and vanquished, is the most powerful part of the picture. The attitude and onward motion of the female figure which represents the fire are admirable; the light from the torches upborne by her fierce arms casts a stern light on the scene in high poetic contrast with the other parts of the picture. Famine and Pestilence are both expressed with great force, and we read with no little interest in this ghostly, soothsaying age, where we totter on the brink of finding the bridge betwixt our inward and our outward destinies, that "for the figure of Famine, following in the train of War, the artist could find no model, though he sought her in many a haunt of Misery, and therefore drew her from his brain; but, strange to say, two weeks after the picture was finished a woman passed his house, who might have been sworn to as the original."

In effective grouping, in the use of lights and shades and in uniting of expression worthy "those creative depths from which comes the fullness of forms" the picture claims honors that declare Rembrandt Peale a Patriarch of American Art, and we hope New-York will not let pass from her this most valued portion of the inheritance he wills to his country.

*

[December 13, 1845]

The Grand Festival Concert at Castle Garden

The evening was fair; the apartment at Castle Garden, full of light, wore the most joyous air; the orchestral platform, when full, had the appearance of a small, but crowded Mount Parnassus; and the nondescript deities, or whatever they were, on the curtain that overhung it, seemed ready to skip and jump with pleasure. All was right, except the audience, which, though good-looking, well-behaved, and quite large enough to make the atmosphere oppressive in the latter part of the evening, was not, alas! satisfactory, viewed in regard to dollars. We fear not more than three or four thousand of those little 'almighties' could have been added to the fund. We suppose the calculation was injudicious and that, in taking so large a hall, the tickets should have been put at a lower rate, for it is well known that the economies of our people lead them to prefer paying eight quarters of a dollar eight times for eight bad books, rather than two whole dollars, all at once, for one good book; and it follows they would prefer paying four half dollars for four ordinary entertainments, rather than two dollars for an excellent one. As for expecting them to act in reference to the future, that can be looked for only from the smallest minority.

The size of the room was a benefit to those who were well seated. Music cannot be equally heard in it, and the more delicate parts are much swallowed up and wasted by its construction. But the grand bursts of sound, the full passages, had, this time, sufficient perspective to give them effect.

The first overture was well performed. Miss Northall followed, but either she was agitated, or did not know how to proportion her voice to the building. Her singing was inefficient, and she fell into her old lachrymose style, from which we hoped she had finally emerged. Perhaps it was straining her voice that destroyed its firmness of tone. We regretted this, as she is becoming, justly, a favorite with the public. An overture of Mozart followed, to which due effect was not given. Then came Madame Otto. She showed skill and practice in making use of her position. We never heard her sing so well, and she was much applauded. But her total want of fire and spontaneity makes her always wearisome to ourselves. We cannot do without the presence of the electric spark of soul in music; mere words do not suffice us.

Then came Mendelssohn's concerto, Mr. Timm at the piano, a truly delightful performance. Mr. Timm's calm elegance and purity of tone are always refreshing. "He is," said one present, "like a rill of pure water," and he was well sustained.

Then came Pico,—dear, honest, generous soul as she seems, in her singing at least; that is all we know of her. She is one of Nature's good ones, and her voice flows forth as the true breath of her being; there is no taught twittering there. Her song was encored, and we were willing, long as the evening necessarily was.

Beethoven's Symphony then came to entrance us. At this first time of hearing, it overshadowed like a tower the wandering mind; we could only feel it, and should need long acquaintance to disentangle our impression. We understood it sufficiently to feel the want in the musicians of a similar apprenticeship to a true and thorough comprehension and rendering of its sense; we felt all along inadequacy, a want of the proper light and shade. This is no disparagement to them; profound study and devotion, no less than capacity, being requisite both for leader and auxiliaries with such a great work. As it was, the impression was almost overpowering, at least to some—not, indeed, to the ladies and gentlemen, who thought that the best time to secure their omnibuses, and who, we do believe, if admitted to the heavenly courts, could not be beguiled from ringing the bell in the midst of Hallelujah to ask if luncheon was ready. Never, never shall we forget one night when Braham was giving forth the sublime remains of his great voice, such tones as none of us will hear again, in Luther's Judgment Hymn, while he was calling upon the trumpets to answer and the dead to arise, the ladies and gentlemen arose instead and began shawling and cloaking lest they should lose the best moment for going out. That was in Boston. Might but such people go out for a permanence, and bear in mind that they have no sense for such things. The ill-breeding that disturbs others is bad enough, but oh the unutterable stupidity! But to return to the symphony. The Ode to Joy was an entire failure owing to the want of voices fitted to sustain such words and such music; still it was very obvious what it must be when adequately given. It was, indeed, a pity to hear such a screeching, shrilling, and jarring, when a world-wide gush of soul, equally magnificent in the post and the musician, demanded the noblest tones, in the most perfect unison of which human nature is capable, still we are glad to have heard it, even so. We mourned to see the weak translation affixed, giving to those who could not read German such a distorted image of the great original where every word is fraught with the inmost fires of the heart. If any were endurable, it would be one verbally exact; it is wicked for common rhymsters to meddle with such things.

We departed at a late hour, fatigued, but grateful for much and high pleasure, and in the opinion that, considering the defects of the apartment and the great number of performers who had to be moulded to a common object with slight and hasty preparation, the success was surprising and the result a great boon.

✳

[May 22, 1846]

Leopold de Meyer

We went to hear Leopold de Meyer on Friday evening prepared for powers of execution entirely new to us and our utmost expectations were realized. We have never taken much pleasure in hearing the piano. It ranks deservedly high among the instruments because it combines so much. It can give us the idea of any kind of music, but, in no kind, the full enjoyment. In rich and complicated music we want the orchestra to satisfy the sense as well as the mind; in simple, deep strains we feel its incompetency of tone to represent what is inmost. From its keys music may be studied and appreciated, but not really heard.

But this poverty disappeared beneath the hands of de Meyer, who draws from the piano surges and torrents of sound, and, by his wonderful energy and fire fills the ear as with twenty instruments.

It was magical when the delicate passages came sparkling like rills and jets to swell the torrent of the main stream. Each note fell like a spark, yet perfectly finished as a flower. The full passages were direct and strong as the storms of Nature herself; it seems as if human hands could hardly do more to subserve the will of a human mind.

But it seems to us not just to speak of the execution of this artist by itself, as if it were a mere knack, or acquired skill, while it is the expression of a powerful individuality, or at least of powerful instincts. There is no spirituality, no deep intellectual expression; those who always seek in music the expression of the more refined and elevated part of our nature, must, of course, go away disappointed. But the range of music is as wide as the world, and those who take pleasure in the flood of vital energy, rising to a very high point—in the triumphs of the will—in sensations of extraordinary richness, fullness and boldness, rapidly accumulated and vigorously dissipated, would find an exhilaration in de Meyer, such as attends the ascent of mountains, the whirl of the dance, or swift career upon a noble steed. In this age of half feelings and low, imperfect organizations, this impression of such fullness of vital energy is to us not oppressive but refreshing. A whimsical introduction to such an entertainment was one of the most sentimental of Italian airs. It seemed when this great horse began to run, he would shake off regret and sadness in a moment, as the hawk might all memory of the song of the nightingale.

We never heard any thing so sustained as the excitement of the Danse du Serail. That dance danced itself dead before the last light went out. The Marche Marocaine is very bold and imposing; it seems like a French conception of savage things, but large in its grasp and crashing in its tread.—Thus does the tramp of cavalry break the silence of the wild caves and tombs of the desert and cymbals clang wild barbaric mourning and the change of eras on the march.

The air and gesture of the musician, as he plays, are as good as the music. His smile is bluff, cordial, a little vain, but not, we should say, with petty vanity. His whole body plays, and his hair sticks out, full of electricity. It is just the right length now; though, indeed, we doubt whether it ever grows any longer; it sympathizes too much with his playing to have time to grow.

*

[November 17, 1845]

*Physical Education and the
Preservation of Health*
By *John C. Warren, M.D. Professor of Anatomy and Surgery in
Harvard University.*
Boston, *William D. Ticknor & Co.* 1846.

*Treatise on the Physiological
and Moral Management of Infancy.*
By *Andrew Combe, M.D. &c. with Notes
and a Supplementary Chapter,
by John Bell, M.D. &c. Fourth Edition.*
New-York, *Saxton & Miles,
Saxton & Huntington,* 1846.

This Lecture of Dr. Warren is printed in a form suitable for popular distribution, while the high reputation of its author insures it respect. Men will expect to find there those rules for daily practice, the plain common-sense which men should possess from Nature, but strangely lose, amid their many inventions, and are obliged to rediscover by aid of experience and science.

There will be found those general statements as to modes of exercise, care of the skin, choice of food and time and circumstances required for its digestion, that might furnish the ounce of prevention that is worth so many pounds of cure. And how much are they needed in this country, where the most barbarous ignorance prevails on the subject of cleanliness, sleeping accommodations, &c. On these subjects improvement would be easy—that of diet is far more complicated, and is, unfortunately, one which it requires great knowledge of the ways in which the human frame is affected by the changes of climate and various other influences, even to discuss. If it is difficult where a race mostly indigenous to the soil feed upon what Mother Nature has prepared expressly for their use, and where excess or want of judgment in its use produces disease, it must be far more so, where men come from all latitudes to live under new circumstances, and need a judicious adaptation of the old to the new. The dogmatism and proscription that prevail on this topic amuse the observer and distress the patient.—"Touch no meat for your life," says one. "It is not meat but sugar that is your ruin," cries another. "No! salt is the ruin of the world," sadly and gravely declares a third. Milk, which once conciliated all regards, has its denunciators. "Water," say some, "is the bliss that shall dissolve all bane. Drink—wash—take to yourself all the water you can get." "That is madness! is far worse than useless," cry others, "unless the water be pure. You must touch none that has not been tested by a chemist." "Yes! you may, at any rate, drink it," say others, "and in large quantities, for the power of water to aid digestion is obvious to every observer."

"No," says Dr. Warren. "Animals do not drink at the time they eat, but some hours after, and they generally take very small quantities of liquid compared with that which is used by man. The savage in his native wilds takes his solid food, when he can obtain it, to satiety, reposes afterwards, and then resuming his chase, through the forest, stops at the rivulet to allay his thirst. The disadvantage of taking a large quantity of liquid must be obvious to all those who consider that the digesting liquid is diluted and weakened in proportion to the quantity of drink."

What wonder is it, if even the well disposed among the multitude, seeing such dissension among the counselors, gathering just enough from their disputes to infer that they have no true philosophical tests for their opinions, and seeing those who would set the example in practice of this art without science of dietetics, generally among the most morbid and ill-developed specimens of humanity, just throw aside all rule[s] upon the subject, partake of what is set before them, trust to air, exercise, and good intentions to ward off the worst effects of the promiscuous fare.

Yet, while hopeless at present of selecting the right articles and building up a pure and healthful body, so far at least as hereditary taint will permit, from feeding on congenial substances, we know at least this much, that stimulants, not food, and over-eating are injurious, and may take care enough of ourselves to avoid these.

The other branches we can really act wisely in. Dr. Warren after giving the usual directions (rarely followed as yet) for airing beds and sleeping-rooms, adds:

"The manner in which children sleep, will readily be acknowledged to be important, yet very little attention is paid to this matter. Children are crowded together in small and unventilated rooms, often two or three in a bed, and on beds composed of half-prepared feathers, from which issues a noxious effluvia, infecting the child at a period when he is least able to resist its influence. So that in the morning, instead of feeling the full refreshment and vigor natural to the age, he is pale, languid, and for some time indisposed to exertion.

"The rooms in which children are brought up, should be well aired, by having a fire-place, which should be kept open the greater part of the year.—There never should be more than one in the same bed, and this remark may be applied with equal propriety to adults. The substance on which they lie should be hair, thoroughly prepared, so that it shall have no bad smell; in Winter it may be of cotton, or of hair and cotton. It would be very desirable, however, whenever practicable, to place them in separate apartments, as well as separate beds.

"It has been justly said, that adults as well as children had better employ single instead of double beds; this remark is intended to apply universally. The use of double beds has been very generally adopted in this country, perhaps in part as a matter of economy, but this practice is objectionable for more reasons than can be stated here."

On the subject of exercise he mentions particularly the Triangle, and we copy what he says because of the perfect ease and convenience with which one could be put up and used in every bed-chamber.

The exercising the upper limbs is too much neglected, and it is important to provide the means of bringing them into action, as well to develop their powers, as to enlarge and invigorate the chest, with which they are connected, and which they powerfully influence. The best I know of is the use of the triangle. This admirably exerts the upper limbs and the muscles of the chest, and, indeed, when adroitly employed, those of the whole body. The triangle is made of a stick of walnut wood, four feet long, an inch and a half in diameter. To each end is connected a rope, the opposite extremities of which being confined together, are secured to the ceiling of a room, at such hight [*sic*] as to allow the motion of swinging by the hands."

We have ourselves derived the greatest benefit from this simple means. Gymnastic exercises, and if possible in the open air, are needed by every one who is not otherwise led to exercise all parts of the body by various kinds of labor. And in this connection we would mention the rooms for Calisthenic exercises now opened by Mrs. Hawley in this city. She is a good instructor, and we wish her rooms may become the haunt of those ladies who need to improve in grace, strength and health. Some, though almost as partial provision, is made for boys by gymnasia and riding schools. In wiser nations such have been the care of the State. And in despotic Governments, the jealousy of a tyrant was never more justly awakened than when the youth of the land, by a devotion to gymnastic exercises showed their aspiration to reach the healthful stature of manhood. For every one who possesses a strong mind in a sane body is heir presumptive to the kingdom of this world; he needs no external credentials, but has only to appear and make his title clear. But for such a princely form the eye searches the street, the mart, and the council-chamber, in vain.

Those who feel as if the game of life was so near up with them that they could not devote much of the time that is left to the care of wise living in their own persons, should, at least, be unwilling to injure the next generation by the same ignorance which has blighted so many of us in our earliest years. Such should attend to this work of Mr. Combe, among other good books. Mr. Combe has done much good already in this country, and this book should be circulated every where, for many of its suggestions are too obviously just not to be adopted as soon as read. Dr. Warren bears his testimony against the pernicious effects that follow upon the use of tobacco, and we cannot but hope that what he says of its tendency to create cancer will have weight with some who are given up to the detestable practice of chewing. This practice is so odious to women, that we must regard its prevalence here as a token of the very light regard in which they are held, and the consequent want of refinement among men. Dr. Warren seems to favor the practice of Hydropathy to some extent, but must needs bear his testimony in full against Homœpathy. No matter; the little doses will insinuate their way, and cure the ills that flesh is heir to,

> "For a' that, and a' that,
> And mickle mair than a' that."

✻

[January 19, 1846]

The Beethoven Monument

With each new arrival from abroad rumors reach us of the ardent expectation which waits upon the ceremony of displaying to the public, for the first time, the Monument to be dedicated to Beethoven in his birth-place. All the musical talent of musical Europe is crowding thither. To be invited to take part in the festival is a certificate of distinction; artists are ashamed to be left out. And there is *living* genius to honor this occasion, genius which will find its highest purpose accomplished by sacrifices on this altar. There is as high a joy in worshiping the hero as in emulating him; his virtue is ours while we know how fervently to love, religiously to prize it. And there are those yet in the world worthy to celebrate the glory of Beethoven in music. It was not so with a similar ceremony which took place several months since in honor of Goethe in *his* birth-place. But one or two of his peers survived, those broken by years, and he had no followers who could step boldly enough to mark where his foot-prints had gone before. It was sorrowful to see how coldly the ceremony in honor of the greatest German writer (for all partisan or obtuse verdicts to the contrary, so he is and so the Ages must unhesitatingly proclaim him,) fell on the heart of Germany. He was not dear to her heart, and her mind had drank, even to oblivion, of his gifts. Beside, he was not in harmony with the great national movement; now Beethoven is. Beethoven is the democratic king, an angel in genius, a priest by gifts and office, a man in his whole nature, fitted alike to command and to obey.

Beethoven would have enjoyed these honors, perhaps will so now. When on earth on the only occasion when adequate honors were paid him, he, in consequence of that calamity, great as ever befel[l] a virtuous mortal, the infirmity which prevented his appreciating how far his thoughts could be realized for the mind of the world, could neither hear the raptures of the audience nor the music that called them forth. When the audience perceived this, there was for once thorough sympathy from lesser men for the woes of a greater, and from rapture they melted into tears. Now he is freed, we trust, from all abstraction in full realization of such serene and blissful energy as is prophesied in his 7th Symphony.

We are reminded on this occasion of the funeral solemnities described by that worthy biographer of genius, Vasari, when all the artists had adorned with trophies from the field of art, such as they had been enabled to win, the bier of Michelangelo. we delight to mention this name in connection with that of Beethoven. They were both in the highest sense Masters; their natures are congenial and their minds of like majestic scope. They belong to that highest class of geniuses of which the world cannot as yet count a score, men whose vast souls and mighty natures prophesy another sphere for human effort, where it shall no longer endure the limitations or suffer the checks which at present leave almost every life a seeming failure. They were both as pure as they were great, of a stern nobleness and sublime determination.

The Queen of England is to be present at this celebration: that is well: England has a title: the generous and prompt sympathy of Englishmen cheered the last days of Beethoven. He died, loving and blessing them, for indeed, as I meant to have said above, though not to be turned aside one hair's breadth by any man's opinion from the purposes and methods which he alone, as is the case with all original genius, could appreciate till fulfilled, yet any intelligent sympathy with what he had done, brought the purest joy to his heart. He wept with pleasure when a stranger adapted words to his music that showed a true, full sense of its meaning, and in his delight at the conduct of the English Philharmonic Society his mind was roused to compose for them what he thought would be the greatest of all his Symphonies. It was with that music still growing in his mind that he took flight from the earth.

But when it is mentioned that the King of Prussia is to be present, we feel indignant that in this connection the old story is revived that he was a natural son of a King of Prussia. This story, one of those fictions by which vulgar minds think to enhance the lustre of genius, gave great pain to Beethoven. To him, as to all great souls, a mother was a patron saint, and those who thought to compensate him for the loss of a pure birthright by giving him a temporal King for a father, especially sinned when the great soul was that of Beethoven, who most of all men despised the dignities conferred by Man, and esteemed alone those from God and Nature. He took the pains, which he never deigned as to calumnies upon himself, to confute this against his mother by every means in his power, even publishing a formal certificate on the subject. Whoever believes in the law of inheritance will not for a moment need evidence that Beethoven sprang from no such stem. There was much talent in the family, even greatness in King Frederic and the Queen, the pupil of Leibnitz, but that very greatness how little beside that of Beethoven! how utterly uncongenial in all its elements with his! When we distill wine from grapes grown on thistles, then may we believe that this full fiery nature, this heart, all solemn enthusiasm and love, came of that narrow, cold, flinty race of which the Great Frederic is the finest type. There is baseness in reviving such a slander at this time.

The following is an interesting description of the Monument:

From the Nürnberg Kurier

"The first thing we saw in the *ateliér* of Burgschmiet was a colossal bust, (it is known that Burgschmiet has cast the statue of the great Master in two parts) which we, even had we met it by accident in any other place, should have instantly recognized as that of Beethoven; so decidedly does it express what is most characteristic in all the portraits we have seen of him.

"This head had an immediate magical effect upon me. It mastered me. I looked at the statue from all sides, sometimes admiring the position, sometimes the arrangement of drapery; looked at it from right and left, from all distances, but always returned to that one spot, where we, the imposing features full in our eye, had before us the front face in its whole effect.

"There is something Titanic—overwhelming, in that earnest countenance. The hair, as if bristling up with the awe of a mighty feeling, displays the commanding forehead in all its breadth and fairness, significant lines mark the cheeks, mouth and chin, and the eye looks straight forward, full of power and thought. We have scarcely ever seen in a statue such marked effect given to the eyes, and the neighboring lineaments of the cheeks and brows. The whole face bears witness of sublime earnestness and transcendent power. There is no sign of misanthropy or chagrin, but there is a certain air of manly defiance, that shows how this mighty soul, consented to what was grand and noble, could be chafed to indignation by social miseries, and the meannesses of daily life, how he could, when his own purposes demanded it, show himself stern, nay, inexorable where he had once been friendly.

"Yet the head as a whole makes a beneficent impression; we feel as much attracted as commanded; we understand that this soul was fitted only for what was noblest, but could find it no less in the tenderest than in the strongest impulses of nature, as the storm which shakes the great trees has murmurs and little streams of refreshment for the leaves and flowers. Nor can one who knows the history of the great Master resist sharing the sadness which filled him beneath the assaults of an unworthy world.

"He is represented in the act of stepping forward; his upper garment falls back. The artist seems to have seized him in the moment of composition, when one of his great ideas was upon him; one of those ideas that affright the unaccustomed ear like a formless chaos, but which, on acquaintance, reveal an unparalleled greatness and beauty. Such an idea he, himself dazzled by its first apparition, is striving to hold fast and embody. One hand holds the pencil, the other, which also carelessly holds his mantle, the score. He has paused in the very act of stepping forward, as if he feared that the slightest approach would banish the vision. For it is said that the slightest motion will affright such heavenly visitants, and they leave the enraptured mortal to sink back into a desert reality.

"Four bas-reliefs will adorn the pedestal of the Monument; one contains the usual dedication; the other three represent mythological music, church music, and that of the symphony. Symphony, a slender form, is playing on the lyre, with the face turned upward. Church Music is seated before an organ. As the one expresses aspiration in her whole aspect and attitude, so does the latter the chaste, pure element of holy tones, looking straight before her, a fair symbol of simple life and passion vanquished.

"But the pleasantest impression is made by the third figure, mythological, or, if you will, worldly music. She sits upon a fabulous animal with a human countenance, which looks up to her, listening, enchanted by the tones. Of singular expression is the look in which the two meet, one serene, enchanting, prodigal of joys, the other conquered, trembling with the pervasive sense of a strange power. It is a successful embodiment of Orphean fable. Each of the bas-reliefs is 6 feet in hight [*sic*], 4 in breadth. The statue of Beethoven is 12 feet in hight [*sic*] and will, with the pedestal, measure 27.

"As to the finish of the whole, it is excellent, and will add to the high reputation of Burgschmiet.—Matter has obeyed his will like a living instrument; the forms are finely discriminated and elegant; as a whole, the work makes a solemn impression, while there is much softness in details. We have mentioned above the great effect produced by the head of the statue; it may easily be seen why it was a first object not to interfere with this. But the drapery is fine, thrown as if in the act of changing position; the elegance of the bas-reliefs remarkable, especially in the bust of Symphony.

"It will be a noble festival, when the statue is unveiled and stands high in the air, beamed upon by the sun, in the Rhineland, that region so rich, so full of life. But when in that hour the men of Bonn hold high their heads proud of their Master, we in Nürnberg will also rejoice that we call Burgschmiet our own."

By what is said in the above of the great ideas coming upon Beethoven we are reminded of a passage in "Festus," that great poem, which we are delighted to see republished here at last, and from which we shall give extracts in a few days.

"Who can mistake great thoughts?
They seize upon the mind,—arrest and search,
And shake it—bow the tall soul as by wind—
Rush over it like rivers over reeds,
Which quaver in the current—turn as cold,
And pale, and voiceless; leaving in the brain
A rocking and a ringing,—glorious,
But momentary,—madness, might it last,
And close the soul with Heaven as with a seal!"

So come the thoughts of Beethoven; such a madness do their burning rays enkindle, the madness of poets and prophets, of the priests of Apollo, into whom the glories of a higher state descend while not strong enough immediately to place and upbear them. And while with many this madness is only the flash of lightning revealing for a moment the celestial hights [sic], with Beethoven the bolt falls

"To close the soul with Heaven as with a seal."

And by the blaze it enkindles we see the triumphs of Faith, Beauty and Love, all consummate—each tear of poor human eyes consecrated to a pearl, and the deepest groan of the breast tuned to the noblest concords of an everlasting Hallelujah.

✢

[September 3, 1845]

Study of the German Language

We wish to call attention to a lecture on this subject which Mr. Ertheiler proposes to deliver preparatory to the forming of classes. We have read it in manuscript and found in it a clear and judicious exposition of the objects and methods of this study.

Mr. Ertheiler gives good reasons, both as to mental culture and practical use, why the study is interesting and important to English and Americans, especially the latter. He alludes to some remarks by Professor Von Raumer as to the advantage of schools where the English and German languages shall be mutually taught, which may be read with advantage in this connection.

He points out the fallacy of the prevalent idea, that a foreign tongue can ever be learnt thoroughly by imitation and practice alone, without understanding of its theory and structure. In this, no less than other matters, he who knows not how to render a reason for the faith that is in him, will be incompetent to teach others, and often at a loss in his own practice when new cases come up. Indeed, without intercourse with natives, and even in the scenes and climate where a language has grown up, neither thorough acquaintance with its idioms and fine meanings, nor full command of it in speech and writing can be attained. But study of it theoretically and in good authors should precede, confirm, and intellectualize this familiar acquaintance.

Mr. Ertheiler points out different means which may be used according to the wants of different minds. We should infer from the lecture that he would be successful in practical teaching through patience, tact, and fixing the attention of the learner on leading points. This last is what most teachers fail in most, especially in the case of the German language, one with which it is easy to become acquainted if attention is directed to its roots, and the principles of its growth; very difficult, if taught by rote, and an accumulation of little rules, as it often is by teachers, either stupid and ignorant, or who, looking on this office merely as a stepping-stone to something better, a temporary means of earning a little money, pay no attention to thinking out a good method; and, by the unnecessary obstacles their carelessness leaves in the way, discourage and disgust the student and excite a prejudice against the study. This prejudice we greatly regret, knowing that many are thus deterred from learning what would most benefit them.

Especially here in New-York, there is no reason why every person, of any pretensions to a liberal education, should not be conversant with French, German and Italian, though the latter is at this moment of less importance. To the acquisition of the two former, motives of practical convenience and of expanding and refining the mind, prompt with equal force. Let the young ladies take from dress and Broadway some mornings for this purpose, the young clerks some evenings from frivolous amusements, and that darling aim of approaching the social standard of Europe would find itself far better served than now.

On those who here pause a moment to think Can I? Shall I? we would urge to listen to Mr. Ertheiler's lecture, and see whether he does not offer powerful inducements, and make plain the way.

To others of more earnest spirit we would say, In no way can you better refine and liberalize taste and fancy than by the comparisons to which you will be led between the gifts of the English and the German Muse. And the language itself, by its great pictorial power and closer representation of what is intimate and homely in life, will refresh you after intimacy with a literature and language where there is a far larger mixture of what is merely conventional, mere phrases, the barren civilities and tactics of literature. Of course this is not true of the productions of great minds any where; such steep anew the dry husk of words in Spirit till every one germinates and blossoms into fresh life. But the stock literature of England and America is amazingly conventional; so much so that you can predict paragraphs and chapters, if you but know the writer and the subject. The writer sleeps, and the reader yawns through the mechanical article or volume.

The Phrase-Book of Mr. Ertheiler has secured a favorable reception, from which his success as a teacher may be inferred.

In mentioning Tschulick, "the inventor of a successful type-composing machine," he says that the name has heretofore been incorrectly printed in The Tribune.

*

[December 11, 1845]

Instruction in the French Language

As every body, with any pretensions to culture, learns French here, the number of persons who offer themselves to teach that language is proportionately great. Still, among these, it must always be the fewest who can be of great value to the pupil. We are subject to such a throng of half-educated or uneducated foreigners, and, any one who speaks French, anyhow thinks it such an easy way of earning a few dollars, that the pupil is subject not only to learn of those who have no method or tact and then make his acquaintance with the language unnecessarily slow and difficult, but to be infected with vulgarities and *mauvais ton*. It is well known what high value the French, in common with all polished nations, set upon a correct and graceful use of their tongue in speech. This was the branch, as we are told, in which the Roman matrons were the special instructors of their sons. From others they learned the arts and bodily exercises, but, from their mothers, to use their native tongue with eloquence, majesty, and persuasive eloquence. To this great art Americans are so indifferent; indeed often appearing to prefer slang, cant phrases, and abrupt or uncouth expressions and intonations; that is not so surprising they do not know, when studying a foreign tongue, whether they have for their master an accomplished *littérateur* or a barber. As, however, the French do not share this indifference, and want of culture both of ear and taste, they are subject, through their carelessness, to become ridiculous the moment they set foot in the city, which is, to the would-be *elegants* and *lions* of New York, the Zion of their hopes, the tabernacle of their faith.

We have the honor of recommending to them a teacher, Prof. J. P. Edwards, who, we are assured by competent judges, will lead them into no such dangers, and has, beside, an excellent, simple method, "joined to extraordinary patience and courtesy as a teacher." A letter of recommendation which he brings hither, signed, among others, by Mr. E. G. Loring of Boston, W. W. Story, and James Russell Lowell, and which gives a more particular notice of his qualifications, may be seen at the counter of the Tribune office. Mr. Edwards is now at Lovejoy's Hotel, where he will remain for a few days, with the purpose of forming classes in New-York.

✻

[March 30, 1846]

Discoveries

Sometimes, as we meet people in the street, we catch a sentence from their lips that affords a clue to their history and habits of mind, and puts our own minds on quite a new course.

Yesterday, two female figures drew nigh upon the street, in whom we had only observed their tawdry showy style of dress, when, as they passed one observed to the other, in the tone of a person who has just made a discovery, "*I* think there is something very handsome in a fine child."

Poor woman! that seemed to have been the first time in her life that she had made the observation.—The charms of the human being, in that fresh and flowerlike age which is intended perpetually to refresh us in our riper, renovate us in our declining years, had never touched her heart, nor awakened for her the myriad thoughts and fancies that as naturally attend the sight of childhood as bees swarm to the blossoming bough. Instead of being to her the little angels and fairies, the embodied poesies which may keep green the humblest lot, they had been to her mere "torments" who "could never be kept still, or their faces clean."

How piteous is the loss of those who do not contemplate childhood in a spirit of holiness. The heavenly influence on their own minds of attention to cultivate each germ of great and good qualities, of avoiding the least act likely to injure, is lost, a loss dreary and piteous! for which no gain can compensate. But how unspeakably deplorable the petrifaction of those who look upon their little friends without any sympathy even, whose hearts are, by selfishness, worldliness and vanity, seared from all gentle instincts, who can no longer appreciate their spontaneous grace and glee, that eloquence in every look, motion and stammered word, those lively and incessant charms, over which the action of the lower motives, with which the social system is rife, may so soon draw a veil.

We can no longer speak thus of *all* children. On some, especially in cities, the inheritance of sin and deformity from bad parents fell too heavily, and encased at once the spark of Soul which God still doth not refuse in such instances, in a careful, knowing, sensual mask. Such are never, in fact, children at all. But the rudest little cubs that are free from taint and show the affinities with Nature and the Soul, are still young and flexible, and rich in gleams of the loveliness to the hoped from perfected human nature.

It is sad that all men do not feel these things. It is sad that they wilfully renounce so large a part of their heritage and go forth to buy filtered water, while the fountain is gushing freshly beside the door of their own huts. As with the charms of children, so with other things. They do not know that the sunset is worth seeing every night, and the shows of the forest better than those of the theatre, and the work of bees and beetles more instructive, if scanned with care, than the Lyceum lecture. The cheap knowledge, the cheap joys, that are spread before every one, they cast aside, in search of an uncertain and feverish joy. We did, indeed, hear our man say that he could not possibly be deprived of his pleasures, since he could always, even were his abode in the narrowest lane, have a blanket of sky above his head, where he could see the clouds pass and the stars glitter. But men in general remain unaware that

> "Life's best joys are nearest us,
> Lie close about our feet."

For them the light dresses all objects in endless novelty, the rose glows, domestic love smiles, and childhood gives out with sportive freedom its oracles in vain. That woman had seen beauty in gay shawls, in teacups, in carpets, but only of late had she discovered that "there was something beautiful in a fine child." Poor human nature! thou must have been changed at nurse by a mad demon at some time, and strangely maltreated to have such blind and rickety intervals as come upon thee every now and then.

*

[April 1, 1846]

Farewell

Farewell to New York City, where twenty months have presented me with a richer and more varied exercise for thought and life than twenty years could in any other part of these United States.

It is the common remark about New-York that it has, at least, nothing petty or provincial in its methods and habits. The place is large enough; there is room enough and occupation enough for men to have no need or excuse for small cavils or scrutinies. A person who is independent and knows what he wants, may lead his proper life here unimpeded by others.

Vice and Crime, if flagrant and frequent, are less thickly coated by Hypocrisy than elsewhere. The air comes sometimes to the most infected subjects.

New-York is the focus, the point where American and European interests converge. There is no topic of general interest to men that will not betimes be brought before the thinker by the quick turning of the wheel.

Too quick that revolution, some object. Life rushes wide and free, but *too fast;* yet it is in the power of every one to avert from himself the evil that accompanies the good. He must build for his study, as did the German poet, a house beneath the bridge, and, then, all that passes above and by him will be heard and seen, but he will not be carried away with it.

Earlier views have been confirmed and many new ones opened. On two great leadings,—the superlative importance of promoting National Education by hightening [*sic*] and deepening the cultivation of individual minds, and the part which is assigned to Woman in the next stage of human progress in this country, where most important achievements are to be effected, I have received much encouragement, much instruction, and the fairest hopes of more.

On various subjects of minor importance, no less than these, I hope for good results from observation with my own eyes of Life in the Old World, and to bring home some packages of seed for Life in the New.

These words I address to my friends, for I feel that I have some. The degree of sympathetic response to the thoughts and suggestions I have offered through the columns of this paper has indeed surprised me, conscious as I am of a natural and acquired aloofness from many, if not most, popular tendencies of my time and place. It has greatly encouraged me, for none can sympathize with thoughts like mine who are permanently ensnared in the meshes of sect or party; none who prefer the formation and advancement of mere opinions to the free pursuit of Truth. I see, surely, that the topmost bubble or sparkle of the cup is no voucher for the nature of its contents throughout and shall, in future, feel that in our age, nobler in that respect than most of the preceding, each sincere and fervent act or word is secure, not only of a final, but a speedy, response.

I go to behold the wonders of art, and the temples of old religion. But I shall see no forms of beauty and majesty beyond what my Country is capable of producing in myriad variety, if she has but the soul to will it; no temple to compare with what she might erect in the Ages, if the catchword of the time, a sense of DIVINE ORDER, should become, no more a mere word or effigy, but a deeply rooted and pregnant Idea in her life. Beneath the light of a hope that this may be, I ask of my friends once more a kind Farewell.

✻

[August 1, 1846]

Notes

Preface
1. Francis Nicoll Zabriskie, *Greeley* (New York: Funk and Wagnalls, 1890), 123.

1. Introducing Margaret Fuller
1. Ralph Waldo Emerson, "Reminiscences," in *Love Letters of Margaret Fuller,* ed. Julia Ward Howe (New York: Appleton, 1903), 197; Edgar Allan Poe, "The Literati of New York City: Sarah Margaret Fuller," 1846, reprint in *Essays and Reviews* (New York: Literary Classics, 1978), 173; Marie Urbanski, *Margaret Fuller's Woman in the Nineteenth Century: A Literary Study of Form and Content, of Sources and Influence* (Westport, Conn.: Greenwood, 1980), 3.
2. Beman Brockway, *Fifty Years in Journalism* (Watertown, Mass., 1891), 157.
3. [Horace Greeley], "Prospectus for the Year 1845," *New York Tribune,* 16 November 1844; Horace Greeley, *Recollections of a Busy Life* (1868; reprint, New York: Arno, 1970), 176; Greeley quoted in Ralph Waldo Emerson, W. H. Channing, and J. F. Clarke, eds., *Memoirs of Margaret Fuller Ossoli* (1852; reprint, Boston: Roberts, 1884), 2: 152.
4. Joel Myerson, *Margaret Fuller: A Descriptive Bibliography* (Pittsburgh: University of Pittsburgh Press, 1978); Horace Greeley, Letter to Schuyler Colfax, 20 February 1846, Horace Greeley Papers, New York Public Library; *Graham's Magazine* quoted by Joel Myerson, *Margaret Fuller: An Annotated Secondary Bibliography* (New York: Burt Franklin, 1977), 15.
5. Margaret Fuller, "Farewell," *New York Tribune* 1 August 1845; Robert N. Hudspeth noted, "A century of scholarship, speculation, and gossip has never been wholly able to untangle the events" surrounding Fuller's relationship with Giovanni Angelo Ossoli. No one has been able to locate a marriage certificate, and Fuller only wrote home that she had married when it was clear that she was going to have a baby (introduction to *The Letters of Margaret Fuller,* ed. Robert N. Hudspeth, Ithaca, N.Y.: Cornell University Press, 1983, 1: 47). Fuller biographies covering the New York period include Margaret Vanderharr Allen, *The Achievement of Margaret Fuller* (University Park: Pennsylvania State University Press, 1979); Katharine Anthony, *Margaret Fuller* (New York: Harcourt, Brace and Harve, 1920); Margaret Bell, *Margaret Fuller* (1930; reprint, Freeport, N.Y.: Books for Free Libraries Press, 1971); Paula Blanchard, *Margaret Fuller* (New York: Delacorte, 1978); Arthur W. Brown, *Margaret Fuller* (New York: Twayne, 1964); Bell Gale Chevigny, *The Woman and the Myth: Margaret Fuller's Life and Writings* (Old Westbury, N.Y.: Feminist Press, 1976); Faith Chipperfield, *In Quest of Love: The Life*

and Death of Margaret Fuller (New York: Coward-McCann, 1957); Thomas Wentworth Higginson, *Margaret Fuller Ossoli* (1884; reprint, New York: Haskell House, 1968); Constance Pentu, "Fuller's Folly: The Eccentric World of Margaret Fuller and the Greeleys," master's thesis, Columbia University, 1960; Amy Slater, *In Search of Margaret Fuller: A Biography* (New York: Delacorte, 1978); Madeleine B. Stern, *The Life of Margaret Fuller* (New York: Putnam, 1946); Mason Wade, *Margaret Fuller: Whetstone of Genius* (New York: Viking, 1940).

6. Margaret Fuller Ossoli, *Woman in the Nineteenth Century and Kindred Papers* (Boston: Jewett, 1855); Margaret Fuller, "The Great Lawsuit," in *Norton Anthology of American Literature*, ed. Ronald Gottesman et al. (New York: Norton, 1979), 1: 1384–1425; Elizabeth Cady Stanton, Susan B. Anthony, and Mitilda Gage, *History of Woman Suffrage* (1889; reprint, New York: Source Book Press, 1970), 801.

7. F. O. Matthiessen, *American Renaissance: Art and Expression in the Age of Emerson and Whitman* (New York: Oxford University Press, 1941); Lurton Ingersoll, *The Life of Horace Greeley* (Chicago: Union, 1873). Fuller bibliographer Joel Myerson has commented, "The most worked over area of Fuller scholarship is that of her published criticism" (introduction to *Critical Essays on Margaret Fuller* (Boston: G. K. Hall, 1980), xv. The many studies of Fuller's literary criticism include Brown, *Fuller;* Wade, *Fuller;* Allen, *Achievement;* Henry L. Golemba, "The Balanced View in Margaret Fuller's Literary Criticism," Ph.D. diss., University of Washington, Seattle, 1971; Perry Miller, *Margaret Fuller: An American Romantic* (Garden City, N.Y.: Anchor, 1963); Patrick Frederick Berger, "Margaret Fuller: Critical Realist as Seen in Her Works," Ph.D. diss., Saint Louis University, 1972; Urbanski, *Fuller's Woman;* Myerson, *Critical Essays;* Barbara Welter, *Dimity Convictions: The American Woman in the Nineteenth Century* (Athens: Ohio University Press, 1976); Karen Ann Szymanski, "Margaret Fuller: The New York Years," Ph.D. diss., Syracuse University, 1980; Susan Phinney Conrad, *Perish the Thought: Intellectual Women in Romantic America, 1830–1860* (New York: Oxford University Press, 1976); Russell E. Durning, *Margaret Fuller: Citizen of the World* (Heidelberg, Germany: Carl Winter, Universitätsverlag, 1969); Wilma R. Ebbitt, "The Critical Essays of Margaret Fuller from the New York 'Tribune,' with Introduction and Notes," Ph.D. diss., Boston University, 1944; Francis M. Fay, "Margaret Fuller," Ph.D. diss., St. John's University, 1951.

8. See Maurine Beasley and Sheila Gibbons, *Women in Media: A Documentary Source Book* (Washington, D.C.: Women's Institute for Freedom of the Press, 1979); Barbara Belford, *Brilliant Bylines* (New York: Columbia University Press, 1986).

9. Robert N. Hudspeth, ed., preface to *Letters,* 4: 7.

10. For more discussion of the Greeley-Fuller friendship, see Szymanski, "New York Years"; Erik S. Lunde, *Greeley* (Boston: Twayne, 1981); Glyndon Garlock Van Deusen, *Horace Greeley: Nineteenth-Century Crusader* (Philadelphia: University of Pennsylvania Press, 1953); and Henry Luther Stoddard, *Horace Greeley: Printer, Editor, Crusader* (New York: Putnam, 1946). For mention of the possibility that Greeley fired Fuller, see Anthony, *Fuller;* Joseph Jay Deiss, *The Roman Years of Margaret Fuller* (New York:

Crowell, 1969); Bernard DeVoto, *The Year of Decision* (Boston: Little, Brown, 1943); Belford, *Brilliant Bylines*.

11. Amy Clampitt, "Margaret Fuller, 1847," *The New Yorker,* 8 September 1986, 38; William Harlan Hale, *Horace Greeley, Voice of the People* (New York: Harper, 1950), 115.
12. Margaret Fuller, *Letters,* 3: 269.
13. Nineteenth-century editions of Fuller's work include Margaret Fuller, *Papers on Literature and Art* (New York: Wiley and Putnam, 1846); Emerson et al., *Memoirs;* Margaret Fuller, *Woman in the Nineteenth Century and Kindred Papers* (Boston: Jewett, 1855); and *Art, Literature and the Drama* (Boston: Brown, Taggard and Chase, 1860). Twentieth-century books containing reprints of Fuller essays include Margaret Fuller, *The Writings of Margaret Fuller,* ed. Mason Wade (New York: Viking, 1941); Miller, *Margaret Fuller;* Chevigny, *Woman and the Myth;* and Margaret Fuller, *Margaret Fuller: Essays on American Life and Letters,* ed. Joel Myerson (New Haven, Conn.: College and University Press, 1978).
14. Four articles printed here have appeared only in the *New York Tribune* itself and in Margaret Fuller, *Life without and Life Within,* ed. Arthur B. Fuller (Boston: Roberts, 1874). Arthur published this volume ten years after his sister's death. Four articles printed here have appeared only in the *Tribune* and in *Woman in the Nineteenth Century and Kindred Papers,* also edited by Arthur Fuller.
15. Edwin L. Godkin, *Life and Letters,* ed. Rollo Ogden (New York: Macmillan, 1907), 167; Brockway, *Fifty Years,* 142.
16. Emerson letter in *The Correspondence of Emerson and Carlyle,* ed. Joseph Slater (New York: Columbia University Press, 1964), 499; Frederic Hudson, *Journalism in the United States 1690 to 1872* (New York: Harper, 1873), 525; Ingersoll, *Greeley,* 129. For more discussion of the *Tribune*'s influence, see Frank Luther Mott, *American Journalism* (New York: Macmillan, 1962); George Brown Tindall, *America: A Narrative History* (New York: Norton, 1984). For information on the influence of the *Tribune*'s essays, see Higginson, *Ossoli;* Warren Bovee, "Horace Greeley and Social Responsibility," *Journalism Quarterly* 63 (1986): 251–59; Bernard A. Weisberger, *The American Newspaperman* (Chicago: University of Chicago Press, 1961); Ingersoll, *Greeley;* Zabriskie, *Greeley;* Godkin, *Life and Letters;* Brockway, *Fifty Years;* Thomas L. Nichols, *Forty Years of American Life,* 2 vols. (1864; reprint, New York: Johnson, 1969); Stoddard, *Greeley;* Hudson, *Journalism.*
17. James Parton, *The Life of Horace Greeley, Editor of the New York Tribune* (New York: Mason, 1855), 263. For more information on the *Tribune* in the 1840s, see Zabriskie, *Greeley;* Hudson, *Journalism;* Hale, *Greeley.*
18. For example, see Higginson, *Ossoli,* 205; Ebbitt, "Critical Essays," v; Anthony, *Fuller,* 119.
19. See Van Deusen, *Greeley;* Hale, *Greeley;* Hudson, *Journalism;* Parton, *Greeley;* Joseph Jay Rubin, *The Historic Whitman* (University Park: Pennsylvania State University Press, 1973), 125.
20. Hudson, *Journalism.*
21. Fuller, *Writings,* 574; Joseph Slater, *Correspondence,* 407; Fuller, *Letters,* 4: 58.
22. The Thursday, 5 January 1854 edition was eight pages long. The Monday, 30 January

1854 edition was also eight pages long. The Friday, 8 April 1854 edition was also eight pages. New York Tribune Association, Printed Bank Checks; Hudson, *Journalism,* 526.

23. For more information on the fire and the newspaper's offices, see Stoddard, *Greeley,* 62; *The New York Tribune: A Sketch of Its History* (New York: 1883, microfilm at New York Public Library, no publisher or author mentioned on document itself or in library's card catalog); Phillip Hone, *The Diary of Philip Hone, 1828–1851,* vol. 1 (New York, 1927), 726; Zabriskie, *Greeley,* 102; Royal Cortissoz, *The New York Tribune: Incidents and Personalities in Its History* (New York: New York Tribune, 1923). For information on the business side of the newspaper, see Horace Greeley's Letter to B. F. Ransom, 13 November 1841, Letter to O. A. Bowe, 30 March 1842, and Letter to Moses A. Cortland, 14 April 1845, Horace Greeley Papers, New York Public Library; Fred C. Shapiro, "The Life and Death of a Great Newspaper," *American Heritage* 18 (1967): 97–112; Michael Schudson, *Discovering the News* (New York: Basic Books, 1978), 20.

24. Fuller was never actually in residence at Brook Farm. Ironically, only one building still stands at the site of Brook Farm in what is now West Roxbury, Mass. That is the Margaret Fuller House. See Henry L. Golemba, *George Ripley* (New York: Twayne, 1977); Golemba, "Balanced View"; Marvin Pave, "Landmark Decays as Agencies Argue," *Boston Globe,* 13 March 1985, 1, 24.

25. Van Deusen, *Greeley;* Lunde, *Greeley;* Stoddard, *Greeley;* Ingersoll, *Greeley;* Sidney Kobre, *Development of American Journalism* (Dubuque, Iowa: Brown, 1969); Mott, *American Journalism;* John Russell Young, *Men and Memories,* ed. May D. Russell Young, 2 vols (New York: Neeley, 1901), 1: 214; Godkin, *Life and Letters,* 167; Ingersoll, *Greeley;* Stoddard, *Greeley.*

26. Brockway, *Fifty Years,* 141; Assignment Log, *New York Tribune* City Department, 1867–68, Special Collections, New York Public Library; Greeley, *Recollections,* 142; Zabriskie, *Greeley.*

27. Zabriskie, *Greeley,* 329–30; Ingersoll, *Greeley,* 130; *Webster's American Biographies* (Springfield, Mass.: Merriam, 1978); Shapiro, "Life and Death," 100. Van Deusen, *Greeley,* says 1846. *Webster's American Biographies* says 1847.

28. Ingersoll, *Greeley;* Solon Robinson, *Hot Corn* (New York: DeWitt and Davenport, 1853).

29. Lunde, *Greeley; National Cyclopedia of American Biography,* 62 vols. (1891; reprint, Clifton, N.J.: White, 1967).

30. Zabriskie, *Greeley;* Mott, *American Journalism;* Caroline Healey Dall, *Margaret and Her Friends* (1895; reprint, New York: Arno, 1972); Golemba, *Ripley.*

31. Parton, *Greeley;* Greeley, *Recollections,* 138; Zabriskie, *Greeley;* Hale, *Greeley;* Stoddard, *Greeley;* and Ingersoll, *Greeley.*

32. [Horace Greeley], "Prospectus of the Semi-Weekly Tribune," *New York Tribune,* 15 April 1845 and 18 April 1845. Hale, *Greeley,* says that by 1845, when Fuller worked at the paper, the editorial staff totaled thirty. However, all other available evidence points to a much smaller staff. Hale's number may include printers as well as writers.

For more information on the size of staffs at New York newspapers in the 1840s, see "The Newspaper Writers of New York," *New York Herald,* 9 November 1842; Shapiro, "Life and Death," 98; *The New York Tribune: A Sketch,* 6; and Rubin, *Historic Whitman,* 105.

33. One can be sure Snow was working for Greeley in 1843 because in a letter to H. Hubbard (6 June 1843, Horace Greeley Papers, New York Public Library) Greeley mentions proofreading Hubbard's manuscript with "Mr. Snow." *The New York Tribune: A Sketch;* Greeley, *Recollections,* 139.

34. Allen Johnson and Dumas Malone, eds., *Dictionary of American Biography* (New York: Scribner, 1928–36), 5: 112; Bayard Taylor, *Life and Letters,* ed. Marie Hansen-Taylor and Horace Scudder (Boston: Houghton, Mifflin, 1884), 1: 114; *National Cyclopedia,* 3: 319.

35. Robert N. Hudspeth, *Ellery Channing* (New York: Twayne, 1973); Emerson, *The Letters of Ralph Waldo Emerson* (New York: Columbia University Press, 1939), 3: 268; Fuller, *Letters,* 4: 44.

36. Horace Greeley, Letter to Moses A. Cortland, 14 April 1845; Greeley, *Recollections,* 140; *National Cyclopedia,* 3: 457.

2. A Journalist at the *Tribune,* 1844–1846

1. Weisberger, *American Newspaperman,* 104; Van Deusen, *Greeley,* 156; Poe, "Literati," 1172; John S. Hart, *The Female Prose Writers of America* (Philadelphia: E. H. Butler, 1852), 237; Joseph Slater, *Correspondence,* 407; Fuller, *Letters,* 4: 58.
2. Margaret Fuller, "Monument to Goethe," *New York Tribune,* 16 December, 1844; Fuller, "Some Items of Foreign Gossip," *New York Tribune,* 2 August 1845.
3. Parton, *Greeley,* 254.
4. The author does not know C. D. S.'s identity.
5. [Horace Greeley], "Magnificent Family Paper," *New York Tribune,* 20 November 1845.
6. Greeley quoted by Hale, *Greeley,* 66; Mott, *American Journalism,* 272.
7. Van Deusen, *Greeley;* "Whigs of New York!" *New York Tribune,* 16 December 1844.
8. [Horace Greeley], "The Texas Iniquity," *New York Tribune,* 9 December 1844; "Our Country, Right or Wrong," *New York Tribune,* 12 May 1846.
9. "The Frauds by Which Polk Was Elected," *New York Tribune,* 17 December 1844; [Horace Greeley], "Texas Matters," *New York Tribune,* 30 July 1845; "Texas Iniquity."
10. "Oregon and War," *New York Tribune,* 13 November 1845; "Oregon and the Chances of War," *New York Tribune,* 22 December 1845; "The Oregon Boundary Settled," *New York Tribune,* 11 June 1846.
11. "A Cruise to Lake Okachobee [sic]," *New York Tribune,* 27 December 1844.
12. "Massachusetts and South Carolina," *New York Tribune,* 10 December 1844; "Massachusetts and South Carolina," *New York Tribune,* 14 December 1844.
13. "Small Business," *New York Tribune,* 6 January 1846; Frederick Douglass, "An American Slave in Great Britain," *New York Tribune,* 2 February 1846.
14. James Grossman, *James Fenimore Cooper* (New York: William Sloane, 1949), 7–8, 197–200.

15. "The Pro and Con of Anti-Rent," *New York Tribune,* 6 September 1845.
16. "The Manorial Tenures," *New York Tribune,* 30 March 1846.
17. "City Items," *New York Tribune,* 2 June 1845.
18. "Destructive Fire—'Dickens Place' Burnt Out," *New York Tribune,* 13 June 1845.
19. "The Fire," *New York Tribune,* 6 February 1845.
20. Grossman, *Cooper,* 5–7, 168–70, 187–88.
21. "A High-Handed Outrage!" *New York Tribune,* 6 March 1846.
22. "Shocking," *New York Tribune,* 3 December 1844; "Lesson of a Peach Skin," *New York Tribune,* 3 December 1844.
23. "Court of Sessions," *New York Tribune,* 24 January 1845.
24. "Aesthetics of Dress: A Case of Hats," *New York Tribune,* 6 February 1845.
25. "Conversational Meetings of the Americas Institute," *New York Tribune,* 17 January 1845.
26. "Oregon and California," *New York Tribune,* 24 June 1845. See Dale Van Every, *The Final Challenge* (New York: William Morrow, 1964), 345; E. N. Feltskog, *The Oregon Trail* (Madison: University of Wisconsin Press, 1969), 24a; DeVoto, *Year of Decision,* 44.
27. For example, see *New York Tribune,* 7 December 1844.
28. *New York Tribune,* 16 December 1844.
29. Ads praising Fuller's work include [Greeley], "Magnificent"; [Greeley], "Prospectus of the Semi-weekly Tribune." Letters with references to the need for Fuller at the *Tribune* include Fuller, *Letters,* 4: 118, 120, 138, 179, 192; Fuller, *Love Letters,* 110.
30. For example, see "Vestiges of the Natural History of Creation," *New York Tribune,* 25 March 1845.
31. "Mary Howitt's Picture and Verse Book," *New York Tribune,* 24 December 1844. The four articles bylined "F" are "Hahnemann on Chronic Diseases," *New York Tribune,* 27 May 1845; "Rokitansky's Pathology" book review of "A Treatise on Pathological Anatomy," *New York Tribune,* 9 June 1845; "Dwellings for the Industrious Poor," 26 February 1846; "Short Elementary Treatise on Homeopathy," *New York Tribune,* 20 September 1845.
32. For example, see a two-column piece, "The Diary of Lady Willoughby," *New York Tribune,* 26 April 1845. It begins with three paragraphs of introduction followed by a long excerpt from the book. Fuller did produce work of this type. "Mrs. Child's Letters" (*New York Tribune,* 10 May 1845) begins with a brief starred introduction followed by two and a half columns of quotes from the book.
33. For instance, see "The Invention of a Type Composing Machine" (*New York Tribune,* 4 November 1845), and "The German Catholics in Baden" (*New York Tribune,* 1 November 1845). Both are translations from the *Schnellpost.*
34. Charles T. Congdon, "Reminiscences," in *Love Letters,* 225; Greeley quoted in Emerson et al., *Memoirs,* 2: 153.
35. Zabriskie, *Greeley,* 326; Stoddard, *Greeley,* 98; Ishbel Ross, *Ladies of the Press* (New York: Harper, 1936), 400–401.
36. Greeley, *Recollections,* 177; Greeley quoted by Emerson et al., *Memoirs,* 2: 155; Greeley, "Her *Tribune* Writing and Concern for Prostitutes," in Chevigny, *Woman and the Myth,* 305.

In one letter Fuller does complain of having violent headaches (*Love Letters*, 75). Emerson also wrote of her headaches (ibid., 206).

37. Brockway, *Fifty Years*, 152; Junius Henri Browne, "Horace Greeley," *Harper's New Monthly Magazine*, April 1873, 740.
38. Zabriskie, *Greeley*; Greeley, Letter to Schuyler Colfax, 1 August 1844, Letter to B. F. Ransom, 2 September 1843, Horace Greeley Papers, New York Public Library; *The New York Tribune: A Sketch*.
39. Brockway, *Fifty Years*, 152–53, 148; Browne, "Greeley," 735; Emerson, *Letters*, 3: 19; Charles Anderson Dana, "Greeley as a Journalist," in *A Library of American Literature*, ed. E. C. Stedman and Ellen M. Hutchinson (New York: Webster, 1889–90), 7: 449. For more information about Greeley's personality, see Hale, *Greeley*; Lunde, *Greeley*; Shapiro, "Life and Death"; Stoddard, *Greeley*.
40. Greeley quoted by Don Carlos Seitz, *Horace Greeley: Founder of the New York Tribune* (1926; reprint, New York: AMS, 1970), 99; Greeley quoted by Hale, *Greeley*, 69; and Ripley quoted by Golemba, *Ripley*, 117.
41. Margaret Fuller, "Darkness Visible," *New York Tribune*, 4 March 1846.
42. Fuller, *Letters*, 3: 269, 4: 46. The following letters show Fuller's preoccupation with the book manuscript: Fuller, *Letters*, 3: 256; Fuller quoted by Higginson, *Ossoli*, 212; Fuller, *Writings*, 574. For more information about the romance with Nathan, see *Love Letters* and the extensive coverage in most of the Fuller biographies.
43. Fuller, *Writings*, 571, 567; Fuller, *Letters*, 3: 202; Higginson, *Ossoli*, 211.
44. Foolscap is a sheet of 13-by-16-inch writing paper.
45. Minion is a type size. It refers to seven-point type.
46. Brockway, *Fifty Years*, 146; Parton, *Greeley*; Nichols, *Forty Years*, 1: 264.
47. Dana, "Greeley as a Journalist," 7: 449; Zabriskie, *Greeley*, 118, 324; Curtis quoted by Stoddard, *Greeley*, 69.
48. Margaret Fuller's friend James Freeman Clarke told her he thought working at the *Tribune* had improved her style (*The Letters of James Freeman Clarke to Margaret Fuller*, ed. John Wesley Thomas (Hamburg, Germany: Cram, deGruyter, 1957), 145. Her writing style has been the subject of extensive literary study. Many scholars have examined her writing style and found it ponderous and preachy, but filled with brilliant ideas. See Allen, *Achievement*; Elizabeth Hardwick, "The Genius of Margaret Fuller," *New York Review of Books*, 4 April 1986, 14–22; Ann Douglas, *The Feminization of American Culture* (New York: Knopf, 1977). Urbanski (*Fuller's Woman*) argued that scholars have underrated Fuller's writing style because they relied too heavily on hostile comments by Ralph Waldo Emerson. Emerson, for instance, told Carlyle in 1843, "She—Margaret Fuller, is an admirable person, whose writing gives feeble account of her" (Joseph Slater, *Correspondence*, 355). At any rate, scholars agree that, under Greeley's tutelage, Margaret Fuller's style became more direct and open.
49. Greeley, "Death of Margaret Fuller," *New York Tribune*, 23 July 1850; Greeley, quoted by Emerson et al., *Memoirs*, 2: 154.
50. Greeley, "Her *Tribune* Writing," 306. See Fuller, *Letters*, 3: 256; Fuller, "Darkness Visible"; and Fuller, *Writings*, 567.

51. Greeley, Letter to H. Hubbard, 12 April 1844, Horace Greeley Papers, New York Public Library; J. S. Bradshaw, "To Correspondents—Horace Greeley," *Journalism Quarterly* 81 (1981): 644–46, 673; Catherine C. Mitchell, "Greeley as Journalism Teacher: 'Give Us Facts, Occurrences,'" *Journalism Educator* 44:3 (1989): 16–19.
52. [Horace Greeley], "To Correspondents," *New York Tribune,* 10 February 1845; Greeley, Letter to H. Hubbard, 24 June 1843, Horace Greeley Papers, New York Public Library.
53. [Greeley], "To Correspondents," 10 February 1845.
54. Ibid.; Greeley, Letter to H. Hubbard, 24 June 1843.
55. Greeley, Letter to H. Hubbard, 12 April 1844, Letter to H. Hubbard, 26 August 1843, Horace Greeley Papers, New York Public Library.
56. For Fuller's praises of Greeley, see Fuller, *Letters,* 4: 40, 46, 56, 58, and 128. For Fuller's comments on Greeley's defects, see Fuller, *Letters,* 3: 256, 4: 46, 56. Fuller was not exceptional in calling Greeley a slattern. His clothing was famous. In his 1852 book, *Crayon Sketches and Off-Hand Takings* ([Boston: Stacy and Richardson, 1852], 31), George W. Bungay described Greeley's "careless, slipshod, slovenly way of dressing." He said this lack of "dignity" and "dandyism" made the editor "popular with the masses" rather than "a great favorite with uppercrustdom." His coworker, Junius Browne, conceded Greeley wore shabby clothes, but argued that "the illustrious editor was simply careless of his attire, though fastidiously neat" ("Greeley," 737).
57. For Fuller's comments on her work at the *Tribune,* see Fuller, *Letters,* 3: 256, 4: 40, 138; letter reprinted in Higginson, *Ossoli,* 212; and Fuller, "Farewell."
58. [Greeley], "Prospectus for the Year 1845"; letter quoted by Szymanski, "New York Years," 139; Greeley quoted by Emerson et al., *Memoirs,* 2: 159; Greeley, "Her *Tribune* Writings," 306; Greeley letter reprinted in Higginson, *Ossoli,* 212; Greeley, *Recollections,* 191.
59. Horace Greeley, Letter to Sarah J. Hale, 3 September 1850, Horace Greeley Papers, New York Public Library; Greeley, quoted by Emerson et al., *Memoirs,* 2: 156; Ingersoll, *Greeley,* 578.
60. Greeley letter in Emerson, *Letters,* 4: 225n; Greeley, "Death"; Greeley, Letter to Sarah J. Hale, 3 September 1850.
61. Greeley, quoted by Emerson et al., *Memoirs,* 2: 156–57.
62. See Barbara Harris, *Beyond Her Sphere: Women and the Professions in American History* (Westport, Conn.: Greenwood, 1978); Regina Morantz-Sanchez, *Sympathy and Science: Women Physicians in American Medicine* (New York: Oxford University Press, 1985); Barbara Welter, "The Cult of True Womanhood," in *Our American Sisters: Women in American Thought and Life,* ed. Jean E. Friedman and William G. Shade (Boston: Allyn and Bacon, 1973); Gerda Lerner, "The Lady and the Mill Girl: Changes in the Status of Women in the Age of Jackson," in *Our American Sisters.*
63. Duncan Crow, *The Victorian Woman* (New York: Stein and Day, 1972); Fuller, *Letters;* Emerson, "Reminiscences," 200.
64. Conrad, *Perish the Thought;* Susan M. Coultrap-McQuin, "Why Their Success? Some Observations on Publishing by Popular Nineteenth-Century Women Writers." *Legacy* 1:2

(1984): 8–9; Welter, "Cult"; Catherine Clinton, *The Other Civil War* (New York: Hill and Wang, 1984).

65. Nathaniel Hawthorne, quoted by Nina Baym, "Rewriting the Scribbling Women," *Legacy* 2:2 (1985): 4; Fuller quoted by Conrad, *Perish the Thought,* 86. See also Douglas, *Feminization.*

66. Clinton, *Other Civil War;* Carroll Smith-Rosenberg, "Beauty, the Beast, and the Militant Woman: A Case Study in Sex Roles and Social Stress in Jacksonian America," *American Quarterly* 23 (1971): 562–84; Jane Grey Swisshelm, *Half a Century* (1880; reprint, New York: Source Book Press, 1970), 92.

67. Sarah J. Hale, *Woman's Record; or, Sketches of All Distinguished Women from "the Beginning" till A.D. 1850* (New York: Harper, 1853), 667.

68. Sandra M. Gilbert and Susan Gubar, eds, *Norton Anthology of Literature by Women* (New York: Norton, 1985), 294; Stanton et al., *Woman Suffrage,* 1: 802; Catherine C. Mitchell, "Horace Greeley's Star: Margaret Fuller's New York *Tribune* Journalism, 1844–1846," Ph.D. diss., University of Tennessee, Knoxville, 1987; Marion Marzolf, *Up from the Footnote: A History of Women Journalists* (New York: Hastings, 1977); Ira L. Baker, "Elizabeth Timothy: America's First Woman Editor," *Journalism Quarterly* 54 (1977): 280–85; Mary Ann Yodelis Smith, "Research Retrospective: Feminism and the Media." *Communication Research* 9 (1982): 145–60.

69. Fuller, *Letters,* 3: 229, 256; Joseph Slater, *Correspondence,* 407; Evart A. Duyckinck and George L. Duyckinck, *Cyclopedia of American Literature* (New York: Scribner, 1856), I: 526; Greeley, *Recollections;* Zabriskie, *Greeley;* Wade, *Fuller;* Richard Kluger, *The Paper: The Life and Death of the New York Herald Tribune* (New York: Knopf, 1986).

70. Fuller, *Letters,* 4: 196, 4: 178–79, 4: 187; Greeley quoted by Stoddard, *Greeley,* 116; Swisshelm, *Half a Century.*

71. Chevigny, *Woman and the Myth;* Madelon Golden Schilpp and Sharon Murphy, *Great Women of the Press* (Carbondale: Southern Illinois University Press, 1983); Dall, *Margaret,* 9.

72. Mitchell, "Greeley's Star"; *Trends in the American Economy in the Nineteenth Century* (Princeton N.J.: Princeton University Press, 1960); Douglas T. Miller, *Then Was the Future: The North in the Age of Jackson, 1815–1850* (New York: Knopf, 1973).

73. *A History of the 100 Years of Unions on the New York Tribune* (New York: Herald Tribune Unit of the Newspaper Guild of New York, Local 3, American Newspaper Guild, 1941); Rubin, *Historic Whitman;* Mott, *American Journalism,* 270; William Hale, *Greeley;* Taylor, *Life and Letters;* and Stoddard, *Greeley.*

74. Ross, *Ladies;* Patricia G. Holland, "Lydia Maria Child as a Nineteenth-Century Professional Author," *Studies in the American Renaissance* (1981): 157–67; Rubin, *Historic Whitman;* Edward T. James, Janet Wilson James, and Paul S. Boyer, eds., *Notable American Women* (Cambridge, Mass.: Belknap, 1971).

75. Mitchell, "Greeley's Star"; *Trends.* Also see Stanley Lebergott, *The Americans: An Economic Record* (New York: Norton, 1984); Stanley Lebergott, *Manpower and Economic Growth* (New York: McGraw-Hill, 1964); Susan Previant Lee and Peter Passall, *A New Economic View of American History* (New York: Norton, 1979); Jeffrey G. Williamson and

Peter H. Lindert, *American Inequality: A Macroeconomic History* (New York: Academic Press, 1980).

76. Swisshelm, *Half a Century*, 91. For instance, see Lydia Maria Child, "Kindness to Criminals—the Prison Association," *New York Tribune*, 10 December 1844.
77. For example, A. R., "Foreign Correspondence of the Tribune: Letter from France," *New York Tribune*, 21 March 1845; Altimira, "How the Poor Live," *New York Tribune*, 15 March 1845; A. D. Dakin, "Memorial to A. Fitch," *New York Tribune*, 13 March 1845.
78. Nichols, *Forty Years*, 1: 330.
79. Greeley letter printed in Taylor, *Life and Letters*, 1: 141.
80. See Stoddard, *Greeley*; Hale, *Greeley*; and Amy Slater, *In Search*.
81. Clinton, *Other Civil War*; Schilpp and Murphy, *Great Women*.
82. Swisshelm, *Half a Century*, 107–8.
83. Ibid., 130–31.
84. Fuller, *Woman*.
85. Fuller, *Letters*, 4: 129.
86. Greeley, *Recollections*, 178; Greeley quoted by Emerson et al., *Memoirs*, 2: 155–56.

3. The Denigration of Margaret Fuller

1. Miller, *Margaret Fuller*, xiii, xx.
2. Urbanski, *Margaret Fuller's Woman in the Nineteenth Century*; Kluger, *The Paper*; Perry Miller, *The American Transcendentalists: Their Poetry and Prose* (Baltimore: Johns Hopkins University Press, 1957), *Margaret Fuller*, and "I Find No Intellect Comparable to My Own," *American Heritage* 8 (1957): 22–25, 96–99. For more discussion of the unflattering image of Fuller in the *Memoirs*, see: Berger, "Margaret Fuller"; Joseph Jay Deiss, "Men, Women and Margaret Fuller," *American Heritage* 23, no. 5 (1972): 42–47, 94–97; Ebbitt, "Critical Essays of Margaret Fuller"; Anthony, *Margaret Fuller*; and Douglas, *Feminization*.
3. Emerson et al., *Memoirs* 1: 236.
4. "Memoirs of Margaret Fuller" (1852; reprinted in Meyerson, *Critical Essays*, 70).
5. Bell Gale Chevigny, "The Long Arm of Censorship: Mythmaking in Margaret Fuller's Time and Our Own," *Signs* 2 (1976): 450–60.
6. Henry James, "Meditation on Her Meaning," in Chevigny, *Woman and the Myth*, 420–21.
7. Myerson, *Fuller: Annotated*, lists three reviews published in 1841 in Greeley's *New Yorker* of Fuller's pieces in the *Dial*. In addition, Myerson lists five pieces in the *Tribune* on Fuller's work, including a review of her book *Summer on the Lakes*.
8. Poe, "Literati," 1172; Joseph Slater, *Correspondence*, 418; Rubin, *Historic Whitman*; Alfred Janson Bloor, "In Memory of Sarah Margaret Fuller d'Ossoli," Bloor Papers, New York Historical Society. For other admiring comments from the 1850s, see Hart, *Female Prose Writers*; Parton, *Greeley*; and Duyckinck, *Cyclopedia*.
9. Edwin A. Studwell and R. A. Canby, *Dottings from the Writings of Margaret Fuller Ossoli* (Brooklyn: Gardner, 1869), 4; Mary B. Temple, *Sketch of Margaret Fuller Ossoli*

(Knoxville, Tenn.: Ossoli Circle, 1886); "In Memoriam: George Ripley," *New York Tribune,* July 1880, extra no. 63, 6.
10. Stanton et al., *Woman Suffrage,* 801; Eleanor Roosevelt, introduction to Bell, *Fuller,* 14; Higginson, *Ossoli;* Anthony, *Fuller.* For other praises of Fuller through the years, see Susan E. Dickinson, "Woman in Journalism," in *Woman's Work in America,* ed. Annie Nathan Meyer (1891; reprint, New York: Arno, 1972); Seth Curtis Beach, *Daughters of the Puritans* (1905; reprint, Freeport, N.Y.: Books for Free Libraries Press, 1967).
11. [George Ripley], "Margaret Fuller Ossoli," *New York Tribune,* 4 September 1850; Hart, *Female Prose Writers,* 267.
12. Longfellow quoted by Wade, *Fuller,* 146; Edgar Allan Poe, *Letters,* ed. John Ward Ostrom (New York: Gordian Press, 1966), 355, 427.
13. [Ripley], "Ossoli"; Ingersoll, *Greeley;* Zabriskie, *Greeley.*
14. Paul Ashdown, introduction to *Selected Journalism,* by James Agee (Knoxville: University of Tennessee Press, 1985).
15. Parton, *Greeley,* 255; Fuller, *Letters,* 4: 39, 138; Fuller, *Papers,* iv.

4. The Rich and the Poor

1. Higginson, *Ossoli,* 216; Ingersoll, *Greeley,* 179.
2. Fuller, *Letters,* 4: 46. See Sharon Kaye George, "Margaret Fuller: American Literary and Social Critic," Ph.D. diss., University of Texas, Austin, 1975; Wade, *Fuller;* Allen, *Achievement;* Amy Slater, *In Search;* Brown, *Fuller;* and Chevigny, *Woman and the Myth;* Francis Edward Kearns, "Margaret Fuller's Social Criticism," Ph.D. diss., University of North Carolina, Chapel Hill, 1961.
3. Douglas T. Miller, *The Birth of Modern America, 1820–1850* (New York: Pegasus, 1970), x; Douglas Miller, *Then Was the Future,* 22.
4. Davy Crockett quoted by Douglas Miller, *Then Was the Future,* 37; Tindall, *America,* 447.
5. Herman Melville, "The Paradise of Bachelors and the Tartarus of Maids," in *Selected Writings of Herman Melville* (New York: Random House, 1952), 201.
6. Ibid., 202.
7. Douglas Miller, *Birth of Modern America,* 103; Charles Dickens, *American Notes and Pictures from Italy* (1842; reprint, New York: Oxford University Press, 1957), 89–90.
8. John Tebbel, *The Media in America* (New York: Thomas Y. Cromwell, 1973), 174; Tindall, *America,* 497.

5. Prison and Asylum Reform

1. Fuller, *Letters,* 4: 45, 46.
2. David J. Rothman, *The Discovery of the Asylum: Social Order and Disorder in the New Republic* (Boston: Little and Brown, 1990) 278, 130–32, 135–37, 147–48, 152.
3. Ibid., 279; Ellen Dwyer, *Homes for the Mad: Life inside Two Nineteenth-Century Asylums* (New Brunswick, N.J.: Rutgers University Press, 1987).
4. Estelle B. Freedman, *Their Sister's Keepers: Women's Prison Reform in America, 1830–1930* (Ann Arbor: University of Michigan Press, 1981), 18, 20.

5. Ibid., 20.
6. Fuller, *Letters,* 4: 46; Greeley, *Recollections,* 180; Greeley quoted by Emerson et al., *Memoirs,* 2: 159.
7. Larry E. Sullivan, *The Prison Reform Movement: Forlorn Hope* (Boston: Twayne, 1990), 9.

6. Equality for Women and African Americans

1. Mott, *American Journalism,* 272; Tindall, *America,* 486; Douglas Miller, *Birth of Modern America,* xi; and Stern, *Fuller,* 231.
2. Tindall, *America,* 454–97.
3. Ibid., 494; Zabriskie, *Greeley.*
4. Hudspeth, preface to *Letters,* 4: 5.
5. Fuller, "Lawsuit"; Fuller, *Woman.*
6. Myerson, *Fuller: Annotated;* Pentu, "Fuller's Folly"; Deiss, *Roman Years,* 19; Briggs quoted by Myerson, *Fuller: Annotated,* 10; Poe, "Literati," 1173; Urbanski, *Fuller's Woman.*
7. Greeley, "Her *Tribune* Writing," 305.

7. The Irish

1. Hasia K. Diner, *Erin's Daughters in America* (Baltimore: Johns Hopkins University Press, 1983), 55; Kerby A. Miller, *Emigrants and Exiles: Ireland and the Irish Exodus to North America* (New York: Oxford University Press, 1985), 280–81.
2. Kerby Miller, *Emigrants,* 193.
3. Dale T. Knobel, *Paddy and the Republic: Ethnicity and Nationality in Antebellum America* (Middletown, Conn.: Wesleyan University Press, 1986), 26.
4. William V. Shannon, *The American Irish* (New York: Macmillan, 1963), 23, 41.
5. Ibid., 44.
6. Parton, *Greeley,* 254.
7. Andrew M. Greeley, *That Most Distressful Nation: The Taming of the American Irish* (Chicago: Quadrangle, 1972), 119.

8. A Miscellany

1. Robert Haven Schauffler, *Thanksgiving: Its Origin, Celebration, and Significance as Related in Prose and Verse* (1907; reprint, New York: Dodd, Mead, 1963).

Bibliography

Abbott, Edith. *Women in Industry: A Study in American Economic History.* 1910. Reprint, New York: Arno, 1969.
Allen, Margaret Vanderharr. *The Achievement of Margaret Fuller.* University Park: University of Pennsylvania Press, 1979.
Anthony, Katharine. *Margaret Fuller.* New York: Harcourt, Brace and Harve, 1920.
Ashdown, Paul. Introduction to *Selected Journalism,* by James Agee. Knoxville: University of Tennessee Press, 1985.
Assignment Log. *New York Tribune* City Department. 1867–68. Special Collections. New York Public Library.
Baker, Ira L. "Elizabeth Timothy: America's First Woman Editor." *Journalism Quarterly* 54 (1977): 280–85.
Baym, Nina. "Rewriting the Scribbling Women." *Legacy* 2, no. 2 (1985): 3–12.
Beach, Seth Curtis. *Daughters of the Puritans.* 1905. Reprint, Freeport, N.Y.: Books for Free Libraries Press, 1967.
Beasley, Maurine, and Sheila Gibbons. *Women in Media: A Documentary Source Book.* Washington, D.C.: Women's Institute for Freedom of the Press, 1979.
Belford, Barbara. *Brilliant Bylines.* New York: Columbia University Press, 1986.
Bell, Margaret. *Margaret Fuller.* 1930. Reprint, Freeport, N.Y.: Books for Free Libraries Press, 1971.
Berger, Patrick Frederick. "Margaret Fuller: Critical Realist as Seen in Her Works." Ph.D. diss., Saint Louis University, 1972.
Blanchard, Paula. *Margaret Fuller.* New York: Delacorte, 1978.
Bloor, Alfred Janson. "In Memory of Sarah Margaret Fuller d'Ossoli." Alfred Janson Bloor Papers. New York Historical Society.
Bovee, Warren. "Horace Greeley and Social Responsibility." *Journalism Quarterly* 63 (1986): 251–59.
Bradshaw, J. S. "To Correspondents—Horace Greeley." *Journalism Quarterly* 81 (1981): 644–46, 673.
Brockway, Beman. *Fifty Years in Journalism.* Watertown, Mass., 1891.
Brown, Arthur W. *Margaret Fuller.* New York: Twayne, 1964.
Browne, Junius Henri. "Horace Greeley," *Harper's New Monthly Magazine,* April 1873, 734–41.
Bungay, George W. *Crayon Sketches and Off-Hand Takings.* Boston: Stacy and Richardson, 1852.
Chevigny, Bell Gale. "The Long Arm of Censorship: Mythmaking in Margaret Fuller's Time and Our Own." *Signs* 2 (1976): 450–60.

———. *The Woman and the Myth: Margaret Fuller's Life and Writings.* Old Westbury, N.Y.: Feminist Press, 1976.
Child, L. Maria. "Kindness to Criminals—the Prison Association." *New York Tribune,* 10 December 1844.
Chipperfield, Faith. *In Quest of Love: The Life and Death of Margaret Fuller.* New York: Coward-McCann, 1957.
Clampitt, Amy. "Margaret Fuller, 1847." *The New Yorker,* 8 September 1986, 38.
Clarke, James Freeman. *The Letters of James Freeman Clarke to Margaret Fuller.* Edited by John Wesley Thomas. Hamburg, Germany: Cram, deGruyter, 1957.
Clinton, Catherine. *The Other Civil War.* New York: Hill and Wang, 1984.
Congdon, Charles T. "Reminiscences." In *Love Letters of Margaret Fuller,* edited by Julia Ward Howe, 223–28. New York: Appleton, 1903.
Conrad, Susan Phinney. *Perish the Thought: Intellectual Women in Romantic America, 1830–1860.* New York: Oxford University Press, 1976.
Cortissoz, Royal. *The New York Tribune: Incidents and Personalities in Its History.* New York: New York Tribune, 1923.
Coultrap-McQuin, Susan M. "Why Their Success? Some Observations on Publishing by Popular Nineteenth-Century Women Writers." *Legacy* 1, no. 2 (1984): 8–9.
Cross, Barbara, ed. *The Educated Woman in America.* New York: Teachers College Press, Columbia, 1965.
Crow, Duncan. *The Victorian Woman.* New York: Stein and Day, 1972.
Dall, Caroline Healey. *Margaret and Her Friends.* 1895. Reprint, New York: Arno, 1972.
Dana, Charles Anderson. "Greeley as a Journalist." In *A Library of American Literature,* vol. 7, edited by E. C. Stedman and Ellen M. Hutchinson, 448–51. New York: Webster, 1889–90.
Deiss, Joseph Jay. "Men, Women and Margaret Fuller." *American Heritage* 23, no. 5 (1972): 42–47, 94–97.
———. *The Roman Years of Margaret Fuller.* New York: Crowell, 1969.
DeVoto, Bernard. *The Year of Decision.* Boston: Little, Brown, 1943.
Dickens, Charles. *American Notes and Pictures from Italy.* 1842. Reprint, New York: Oxford University Press, 1957.
Dickinson, Susan E. "Woman in Journalism." In *Woman's Work in America,* edited by Annie Nathan Meyer. 1891. Reprint, New York: Arno, 1972.
Diner, Hasia K. *Erin's Daughters in America.* Baltimore, Md.: Johns Hopkins University Press, 1983.
Douglas, Ann. *The Feminization of American Culture.* New York: Knopf, 1977.
Durning, Russell E. *Margaret Fuller: Citizen of the World.* Heidelberg, Germany: Carl Winter, Universitätsverlag, 1969.
Duyckinck, Evart A., and George L. Duyckinck, *Cyclopedia of American Literature.* 2 vols. New York: Scribner, 1856.
Dwyer, Ellen. *Homes for the Mad: Life inside Two Nineteenth-Century Asylums.* New Brunswick, N.J.: Rutgers University Press, 1987.

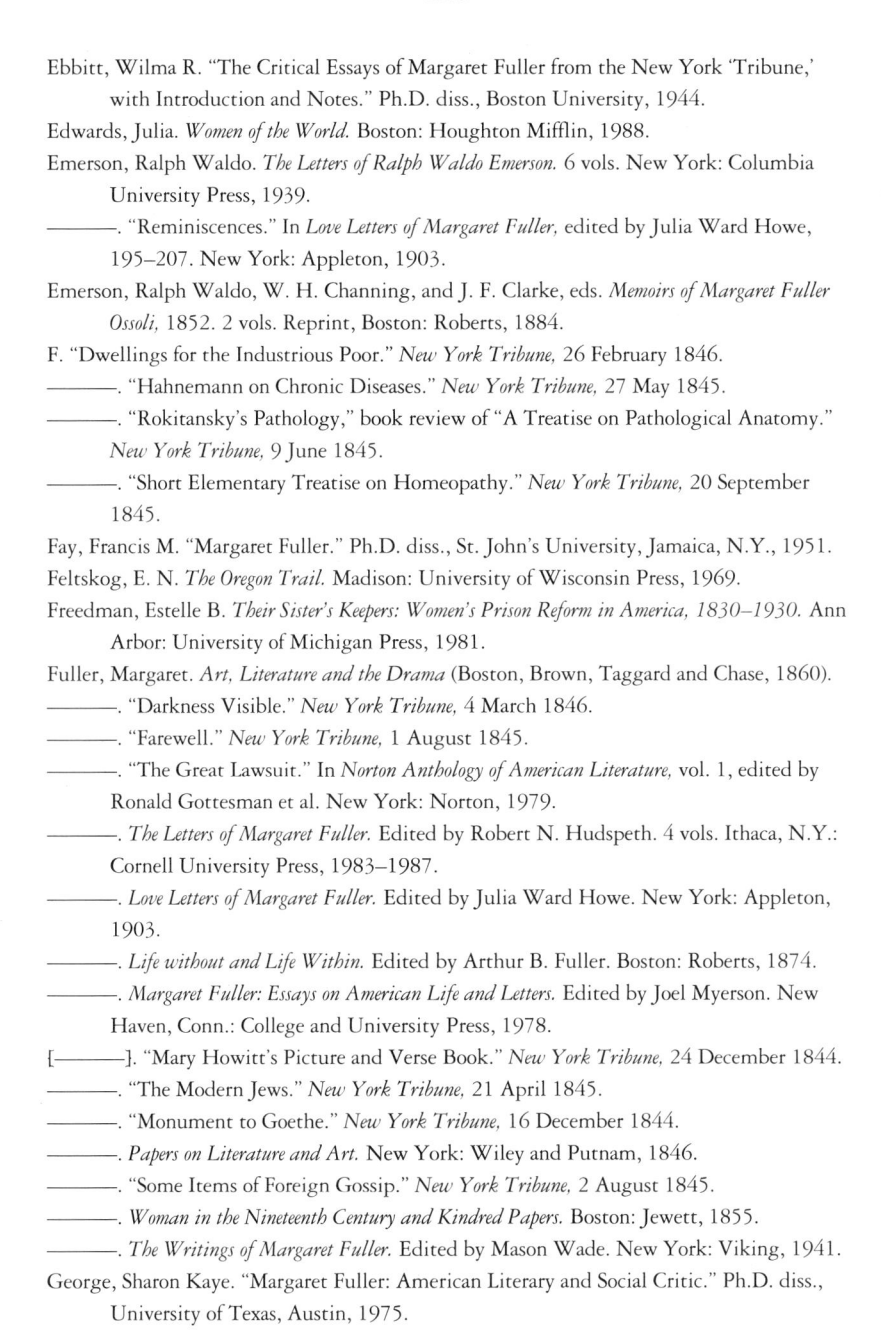

Ebbitt, Wilma R. "The Critical Essays of Margaret Fuller from the New York 'Tribune,' with Introduction and Notes." Ph.D. diss., Boston University, 1944.
Edwards, Julia. *Women of the World.* Boston: Houghton Mifflin, 1988.
Emerson, Ralph Waldo. *The Letters of Ralph Waldo Emerson.* 6 vols. New York: Columbia University Press, 1939.
―――. "Reminiscences." In *Love Letters of Margaret Fuller,* edited by Julia Ward Howe, 195–207. New York: Appleton, 1903.
Emerson, Ralph Waldo, W. H. Channing, and J. F. Clarke, eds. *Memoirs of Margaret Fuller Ossoli,* 1852. 2 vols. Reprint, Boston: Roberts, 1884.
F. "Dwellings for the Industrious Poor." *New York Tribune,* 26 February 1846.
―――. "Hahnemann on Chronic Diseases." *New York Tribune,* 27 May 1845.
―――. "Rokitansky's Pathology," book review of "A Treatise on Pathological Anatomy." *New York Tribune,* 9 June 1845.
―――. "Short Elementary Treatise on Homeopathy." *New York Tribune,* 20 September 1845.
Fay, Francis M. "Margaret Fuller." Ph.D. diss., St. John's University, Jamaica, N.Y., 1951.
Feltskog, E. N. *The Oregon Trail.* Madison: University of Wisconsin Press, 1969.
Freedman, Estelle B. *Their Sister's Keepers: Women's Prison Reform in America, 1830–1930.* Ann Arbor: University of Michigan Press, 1981.
Fuller, Margaret. *Art, Literature and the Drama* (Boston, Brown, Taggard and Chase, 1860).
―――. "Darkness Visible." *New York Tribune,* 4 March 1846.
―――. "Farewell." *New York Tribune,* 1 August 1845.
―――. "The Great Lawsuit." In *Norton Anthology of American Literature,* vol. 1, edited by Ronald Gottesman et al. New York: Norton, 1979.
―――. *The Letters of Margaret Fuller.* Edited by Robert N. Hudspeth. 4 vols. Ithaca, N.Y.: Cornell University Press, 1983–1987.
―――. *Love Letters of Margaret Fuller.* Edited by Julia Ward Howe. New York: Appleton, 1903.
―――. *Life without and Life Within.* Edited by Arthur B. Fuller. Boston: Roberts, 1874.
―――. *Margaret Fuller: Essays on American Life and Letters.* Edited by Joel Myerson. New Haven, Conn.: College and University Press, 1978.
[―――]. "Mary Howitt's Picture and Verse Book." *New York Tribune,* 24 December 1844.
―――. "The Modern Jews." *New York Tribune,* 21 April 1845.
―――. "Monument to Goethe." *New York Tribune,* 16 December 1844.
―――. *Papers on Literature and Art.* New York: Wiley and Putnam, 1846.
―――. "Some Items of Foreign Gossip." *New York Tribune,* 2 August 1845.
―――. *Woman in the Nineteenth Century and Kindred Papers.* Boston: Jewett, 1855.
―――. *The Writings of Margaret Fuller.* Edited by Mason Wade. New York: Viking, 1941.
George, Sharon Kaye. "Margaret Fuller: American Literary and Social Critic." Ph.D. diss., University of Texas, Austin, 1975.
Gilbert, Sandra M., and Susan Gubar, eds. *Norton Anthology of Literature by Women.* New York: Norton, 1985.

Godkin, Edwin L. *Life and Letters*. Edited by Rollo Ogden. New York: Macmillan, 1907.
Golemba, Henry L. "The Balanced View in Margaret Fuller's Literary Criticism." Ph.D. diss., University of Washington, Seattle, 1971.
———. *George Ripley*. New York: Twayne, 1977.
Gottesman, Ronald, et al., eds. *Norton Anthology of American Literature*, vol. 1. New York: Norton, 1979.
Greeley, Andrew M. *That Most Distressful Nation: The Taming of the American Irish*. Chicago: Quadrangle, 1972.
[Greeley, Horace]. "Death of Margaret Fuller." *New York Tribune*, 23 July 1850. This article in the *Tribune* is unsigned. However, attribution to Greeley is based on a 2 September 1850 letter to Sarah J. Hale, in Horace Greeley Papers, New York Public Library. Greeley told Hale, "My own article concerning her [Fuller] may be found in the *Tribune* of the 23rd or 24th July."
———. "Her *Tribune* Writing and Concern for Prostitutes." In *Woman and the Myth*, edited by Bell Gale Chevigny. Old Westbury, N.Y.: Feminist Press, 1976.
———. Introduction to *Woman in the Nineteenth Century and Kindred Papers*, by Margaret Fuller Ossoli. Boston: Jewett, 1855.
———. Letters. Horace Greeley Papers. New York Public Library.
[———]. "Magnificent Family Paper." *New York Tribune*, 20 November 1845.
[———]. "Prospectus for the Year 1845." *New York Tribune*, 16 November 1844.
[———]. "Prospectus of the Semi-Weekly Tribune." *New York Tribune*, 15 April 1845 and 18 April 1845.
———. *Recollections of a Busy Life*. 1868. Reprint, New York: Arno, 1970.
———. "Reminiscences." In *Love Letters of Margaret Fuller*, edited by Julia Ward Howe, 208–22. New York: Appleton, 1903.
[———]. "To Correspondents." *New York Tribune*, 10 February 1845.
[———]. "To Correspondents." *New York Tribune*, 18 February 1846.
Grossman, James. *James Fenimore Cooper*. New York: William Sloane, 1949.
Hale, Sarah J. *Woman's Record; or, Sketches of All Distinguished Women from "the Beginning" till A.D. 1850*. New York: Harper, 1853.
Hale, William Harlan. *Horace Greeley, Voice of the People*. New York: Harper, 1950.
Hardwick, Elizabeth. "The Genius of Margaret Fuller." *New York Review of Books*, 4 April 1986, pp. 14–22.
Harris, Barbara. *Beyond Her Sphere: Women and the Professions in American History*. Westport, Conn.: Greenwood, 1978.
Hart, John S. *The Female Prose Writers of America*. Philadelphia: E. H. Butler, 1852.
Higginson, Thomas Wentworth. *Margaret Fuller Ossoli*. 1884. Reprint, New York: Haskell House, 1968.
A History of the 100 Years of Unions on the New York Tribune. New York: Herald Tribune Unit of the Newspaper Guild of New York, Local 3, American Newspaper Guild, 1941.
Holland, Patricia G. "Lydia Maria Child as a Nineteenth-Century Professional Author." *Studies in the American Renaissance* (1981): 157–67.

BIBLIOGRAPHY

Hone, Phillip. *The Diary of Philip Hone 1828–1851*, vol. 1. New York, 1927.
Hudson, Frederic. *Journalism in the United States 1690 to 1872*. New York: Harper, 1873.
Hudspeth, Robert N. *Ellery Channing*. New York: Twayne, 1973.
———, ed. *The Letters of Margaret Fuller*. 4 vols. Ithaca, N.Y.: Cornell University Press, 1983–87.
"In Memoriam: George Ripley." *New York Tribune,* July 1880, extra no. 63.
Ingersoll, Lurton. *The Life of Horace Greeley*. Chicago: Union, 1873.
James, Edward T., Janet Wilson James, and Paul S. Boyer, eds. *Notable American Women*. 4 vols. Cambridge, Mass.: Belknap, 1971.
James, Henry. "Meditation on Her Meaning." In *The Woman and the Myth,* edited by Bell Gale Chevigny. Old Westbury, N.Y.: Feminist Press, 1976.
Johnson, Allen, and Dumas Malone, eds. *Dictionary of American Biography*. 20 vols. New York: Scribner, 1928–36.
Kearns, Francis Edward. "Margaret Fuller's Social Criticism." Ph.D. diss., University of North Carolina, Chapel Hill, 1961.
Kluger, Richard. *The Paper: The Life and Death of the New York Herald Tribune*. New York: Knopf, 1986.
Knobel, Dale T. *Paddy and the Republic: Ethnicity and Nationality in Antebellum America*. Middletown, Conn.: Wesleyan University Press, 1986.
Kobre, Sidney. *Development of American Journalism*. Dubuque, Iowa: Brown, 1969.
Lebergott, Stanley. *The Americans: An Economic Record*. New York: Norton, 1984.
———. *Manpower and Economic Growth*. New York: McGraw-Hill, 1964.
Lee, Susan Previant, and Peter Passall. *A New Economic View of American History*. New York: Norton, 1979.
Lerner, Gerda. "The Lady and the Mill Girl: Changes in the Status of Women in the Age of Jackson." In *Our American Sisters: Women in American Life and Thought,* edited by Jean E. Friedman and William G. Shade, 82–95. Boston: Allyn and Bacon, 1973.
Lunde, Erik S. *Horace Greeley*. Boston: Twayne, 1981.
Marzolf, Marion. *Up from the Footnote: A History of Women Journalists*. New York: Hastings, 1977.
Matthiessen, F. O. *American Renaissance: Art and Expression in the Age of Emerson and Whitman*. New York: Oxford University Press, 1941.
Melville, Herman. "The Paradise of Bachelors and the Tartarus of Maids." In *Selected Writings of Herman Melville,* 185–212. New York: Random House, 1952.
"Memoirs of Margaret Fuller." *New Quarterly Review* 1 (1852): 168–70. Reprinted in *Critical Essays on Margaret Fuller,* edited by Joel Myerson, 70–72. Boston: Hall, 1980.
Miller, Douglas T. *The Birth of Modern America 1820–1850*. New York: Pegasus, 1970.
———. *Then Was the Future: The North in the Age of Jackson, 1815–1850*. New York: Knopf, 1973.
Miller, Kerby A. *Emigrants and Exiles: Ireland and the Irish Exodus to North America*. New York: Oxford University Press, 1985
Miller, Perry. *The American Transcendentalists: Their Poetry and Prose*. Baltimore: Johns Hopkins University Press, 1957.

———. "I Find No Intellect Comparable to My Own." *American Heritage* 8 (1957): 22–25, 96–99.

———. *Margaret Fuller: An American Romantic*. Garden City, N.Y.: Anchor, 1963.

Mitchell, Catherine C. "Greeley as Journalism Teacher: 'Give Us Facts, Occurrences.'" *Journalism Educator* 44 (Autumn 1989): 3, 16–19.

———. "Horace Greeley's Star: Margaret Fuller's New York *Tribune* Journalism, 1844–1846." Ph.D. diss., University of Tennessee, Knoxville, 1987.

Morantz-Sanchez, Regina. *Sympathy and Science: Women Physicians in American Medicine*. New York: Oxford University Press, 1985.

Mott, Frank Luther. *American Journalism*. New York: MacMillan, 1962.

Myerson, Joel. *Margaret Fuller: An Annotated Secondary Bibliography*. New York: Burt Franklin, 1977.

———. *Margaret Fuller: A Descriptive Bibliography*. Pittsburgh, Pa.: University of Pittsburgh Press, 1978.

———, ed. *Critical Essays on Margaret Fuller*. Boston: G. K. Hall, 1980.

National Cyclopedia of American Biography. 1891. 62 vols. Reprint, Clifton, N.J.: White, 1967.

New York Tribune, 29 November 1844 to 11 August 1845.

New York Tribune: A Sketch of Its History. New York, 1883. (Microfilm at New York Public Library. No publisher or author mentioned on document itself or in library's card catalog.)

New York Tribune Association. Printed bank checks. Horace Greeley Papers. New York Public Library.

"The Newspaper Writers of New York." *New York Herald*, 9 November 1842.

Nichols, Thomas L. *Forty Years of American Life*. 1864. 2 vols. Reprint, New York: Johnson, 1969.

Parton, James. *The Life of Horace Greeley, Editor of the New York Tribune*. New York: Mason, 1855.

Pave, Marvin. "Landmark Decays as Agencies Argue." *Boston Globe*, 13 March 1985, pp. 1, 24.

Pentu, Constance. "Fuller's Folly: The Eccentric World of Margaret Fuller and the Greeleys." Master's thesis, Columbia University, 1960.

Poe, Edgar Allan. *Letters*. Edited by John Ward Ostrom. 2 vols. New York: Gordian Press, 1966.

———. "The Literati of New York City: Sarah Margaret Fuller." 1846. Reprinted in *Essays and Reviews*. New York: Literary Classics, 1978.

[Ripley, George]. "Margaret Fuller Ossoli." *New York Tribune*, 4 September 1850. In a 3 September 1850 letter to Sarah Josepha Hale, Horace Greeley recommends that she read an article which he said George Ripley wrote on Fuller in the *Southern Literary Messenger* of September 1850. The unbylined *Tribune* obituary headed "Margaret Fuller Ossoli" on 4 September 1850 said it is a reprint from the *Southern Literary Messenger*.

Robinson, Solon. *Hot Corn*. New York: DeWitt and Davenport, 1853.

Roosevelt, Eleanor. Introduction to *Margaret Fuller*, by Margaret Bell. New York: Freeport, 1930.

BIBLIOGRAPHY

Ross, Ishbel. *Ladies of the Press.* New York: Harper, 1936.

Rothman, David J. *The Discovery of the Asylum: Social Order and Disorder in the New Republic.* Boston: Little and Brown, 1990.

Rubin, Joseph Jay. *The Historic Whitman.* University Park: Pennsylvania State University Press, 1973.

Schauffler, Robert Haven. *Thanksgiving: Its Origin, Celebration, and Significance as Related in Prose and Verse.* 1907. Reprint, New York: Dodd, Mead, 1963.

Schilpp, Madelon Golden, and Sharon Murphy. *Great Women of the Press.* Carbondale: Southern Illinois University Press, 1983.

Schudson, Michael. *Discovering the News.* New York: Basic Books, 1978.

Seitz, Don Carlos. *Horace Greeley: Founder of the New York Tribune.* 1926. Reprint, New York: AMS, 1970.

Shannon, William V. *The American Irish.* New York: Macmillan, 1963.

Shapiro, Fred C. "The Life and Death of a Great Newspaper." *American Heritage* 18 (1967): 97–112.

Slater, Amy. *In Search of Margaret Fuller: A Biography.* New York: Delacorte, 1978.

Slater, Joseph, ed. *The Correspondence of Emerson and Carlyle.* New York: Columbia University Press, 1964.

Smith, Mary Ann Yodelis. "Research Retrospective: Feminism and the Media." *Communication Research* 9 (1982): 145–60.

Smith-Rosenberg, Carroll. "Beauty, the Beast, and the Militant Woman: A Case Study in Sex Roles and Social Stress in Jacksonian America." *American Quarterly* 23 (1971): 562–84.

Stanton, Elizabeth Cady, Susan B. Anthony, and Mitilda Gage. *History of Woman Suffrage.* 1889. 3 vols. Reprint, New York: Source Book Press, 1970.

Stern, Madeleine B. *The Life of Margaret Fuller.* New York: Putnam, 1946.

Stoddard, Henry Luther. *Horace Greeley: Printer, Editor, Crusader.* New York: Putnam, 1946.

Studwell, Edwin A. and R. A. Canby. *Dottings from the Writings of Margaret Fuller Ossoli.* Brooklyn: Gardner, 1869.

Sullivan, Larry E. *The Prison Reform Movement: Forlorn Hope.* Boston: Twayne, 1990.

Swisshelm, Jane Grey. *Half a Century.* 1880. Reprint, New York: Source Book Press, 1970.

Szymanski, Karen Ann. "Margaret Fuller: The New York Years." Ph.D. diss., Syracuse University, 1980.

Taylor, Bayard. *Life and Letters.* Edited by Marie Hansen-Taylor and Horace Scudder. 2 vols. Boston: Houghton, Mifflin, 1884.

Tebbel, John. *The Media in America.* New York: Thomas Y. Cromwell, 1973.

Temple, Mary B. *Sketch of Margaret Fuller Ossoli.* Knoxville, Tenn.: Ossoli Circle, 1886.

Tindall, George Brown. *America: A Narrative History,* vol. 1. New York: Norton, 1984.

Trends in the American Economy in the Nineteenth Century, vol. 26. Princeton N.J.: Princeton University Press, 1960.

Urbanski, Marie. *Margaret Fuller's Woman in the Nineteenth Century: A Literary Study of Form and Content, of Sources and Influence.* Westport, Conn.: Greenwood, 1980.

Bibliography

Van Deusen, Glyndon Garlock. *Horace Greeley: Nineteenth-Century Crusader.* Philadelphia: University of Pennsylvania Press, 1953.
Van Every, Dale. *The Final Challenge.* New York: William Morrow, 1964.
Wade, Mason. *Margaret Fuller: Whetstone of Genius.* New York: Viking, 1940.
———, ed. *The Writings of Margaret Fuller.* New York: Viking, 1941.
Webster's American Biographies. Springfield, Mass.: Merriam, 1978.
Weisberger, Bernard A. *The American Newspaperman.* Chicago: University of Chicago Press, 1961.
Welter, Barbara. "The Cult of True Womanhood." In *Our American Sisters: Women in American Thought and Life,* edited by Jean E. Friedman and William G. Shade. Boston: Allyn and Bacon, 1973.
———. *Dimity Convictions: The American Woman in the Nineteenth Century.* Athens: Ohio University Press, 1976.
Williamson, Jeffrey G., and Peter H. Lindert. *American Inequality: A Macroeconomic History.* New York: Academic Press, 1980.
Young, John Russell. *Men and Memories.* Edited by May D. Russell Young. 2 vols. New York: Neeley, 1901.
Zabriskie, Francis Nicoll. *Horace Greeley.* New York: Funk and Wagnalls, 1890.

Index

Abolitionism, 18, 19, 36, 127
Akerly, Samuel, 117
Anthony, Katharine, 45
anti-rent violence, 19–20

Beecher, Catherine, 128, 133
Bellevue Alms House, 51, 78
Birch, William Y., 116
Bloomingdale Asylum, 76–77
Bloor, Alfred Janson, 45
Brigham, Amariah, 111

Canby, R. A., 45
Carlyle, Thomas, 44, 122
Catholicism, 164, 170
Channing, William Ellery, 12–13
Child, Lydia Maria, 38
Clay, Henry, 17
Cooper, James Fenimore, 21

Dana, Charles, 11
Dial, The, 11, 44, 126
Dix, Dorothea, 77
Douglass, Frederick, 19, 127

Earle, Pliny, 76, 79, 83
Emerson, Ralph Waldo, 143–44, 151
environmental portrait, 7

Fillmore, Millard, 41
fire: in New York City, 20; at *New York Tribune,* 10, 21

Five Points slum, 54
Florida Indian War, 18
Fourier, Charles, 125
Fuller, Margaret: admirers of, 44–46; attitude towards work, 5, 7, 29, 33, 47, 52; byline, 3–5, 25, 39–40; detractors of, 43–44, 46; and *The Dial,* vii; duties at *Tribune,* 5, 7, 14, 24–26, 175; effort at work, 26–27, 30, 40–41; on "female scribblers," 35–36; and Horace Greeley, 6, 26, 32–34; importance of, 5, 36, 37; and George Ripley, vii; on reform, 51–52, 54, 77–78, 125–27; and romance, 6; *Tribune* advertising about, 3, 16, 24–25; wages, 37–38; writing style, 26, 31, 51–52

Graham, Sylvester, 125
Greeley, Horace: advice on writing, 31–32; articles by, 25; byline policy, 40; as an employer, 27–29; fame of, 8; as a fast writer, 26, 30–31; and Margaret Fuller, 3, 6, 26, 33–34; income, 38; letters of, viii; personality, 27–28; as reformer, 16–17, 54, 125; on woman's rights, 41–42
Greeley, Molly, 3, 6

Hart, John S., 45
Hastings, Lansford W., 23
Hawthorne, Nathaniel, 35, 38
Higginson, Thomas Wentworth, 45

Index

Industrial Revolution, 53–54

Johnson, Oliver, 12, 39
journalism: controversial nature of, 46–47; low status of, 47–48

Know Nothings, 164

Lee, Mrs. George, 131
Longfellow, Henry Wadsworth, 46
Lowell, James Russell, 46

Massachusetts, conflict with South Carolina, 18
McElrath, Thomas, 13
Memoirs of Margaret Fuller Ossoli, 43–44
Mexican-American War, viii, 18–19
Miller, Perry, 43

Nathan, James, 6
New York Alms House, 118
New York City: everyday life, 21–22; fires, 20; social conditions, 51
New York Courier and Enquirer, 161–62
New York State Lunatic Asylum, 111
New York Tribune: advertising, 15, 23–24; assignment log, viii; beginnings, 9–10; byline policy, 39–40; circulation, 9–10; conflict with U.S. Congress, 21; contents of, 15–16; and Cooper libel suit, 21; fame of, 8; fire, 10, 21; house ads about Fuller, 3, 16, 24–25; literary section, 15–16; number of pages, 15; page make-up, viii; staff, 10–13

Olin, Rev. Stephen, 66
Oregon Territory, 18
Ossoli Circle, 45

Peet, Harvey P., 97ff
Perkins, T. K., 116
Poe, Edgar Allan, 2, 24, 38, 44, 46
Polk, James K., 18

Raymond, Henry J., 12, 29, 38
reform movements, 54, 78, 125–27
Ripley, George, vii, 11, 29, 38, 45, 46
Robinson, Solon, 11
Roosevelt, Eleanor, 45

Sing Sing Prison, 76, 106
slavery. *See* Abolitionism
Snow, George, 12, 39
South Carolina, conflict with Massachusetts, 18
Stanton, Elizabeth Cady, 45
Stowe, Harriett Beecher, 128, 133
Stowe, Rev. Calvin, 132
Studwell, Edwin, 45
strait jackets, 77
Sumner, Charles, 151
Swisshelm, Jane Grey, 36–39 passim

Taylor, Bayard, 11, 29, 38, 40
Texas, annexation of, 17
Transcendentalists, 11
Tyler, John, 19

wages in the 1840s, 38
Walter, Cornelia, 36, 38, 40
Whig Party, 17
Whitman, Walt, 38, 44
Woman in the Nineteenth Century, 45, 126, 133
woman's sphere, 35–36
women: factory workers, 53; prisons for, 77; proper role of, 35–36; in public life, 36; working in offices, 40–41
Wood, Samuel, 117

PS 2502 .M56 1995